Understanding
Psychotherapy

Also by Michael Franz Basch

Doing Psychotherapy

Understanding Psychotherapy

The Science Behind the Art

Michael Franz Basch

Basic Books, Inc., Publishers

NEW YORK

Photographs in figure 4.1 © Joe McNally/Wheeler Pictures.

Photographs in figure 4.2 originally appeared in Tiffany M. Field et al., "Discrimination and Imitation of Facial Expressions by Neonates," *Science* 218 (8 October 1982): 179–81. Copyright 1982 by the AAAS.

Library of Congress Cataloging-in-Publication Data
Basch, Michael.
  Understanding psychotherapy.
  Bibliography: p. 315
  Includes index.
  1. Psychotherapy. I. Title.
RC480.B3174 1988   616.89'14   88–47763
ISBN 0–465–08863–5

PTBC offers cassettes and books. For information and catalog write to PTBC, 230 Livingston Street, Northvale, NJ 07647.

Dedicated to the memory

of my grandmother

Gertrud Hess née Engelmann-Ullstein

Contents

List of Figures

Preface

THIS BOOK is addressed not only to the student, the teacher, and the practitioner of psychotherapy, but also to those readers who have an interest in and/or a need for a working knowledge of psychological development as it influences everyday behavior. In order to be accessible, useful, and readily understandable, I have done my best to define my terms clearly and to explain their significance in the context of my clinical work. The case examples that I give are disguised reconstructions from notes and from memory of patients in my own practice, as well as from cases that I have supervised or discussed in seminars. Because this material is adduced to illustrate how a comprehensive theory of psychotherapy can be formulated and applied rather than to describe the treatment of any particular individual, I have not hesitated to combine material from different cases and to abbreviate the record once I have made my point. Although my case material is disguised, my participation is not. What I say I said to a patient accurately reflects what I have said in these or similar circumstances. I have no doubt that other therapists might well have chosen to intervene differently; it should be understood that my purpose is not to advocate particular things I said or the style I use, but to clarify the underlying principles of development that I am addressing by my interventions—principles that, when taken together, form a scientifically valid and practically applicable theory of mental functioning.

Useful as I hope it will be, what I have written is in no way intended to be final or complete. Rather, I would feel amply rewarded if the synthesis made here were to serve as a useful step both in the continued refinement that psychotherapy has undergone since Freud first visited the clinic of Charcot, and in the contribution that psychotherapy can make to the understanding and practice of human communication generally.

Acknowledgments

THE DISCREPANCY between what theories of psychotherapy predict should take place and what actually happens in practice already troubled me in my early days as a student in the field. Many people helped me to find a way out of this dilemma. I regret that I cannot thank all of them individually. I do want to acknowledge my indebtedness to my patients for giving me the opportunity to experience the resourcefulness and versatility with which we human beings are able to overcome the obstacles that stand in the way of our well-being; to the many colleagues who helped me to refine and shape my ideas in workshops, at professional meetings, and in informal discussions; and to my students, who gave me the opportunity to learn how I might convey in reasonably coherent fashion what I found useful.

I am very grateful to my daughter, Gail Basch, M.D., and to my colleagues Miriam Elson, M.A., A.C.S.W., Michael Gribetz, M.D., Csaba Hegyvary, M.D., and George Klumpner, M.D.—all of whom gave me valuable suggestions as the manuscript began to take shape.

In our semimonthly meetings, later drafts of the manuscript were thoughtfully reviewed by the following members of the Faculty Seminar of the Department of Psychiatry, Rush Medical College: Katie Busch, M.D., Suzanne Cooperman, M.D., Lionel Corbett, M.D., James Crawford, M.D., Peter Fink, M.D., Paul Holinger, M.D., Charles Jaffe, M.D., Hartmut Mokros, Ph.D., Karen Pierce, M.D., Janice Swope, M.D., Judith Tellerman, Ph.D., Ruth Westheimer, M.D., and Robert Zadylak, M.D. Their comments were most helpful, and I implemented many, perhaps most, of their suggestions.

I also wish to express my appreciation to the following colleagues: Beatrice Beebe, Ph.D., who not only put at my disposal her encyclopedic knowledge of infant research but also made many valuable suggestions regarding the style and content of the manuscript; Douglas Detrick, Ph.D., for his thoughtful comments and his help with the book's index; Arnold Goldberg, M.D., and Constance Goldberg, M.S.W., who were, as always, encouraging and helpful throughout the years it took to complete this project; Alan Kindler, M.D., for his stimulating and insightful discussions of many parts of the manuscript; and Roy R. Grinker, Jr., M.D., and Virginia Saft, M.D., who were kind enough to give me an invaluable line-by-line critique of the penultimate draft of this work.

Jan Fawcett, M.D., chairman of the Department of Psychiatry, Rush Medical College, and Robert Zadylak, M.D., its director of Psychiatric Education and Training, have been most forthcoming and generous in giving me the time and the opportunity to develop and formulate the concepts I am presenting here. The administrative secretaries of the department, first Lanette Stigsen and then Therese Molyneux, were more than helpful in preparing charts and illustrations necessary to my work, and in managing the innumerable details involved in bringing my students and me together.

Gilbert Levin, Ph.D., director of the Cape Cod Institute, sponsored by the Department of Psychiatry of the Albert Einstein College of Medicine, offered me repeated and welcome opportunities to conduct summer seminars that let me exchange ideas with and benefit from the reactions of fellow professionals from all areas of the country.

My thanks to the Benedek Research Fund of the Institute for Psychoanalysis, Chicago, for its assistance while my manuscript was in preparation.

While preparing my final draft, I profited greatly from the editorial advice of Natalie Altman. Rigorous and uncompromising when it comes to her craft, Natalie brought out the best I had to offer— more than that no one can do, and I am extremely grateful to her.

At Basic Books, Jo Ann Miller, senior editor, was a source of strength and gave me many valuable suggestions; Phoebe Hoss miraculously transformed my manuscript into a book; and Suzanne Wagner was an ever cheerful and efficient shepherd, seeing that everything got between two covers.

There are two people without whom this book would not have

seen the light of day. Eva Sandberg has, once again, stood by me, typing and retyping, from early sketches to the final draft—the many versions of my manuscript. By now our relationship goes back many years, but I am no less appreciative of Eva's help and expertise than when I first had the good fortune to enlist her in my efforts. I am most grateful to my wife, Carol, who supported me in my quest, held firm when my resolve flagged, and, as she has throughout our married life, gave me reason to believe that I could indeed accomplish what I had set out to do.

Understanding
Psychotherapy

Introduction

Psychotherapy and Science

A CENTURY AGO, Freud recognized the unconscious well-springs of human motivation—an insight that has shaped education, politics, business, our attitudes toward child rearing, our understanding of history, and literary criticism. Indeed, we all think of ourselves and of one another in terms that Freud first formulated. Nonetheless, in devising and promoting psychoanalysis as a research method into human motivation, Freud fell short of his goal. He was unable to establish a theory that would serve both as a scientific basis for psychotherapy generally as well as a foundation for the investigation of human nature.

Nor has a generally useful theory of psychotherapy been developed since Freud's time. Instead, competing but also limited theories were generated as it was found that the psychoanalytic method, as formulated by him for the treatment of psychoneurotic patients, was applicable to few of the patients who began to look for help from psychotherapy. What usually happened was that an innovative therapist was able to set aside the prejudices of his or her training, listen to a patient who presented a particular problem, and, through trial and error, find a way to help that person and then other patients suffering from similar difficulties. Then history would repeat itself. Very much as in Freud's case, an approach successful in dealing with particular problems became transformed in the hands of its innovator and his or her students into a theory purporting to explain the human mind *in toto* and advanced as a universally applicable therapeutic technique that would replace whatever had gone before. In this way, competing schools of psychotherapy evolved—dynamic, cognitive, and behavioral—only to split again and again as clinical advances were made that could not be related to an overarching theory which might have been able to encompass them and explain their efficacy. In the last forty or fifty years, however, progress in related fields, as well as in dynamic psychotherapy,* has gone a long way toward correcting this situation. The formulation of a valid and useful approach toward integrating what the various schools of psychotherapy have to offer is now a real possibility. This union of the art of psychotherapy—the discovery of therapeutic techniques and their skillful application—with the scientific basis that explains how and why any particular technique works—and what that can tell us about human nature generally—is the subject of my book.

Let me now introduce in greater detail the rationale for what I have tried to do, beginning—since I was fortunate enough to grow up as a professional during this time of ferment in the field—with some personal experiences from my student days.

The Scientific Method

THE "SHIRT-CARDBOARD" EXERCISE

On my first day at the small midwestern college I attended in the 1950s, I was one of about a hundred freshmen who, having expressed interest in the premedical program, were brought together

---

Psychoanalysis, as Freud used the term and as it is still used today, refers to a research method into human motivation, to a particular form of intensive psychotherapy, and to his proposed general theory of mental functioning. Here, unless there is reason to single out psychoanalysis in order to emphasize its differences from other forms of psychotherapy (as I do in chapter 10), I use *psychotherapy* as a generic term subsuming psychoanalysis as one member of the class of insight or dynamic therapy; and, unless otherwise specified, use *psychotherapist* to include *psychoanalyst.*

in a large lecture hall for a special meeting. My father was a physician, and I was sure I was meant to be one. But only that day did it dawn on me that admission to medical school required more than that conviction. One by one the various representatives of both the faculty and the administration told us that we were in a competitive situation and that the curriculum was Darwinian—designed to ensure the survival of the fittest, and the fittest only. There were, we were told, seven qualified applicants for every opening in a medical school. And we were competing not only against each other but also against students from prestigious universities in the East and elsewhere who, it was implied, possessed minds far superior to any of ours.

After I had been further frightened out of my wits by assorted deans, department heads, and senior professors, all of whom did their best to persuade us to abandon our ambition and aim for a more attainable career, the chairman of the meeting announced that the final speaker would be the instructor in Biology 101—the beginners' course. Now came to the podium a rumpled, dumpy, balding man, puffing asthmatically and looking for all the world like a walrus with his red toothbrush moustache, oversized teeth, and receding chin. Any one of us who, judging him by his appearance and lack of advanced academic degrees, was ready to mistake John W. Hudson for a comic or inconsequential figure was quickly disillusioned. Wheezing more than speaking, he came directly to the point. Admission to and graduation from a medical school, he informed us, required nothing more, but nothing less, than giving absolute attention to everything he said in his lectures and the willingness to follow his instructions to the letter. Those who succeeded in his class became physicians; those who did not, did not. I clung to those words, with their unmistakable air of certainty, like a drowning man to a raft, and am today a living testimonial to their truth. I remember Mr. Hudson fondly and try not to think of what might have happened to me had not chance brought me into his orbit.

I spent the next year in Mr. Hudson's biology class writing on shirt-cardboards, which laundries use to keep a freshly washed and ironed shirt from wrinkling. Each of these rectangles, fourteen inches long and eight inches wide, was divided precisely, as per instructions, into nine columns: the first was devoted to the Linnean classification of the animal being studied; the second, to a description of its gross and microscopic anatomy; and then each of the next seven was used to summarize the manner in which this organism carries out one of the functions of protoplasm necessary for animal life—respiration, digestion, circulation, excretion, reproduction, locomotion, and communication. We were required to fill in from lecture notes and textbooks the details of the basic life processes as they occur in a representative of each animal phylum. All this had to be done in microscopically fine print, for everything had to fit on one side of the cardboard.

Mr. Hudson collected our cardboards as they became due, read every word, and noted errors of omission and commission in red pencil. Any assignment that rated less than a "B" had to be completely redone. In the laboratory, we dissected our specimens and reinforced through touch and vision the accuracy of what we were summarizing on our cards. Perfection was expected, and good work was not acknowledged by so much as a smile or a word of praise. But I soon learned that I would find a minimum, at times even an absence, of red pencil and an "A" in the upper left-hand corner if I heard a little premonitory wheeze as he paused briefly at my desk to hand my assignment back to me. I worked harder than I ever imagined I could for those wheezes, and lived in fear that, in spite of my best efforts, I would not hear one when the next unit of work was completed.

By the time Mr. Hudson was satisfied that one had extracted, and briefly but comprehensively presented, the pertinent facts about each animal phylum, the conscientious student, one who had done his or her own work and not cribbed from that of others, had a working mastery not only of what one needed to know to pass an examination with flying colors, but of an approach to the study of science that went far beyond the subject matter at hand.

I am sure that Mr. Hudson realized that he was teaching us not just basic biology but the proper approach to mastering Cartesian mechanism, the philosophical approach that has defined for almost four hundred years what falls within the boundaries of science. Essentially, mechanism tells us that no matter what the subject may happen to be, it is part of science if we can reach an understanding of the whole by first subdividing it and then studying the interaction between the parts so as to lead to a chain of cause-and-effect statements that can be actually—or, at least, potentially—validated through observation or experimentation. Within this paradigm, Mr. Hudson's training worked beautifully. Advanced courses, such as physiology, histology, and embryology, were essentially extensions in depth of one or another of the columns of facts we had laboriously inscribed on one cardboard after another, and their subject matter could be extracted, fractionated, and summarized in similar fashion.

My father's patients dutifully delivered up the shirt-cardboards collected since their last visit to his office, and I kept on accumulating "A's" until, three years from that inauspicious beginning, the doors to the promised land opened and I became a medical student. The first year of medical school was essentially a repetition of what I had already learned about the life processes in lower animals, but now focused on the complex interactions of the organ systems that make up the human body. The last three years were spent learning what, why, and how things can go wrong with the various pipes, pumps, filters, cables, levers, and whatnot that keep us going, and how the physician, using the arts of pharmacy and surgery, can apply the knowledge supplied by research in chemistry and physics to maintain and repair this exquisite machine. As Mr. Hudson had promised, the approach to science that he taught worked as effectively in medical school as it had before, and in due time I became a licensed physician.

It was when I entered my psychiatric residency that, for the first time, the shirt-cardboard method failed me. Here was no fund of knowledge that could be subdivided into ever-smaller parts whose study would eventually clarify the function of the whole. The human mind, unlike the human body, seemed to defy Cartesian mechanism, an approach that over a span of seven years had become second nature to me.

Nor was I reassured when—only a few weeks after I had begun my residency in psychiatry—in response to a lecture given by the head of the department, a lecture that dealt with Freud's concept of infantile sexuality as the prime motivator of human behavior, I innocently asked how one could know that, for example, the infant's sucking was a manifestation of sexuality when the infant could not tell us what he or she was experiencing. I was shocked by my chief's outraged response. He ended his tirade by suggesting that if I was not prepared to accept the fundamental truths on which the science of psychoanalysis was built, I knew where the door was and should use it. Though I did take the earliest opportunity to switch training programs, I did not accept the invitation to seek a different profession. Still, I did have second thoughts about the field I had chosen. Why, I wondered, would a person of such eminence bother to get upset with a mere beginner like me instead of simply answering my question? Some years passed before I realized that there were no epistemologically acceptable answers to such questions. All that Freud himself could offer was that the positive results obtainable with the psychoanalytic *method* constituted the proof that the *hypotheses* said to account for those results must also be valid. It was this circular reasoning that I had innocently challenged with my query—thereby threatening to call attention to the fact that the Emperor was scantily clad.

Freud himself was aware of many of the shortcomings of his theory and saw his explanations of mental functioning only as attempts to be replaced as soon as better ones were available. Indeed, given the conception of mind and mental work in Freud's day, one that is only now gradually beginning to change, there was no way in which psychology could qualify as a scientific endeavor.

DESCARTES AND THE ORIGIN OF THE MIND–BRAIN DICHOTOMY

The great French philosopher René Descartes (1586–1650) inadvertently set the stage for the problems with which psychology is still grappling. For replacing the animistic approach to the study of the human body with a mechanistic one, Descartes, among many other achievements, must be honored as the father of modern medical practice. Up till his time, what prevailed was the idea of the ancients that life and bodily health depend on the presence of a spiritual essence or soul, the *anima.* Animism took different forms, evolving from early priestly efforts to pacify and influence the gods who controlled the life-giving spirits, to the physicians' efforts to detect and determine the nature of the humors or essential fluids

whose balance, it was believed, accounted for the proper functioning of bodily organs. Descartes, using the analogy of the recently
invented mechanical clock, suggested that the difference between
health and disease depends not on unseen essential forces, but on
whether the body's constituent parts are working harmoniously. To
this hypothesis, however, he posited one exception—the brain.

A mechanistic view of human functioning threatened to make
man out to be just one more kind of animal, complex to be sure, but
only an animal; a heretical position in the eyes of the Church, and
likely to bring its creator fatally unfavorable attention from the
Inquisition. Descartes dealt with this problem by declaring that six
weeks after conception, as a consequence of a divine intervention,
there was implanted in the human brain's pineal gland a spirit or
soul, which in certain respects controlled the brain's power to initiate behavior. The soul, Descartes postulated, in keeping with the
doctrine of his church, differentiated human beings from all other
earthly creatures by instilling in them both a sense of morality and
the ability to reason, therewith gifting us alone with the ability to
know and, potentially, choose good rather than evil—that is, to will
freely. The soul's control over the brain then ensured that, once
made, voluntary choices could be activated through behavior. Such
behavior having been chosen or freely willed by the person engaged
in it, rather than having been forced or determined by bodily or
other environmental circumstances, could then be judged by the
Giver of the soul as bringing the actor closer either to heaven or to
hell.

To this explanation, Descartes added a series of further assumptions. He equated reason with thought, thought with consciousness,
and consciousness with the experience of self-awareness. Because
it was taken for granted that only humans are self-aware, it followed that we alone are capable of thinking reasonably. The corollary was that unconscious activities of the brain are animalistic
automatisms and cannot be attributed to reason. This dictum satisfied the requirements of the Church that man be fundamentally
differentiated from all other creatures; it resulted, however, in the
brain remaining the last "animated" organ in the body, one still
directly controlled, at least in part, by supernatural forces. This
belief was in keeping with the concept of the time that behavior we

would today call psychotic or neurotic was due to possession or some other aberration of the soul and therefore within the purview of the priest.

L. L. Whyte, in his *The Unconscious Before Freud* (1960), documents that Descartes's scholarly contemporaries were by no means unanimous in accepting his position. Immediate objections were raised to his equation of consciousness with thinking. It was obvious to many philosophers that, among other things, this equation contradicted everyday experience. For instance, we have all tried to recall a name, only to find ourselves unable to do so. When we give up trying, we find it comes to us "out of the blue" some hours later when we have long "stopped thinking" about it—that is, are not conscious of trying to remember it. If we attribute to thought our conscious efforts to remember, to what powers shall we attribute the actual remembering that suddenly brings into consciousness the heretofore-elusive name? We must have reasoned our way to that memory unconsciously. But, according to Descartes, to do this is not possible.

Nevertheless, in spite of evidence and arguments to the contrary, Descartes's concept was apparently sufficiently persuasive to the majority and carried the day. Its origins were soon forgotten, and what had been a hypothesis came to be accepted as self-evident fact.

Descartes's simplistic—in retrospect—comparison between the human body and the spring-wound clock, and his crude speculations about the manner in which the body's parts interacted (he suggested, for example, that the nerves were hollow tubes used by the brain to initiate movement as it selectively forced air into the muscles), soon were replaced by the knowledge gained from more accurate observation and from experimentation. The rise of physics and its postulation of energy as a quantifiable force capable of performing work—that is, moving mass through distance—and the chemical studies showing how matter can be transformed into energy, explained a great deal about the physiology or functioning of the interacting bodily parts. As we students filled out Mr. Hudson's columns on digestion, respiration, and other bodily functions, we gained an understanding of how every living organism, from the simplest one-celled creature to the most complex of mammals, can be looked upon as functioning essentially as if it were a steam engine, a machine in which the conversion of the potential energy of fuel into heat can be harnessed to produce work. Foodstuffs taken in by the animal are degraded, and the energic potential released in the process is stored until it is used to support various bodily activities that bring the organism into contact with new fuel supplies. It is on knowledge of this sort that scientific medicine was built. When the machine fails in some aspect of the energy-conversion process, the result is called an illness. If enough is understood about the physics and chemistry behind the affected part of the process, one can determine hypothetically what needs to be done to repair the damage. This is the model of functioning available to Freud, and he did what he could with it.

Today Descartes's soul-brain dichotomy is no longer an issue for most of us, and philosophers and psychologists have long since replaced it with a mind-brain, or mind-body dichotomy. However, substituting *mind* for *soul* has changed nothing: thought continues to be attributed to a supranatural source: that is, to a *mind* that, though it is associated with the brain, is not part of the brain; an immaterial entity with great influence, whose origin is unknown and whose nature cannot be further studied or understood.

Though, as far as we know, Freud was not aware of this philosophical historical issue—which had taken psychology out of the realm of natural science—it was left for him implicitly to challenge this dichotomy by systematically demonstrating through his clinical discoveries that the equation of consciousness with reason and thought was false. And so began the slow process, not yet completed by any means, of undoing the long-standing reification of *mind* and deanimating the brain.

FREUD'S EFFORT AT A SCIENTIFIC PSYCHOLOGY

Modern psychotherapy and the mental health professions had their origin in 1885 when Sigmund Freud, then a young physician but already a highly regarded neurophysiological researcher, visited Paris and the clinic of the most renowned neurologist of the day, Jean-Martin Charcot. Although Freud's interests lay elsewhere, he soon found intriguing Charcot's investigation of neurotic phenomena through the use of hypnosis. Unlike most physicians of that time, Charcot did not think of the bizarre rituals of the obsessive-compulsive, the inexplicable paralysis of the hysteric, or the irrational fears of the phobic patient as evidence of malingering or fraud. Charcot, using the method of time regression under hypnosis, established that neurotic symptoms were the result of highly emotionally charged, seemingly irrational, fixed ideas outside of adult consciousness—ideas that had been acquired in earlier years and that, under stress, took over and controlled a person's personality.

When Freud, following Charcot, first studied the hypnotic investigation and treatment of neuroses—more than ten years before he was to discover the method of psychoanalysis—it occurred to him that since the study of the functioning of a diseased organ elsewhere in the body could shed light on its normal functioning and development, why should this not be true for the brain? Since the neurotic patient gave clear evidence for the existence of unconscious thought processes, perhaps, he reasoned, the study of neurotically disturbed persons could provide an entrée to learning how the brain gives rise to thought processes in general. And though, after 1900, he continued for the rest of his life to perfect psychoanalysis as a method of treatment for emotional disorders, he considered that therapeutic work to be secondary to the goal of using what he learned from it to establish a scientific psychology that would serve as the basic science for the study of human nature. However, Freud's wish to go beyond an understanding of the motivation for behavior to the nature of the thought process itself was premature, and it sowed the seeds for the confusion and discord that plagues the field of psychotherapy to this day.

During the late nineteenth century when Freud began this work, the study of brain anatomy and physiology was in its infancy, and Freud's attempt at finding a biological explanation for his clinical findings failed. *The Project for a Scientific Psychology*, written in 1895 but never published during Freud's lifetime, is a prescient tour de force in which he did his best, given his knowledge of the brain's anatomy and its functioning, to create a neurological model that would explain what he had discovered about thought formation through working with neurotic patients.

In making this attempt at a general theory, Freud posed all the right questions. So, for example, he asked himself whence neurotic thought attains the power to dominate an otherwise reasonable person's mental life, and recognized that the force excited by such thought was related to the degree of affect attached to it. As yet, however, no viable theory regarding the origin and nature of affect existed, and he could not further explain his observations. Instead, he tried to reduce psychology to physics, thinking of thought as a form of instinctually generated "psychic" energy that strove for discharge. Reasoning from the clinical finding that the unconscious motivation behind neurotic thoughts originated in the sexual life of the patient's childhood years, Freud hypothesized that the source of this *psychic energy* was a sexual drive or instinct; and, extrapolating from this hypothesis, that the discharge of accumulated sexual instinctual energy was fundamental for human behavior generally.

In all of Freud's (1895, 1900, 1923) models of motivation, the brain functions like a steam boiler that is constantly under excess pressure and needs to discharge continuously through thought or action the excess energy produced by the sexual instinct and by the (later postulated) aggressive instinct. In health, this excess energy is channeled productively in a culturally acceptable manner. In disease, the energy is either dammed up, giving rise to discomfort in feeling and thought, or channeled into activities that are counterproductive for the individual and/or lead one into conflict with what one has learned are the acceptable modes of instinctual discharge. Freud's valiant attempt at creating a mental machine survives to this day; but in spite of the tinkering that it has undergone in the last hundred years, it still does not run and never will. The problem is that Freud's model of the brain, or mental apparatus as he later called the motivational engine, has no explanatory value. It is only an analogy, and not an apt one at that, for it can be used to illustrate only neurotic psychopathology, and no other.* Freud knew this: he himself referred to the instinct theory as the "mythology" of psychoanalysis (1933, p. 95). His pessimism regarding the validity and usefulness of his explanatory theory—his *metapsychology*, as he called it—and his eventual retraction of its basic tenets (1940, pp. 162–64) arose from his knowledge that his attempt to use the

---

*My own work in exploring both the history and the present-day meaning of Freud's work has led me to publish some forty articles dealing with various facets of his theory. In this book, I will only use the conclusions at which I arrived without repeating the detailed arguments necessary to justify them; the interested reader will find these in the papers referred to.

laws of nineteenth-century physics and biology to explain mind by connecting it with the functions of the brain had not succeeded and could not be used to explain the clinical findings he continued to accumulate.

Today we are no longer caught in Freud's dilemma—that is, of having perfected a method of investigation that far outstripped the ability to explain what it was uncovering.

A Scientific Basis for Psychotherapy

Psychotherapy is about communication and failures of communication—the last column on Mr. Hudson's shirt-cardboards. Since on neither the cellular nor the interpersonal level can physics and chemistry explain the nature of information or how it is processed, psychotherapy had to wait for other sciences to catch up with Sigmund Freud. In the last forty years, advances in several fields— from within psychoanalysis and psychotherapy, from infant obser- vation, from research in perceptual, cognitive, and affective psy- chology, from neurobiology and scientific philosophy, as well as from such new sciences as cybernetics, systems theory, and infor- mation theory—have combined to make possible, for the first time, the construction of a theory that encompasses what is important for *human* development: a theory that can take into account the signifi- cance of how we think and how we interact. And, unlike what has gone before, it is a theory not simply based on retrospective specu- lation from the treatment situation.

We are now able to supplant Freud's evocative language with appropriate concepts drawn from the sciences that investigate the various aspects of communication. Thus, I replace Freud's idea— that the underlying motivation for all behavior is the discharge of *instinct*—with the striving for *order, competence,* and *self-esteem,* a predis- position which is already experimentally demonstrable in infancy; while Freud suggested that a *psychic energy* is responsible for the intensity of thought, I attribute that intensity to the force of infor- mation in the form of *affect, feeling, emotion,* or *empathy;* where Freud spoke of *psychic structure,* I talk about *feedback* and *pattern matching;* and instead of falling back on Freud's postulation of a *mental apparatus* composed of imaginary agencies like *ego* and *id,* I refer to the *decision-making* functions of the brain and to the *self system*—the latter being a concept that bridges a long-standing and counterproductive gap between psychology and biology. These new, and scientifically based, concepts are part of a unified, and unifying, theory of psychotherapy which both explains and transcends the vicissitudes and aberrations of any one person's development.

Twenty years ago at a research meeting of my analytic institute, I, only recently graduated, presented a paper outlining some of the discrepancies between Freud's clinical findings and his explanatory theory. I was taken aback when apparently taking my scholarly interest to be an attack on Freud—a senior member of the faculty sarcastically, and with an air of finality, commented that if I was dissatisfied with what Freud had to offer why did I not come up with something better? It seems that, just as at the beginning of my psychiatric training, I had once again inadvertently upset the establishment by challenging received wisdom.

Today my former teacher's challenge can be met. The building blocks for the construction of a valid, unifying, and useful explanatory theory for psychotherapy now lie all around us—one need only put them in place, and then demonstrate how such a theory may be profitably applied. That is what I intend to do in the chapters that follow.

1

The Goal of Psychotherapy: Self-Image and the Search for Competence

The Six Phases of Treatment: Al Gertz

On a cold, snowy winter day I found myself looking for a taxi. As is always the case when one is in a hurry, none was immediately at hand. After standing on a windy corner for what seemed to be an awfully long time, I was finally successful in flagging down an empty cab and gratefully plopped into the seat, giving the driver the address of my office.

DRIVER: Want I should take Michigan Avenue or the Outer Drive?
ME: Whatever way you think is faster.
DRIVER: [*In an angry voice*] Nothing's fast on a day like this. It's bad enough, when the weather's good. Damn street's ripped up from ass to appetite.

I felt somewhat anxious to find myself at the mercy of this rough, angry fellow, especially on a day when ice had made the roads dangerous enough. Checking the identification card on the back of the taxi's front seat, I was not at all reassured by the villainous passport photo displayed there purporting to be the likeness of one Al Gertz.

ME: I understand that. Just go whichever way you think is best.
DRIVER: You a doctor?
ME: Yes, I am.
DRIVER: I knew that when I saw you standing in front of the hospital. That's a fancy coat you got on. I figured only a doctor could afford something like what you're wearing.
ME: [*Still trying to be conciliatory and ignoring the anger and envy of his comment*] It's warm, but nothing helps much with the wind we have today.

There was a long silence as Al skillfully negotiated the slippery, crowded street. I now felt quite safe and began to admire his expertise: though an angry man, he really knew what he was doing.

DRIVER: You some kind of surgeon, maybe doing one of them high-price heart operations?

I felt that my attempt to mollify him had been unsuccessful—he was just bound and determined to put me on the defensive. Still, I had no wish to get into a verbal argument with him; he was doing a fine job, and I was prepared to be friendly. So I tried again.

ME: No, I'm not a surgeon. As a matter of fact, I was visiting a colleague of mine who just had an operation on his back.
DRIVER: Probably hurt himself skiing. . . . [*Pause*] I was laid up with a bum leg for three months, but not on no fancy vacation.
ME: Oh?
DRIVER: Vietnam. Shell fragment.
ME: Sorry to hear it. Is it all right now?

DRIVER: Good enough, I guess. Still bothers me when it's raining or after twelve hours in this buggy.

ME: I can imagine.

DRIVER: People look at you funny when you tell 'em you were in Nam—like you're some kind of dummy to have gotten caught in that mess. Bet you didn't have to go, Doc.

ME: Not that one I didn't.

DRIVER: You were in before?

ME: Korea, but I was luckier than you. The shooting had stopped by the time I got there.

DRIVER: You go to school on the G.I. Bill?

ME: No, I was a physician when I went in.

DRIVER: I ought to do something like that. Go to school, get good at something, so's I can kiss this fucking job good-bye— get some class, maybe be like you, Doc. Funny, huh? Well, anyway, d'you mind if I let you off here so's I don't have to go around and get caught in that mess on Wabash? Four-fifty, you owe me.

ME: Fine. Here you go [*handing over the money owed and a tip*]. You know, I don't know what you plan to do with your life, but as far as having class goes, you've got it!

DRIVER: Yeah? Wa'd you mean?

ME: You're a terrific driver. I never thought I'd make it here on time in this kind of weather, but you got me here faster than it takes when the streets are clear and without taking chances. That's class in my book.

DRIVER: [*With a big smile and a warm, friendly tone that had been nowhere in evidence before*] Well, thanks, Doc. Have a good day.

ME: You, too. Take care.

Not so many days later, I stepped into a cab outside my office building. As I gave the address to the driver, we recognized each other.

DRIVER: Hey Doc, how you doing?

ME: Fine, thanks, Al. Better weather today, thank God.

DRIVER: Yeah, I can do without the snow. Wish it'd warm up though.

ME: That makes two of us.

DRIVER: Funny I should see you just now, Doc. I was thinking of
        you last night.

ME: Oh?

DRIVER: Yeah, I was in this bar where I hang out, and they were
        starting to give me the business—you know, calling me a
        baby killer, 'cause I was in 'Nam. Egging me on to get into
        a fight, like they always do. But this time I thought, "Fuck
        'em, I don't have to crawl in the mud with these pigs. I
        didn't do nothing wrong. I was a good soldier and done my
        job, and I'm doing my job now, and I don't have to take
        shit from nobody." So's I just drunk my beer and left and
        went home. I was thinking of you and what you said. I
        mean, coming from somebody like you, I mean a guy don't
        forget that.

ME: I meant what I said. And you're absolutely right. Why
        bother with people who won't take the trouble to find out
        where you're coming from, what kind of a person you are,
        or what you stand for.

Obviously, this was not a clinical situation. Functioning as a
psychotherapist was the furthest thing from my mind when I first
encountered Al Gertz, but I think it fair to say that incidental to our
respective goals in coming together—his to earn a living, mine to get
to my office—something that deserves to be called psychotherapeutic took place in my interaction with him. By *psychotherapeutic* I mean that through our transaction Al got a picture of
himself different from the one he had had before; that is, he got a
new self-image, one that had a beneficial effect on his life, changing
his feelings about himself and his behavior with others.

This vignette contains the core of what dynamic psychotherapy
is all about. It is a person's self-image, or self-concept, that furnishes
both the potential and the limits of individual existence. Psychotherapy focuses on the aspect of a person's self-concept that is
either frustrating that potential or is leading the patient into an
inappropriate and counterproductive attempt to breach those limits,
and then tries to help the patient resolve those problems.

My encounter with Al Gertz illustrates what I think of as the six phases of psychotherapy: orientation, consternation, reorientation, collaboration, integration, and transformation.

Orientation, or sizing up a patient: What is that person's self-image like? What is his or her level of self-esteem? And upon what is that self-evaluation based?

Consternation, or recognition of disorientation: I thought I understood what was going on, but this doesn't make sense. Now I can't seem to understand why this person is functioning the way he does. What makes him behave this way? Why is he saying what he is saying?

Reorientation, or grasping the material from the patient's point of view: Oh, *that's* what it's all about! Now I think I know again what's going on. Let's check it out.

Collaboration, or therapist and patient communicating effectively with one another: Now that we're on the same track, how can I help him to use me to solve the problems that seem to be hindering him?

Integration, or what has transpired in the therapeutic dyad now becomes the patient's own: The patient now seems to understand both what is troubling him and something about how and why this came about.

Transformation, or a permanent change in the patient's manner of coping: In some significant respect the patient is no longer the same person as before and can, as a result, now deal differently and more effectively with what bothered him than when he first came for treatment.*

In the first, or orienting phase, the two participants in the transaction size each other up, and each comes to some preliminary conclusions about the other and their common situation. These can lead to a harmonious therapeutic "honeymoon," each satisfied with the other and working together as a team. But, inevitably, this blissful state is disrupted when the vulnerable, problematic aspects of the patient's personality become directly involved in the therapeutic process. Usually, neither patient nor therapist understands what is happening. Often the patient experiences mounting anxiety at that point, and, though unable yet to identify its source, reacts by faulting the therapist and/or the therapeutic process. Sometimes an ad-

---

*One important form of transformation is what Kohut (1971) has called transmuting internalization (see pages 143–44).

versarial feeling enters the relationship much sooner. That is what happened to Al and me: he was apparently all set to dislike me the minute he laid eyes on me; the way I dressed automatically meant, given the way he felt about himself, that I belonged to those who looked down on him.

What follows is consternation on the part of the therapist, who wonders whether a therapeutic relationship will be at all possible, or, if things have been going well, whether it can continue.

In retrospect, it seems clear that Al, in his anger about his life situation, was going to involve me in a self-fulfilling prophecy. By his gruff, challenging behavior, he implicitly invited me to respond in kind, to defend myself against his slurs by becoming angry and arrogant—indirectly confirming his self-image of a person who had failed to accomplish anything worthwhile and deserving of respect. I might, for example, have been provoked into saying, "What are you so hot under the collar for? If you want a coat like this, all you have to do is work for it—I did"; or, "Listen, pal, I didn't do anything to you except hail your cab. Just get me where I want to go in one piece, if that's O.K. with you"; or, "You want to be a doctor, go to medical school, then talk to me about the soft life I have"; and so on.

Instead, I made a decision—initially probably in the interest of my own safety, since the angrier Al got, the more likely was an accident on the hazardous ice-covered streets—not to rise to the bait; I would ignore the nastiness of his envious comments. He, however, would have none of it and mounted another attack on physicians and their life style as he imagined it to be.

My interaction with Al Gertz also illustrates how one's picture of oneself tends to shape one's experience of the world, literally determining what one sees and hears and what that information signifies. Without knowing me, Al had made up his mind that I was a successful person and would therefore naturally despise him. He reacted to his assumption by treating me immediately in an angry fashion, trying to turn the tables and make me ashamed of myself and my profession.

If the therapist's consternation does not result in an empathic break with the patient—that is, if the therapist continues to make an effort to hear the meaning of what the patient is trying to communicate—then there is usually a phase of reorientation during which the therapist gains empathic insight into what the patient seems to be trying to accomplish through particular behaviors and attitudes. (Empathy—what it encompasses and how empathic understanding may be attained—is discussed in chapter 6.) In this stage, the therapist is able to recognize that, whatever the nature of the struggle, it is taking place within the patient and not primarily between patient and therapist, the latter's presence and whatever he or she brings to the transaction providing an opportunity for *the patient* to play out in some form what he or she is impelled to do in order to maintain a shaky self-esteem.

With Al it was not what he said but what he did that marked the turning point in our relationship. Once I realized what an expert driver he was, I was no longer afraid for my life. I now saw him in a much more favorable light than he saw himself. I became more curious about his anger than offended by it: why was he so bitter? When he spoke of his war wound and the lack of respect for his sacrifice, I felt empathic with his plight: that is, I thought I could appreciate how he felt, having risked his life and suffered wounds in the service of his country only to find that, when he came home, instead of getting the kind of recognition that would have enhanced his self-image, he got the opposite message.

The therapist who is not concerned for his or her own self-esteem when working with an antagonistic patient can remain alert for the opportunity that usually presents itself somewhere along the line to bridge the gap that was either there initially or has come into being between them. I was able to draw closer to Al when I let him know that I, too, had been in uniform. Apparently deciding that I was not all that bad if I had been in the service, he stopped trying to make me feel guilty for being a physician and made a 180-degree turn by telling me how ashamed he felt for not having attained professional status himself. It was the pain of his own sense of worthlessness, accentuated by the contrasting picture he drew for himself of my life, that had heightened what seemed to be his chronically angry, resentful emotional set.

Reorientation, coming to understand what the patient is saying from the *patient's* point of view, restores harmony and leads to collaboration—patient and therapist working together to reach a therapeutic goal. Sooner or later this process permits the therapist to make interventions that lead to integration; to make interpretations, clarifications, or other empathically guided comments that either let the patient see himself or herself in a new light or set in motion the process that leads to that result. So, for example, I was able to tell Al that my picture of him, based on the evidence he had given me of his expertise, was very different from his own. I valued him for the job he did, not for the nature of his occupation, or for the amount of money he earned doing it. Al, having previously dropped his defensive anger and acknowledged that, far from despising me, I represented an ideal, had opened himself up and was implicitly asking to be understood and helped. Under these circumstances, the sincerity of my compliment brought about a dramatic change in him, and we parted with mutual good feelings.

That our exchange had had more than a transitory effect, that it had led to the final, consolidating phase of psychotherapy—that is, transformation—I learned a few days later when we chanced to meet again. To some extent, apparently as a result of the picture *I* had of him, *his* view of himself had changed sufficiently to enable him, at least on the occasion he recounted, to mobilize and maintain a self respecting attitude, rejecting the temptation to fall back into the familiar but counterproductive, shame-producing pattern that his tavern companions sought to provoke. Al was now able on the basis of his improved self-concept to make choices, to decide how he would behave under stress, rather than finding himself willy-nilly reacting violently when tempted to do so by others who knew of his vulnerability. Exercising such control, in turn, enhanced his self-esteem and will—I can only hope, since I have not seen him again—enable him to make decisions that will further his development and improve his self-image. This is the goal for all patients in psychotherapy.*

*I do not want to leave the impression that psychotherapy inevitably moves in lockstep according to the six steps of this schema. Once the treatment is finished, one can usually organize, in retrospect, its course along these lines; however, while therapy is proceeding, phases overlap, and the patient, when under stress, may well retreat to earlier positions. Indeed, in each session and/or group of sessions, therapist and patient may find themselves going through minicycles of the various steps of psychotherapy described here (chapter 8 provides an extensive clinical illustration of this process).

The Search for Competence

A patient some months into treatment with me reacted with anger when, as I had done with Al Gertz, I pointed out to him that his self-depreciation seemed to have no basis in fact. He felt ashamed, he said, that I was being nice to him only because I had to be. As far as he was concerned, he had come to me feeling lonely and miserable and had hired me essentially as a "paid friend"; and, like a prostitute with a customer, I had to give him what he needed, including a pretense of interest in and affection for him that he was sure I did not feel. Apart from this man's belief that he was unlikable, his comment raised an interesting issue. Is being "nice," or "loving," or "understanding," or "empathic," the essential ingredient that makes for positive changes in psychotherapy?

Once I understood what was going on with Al Gertz, I could be empathic with the desperation he communicated, and certainly would have felt remiss had I not tried to help him by conveying my appreciation for his skill. I suppose one could say that was a "nice" or a "loving" thing to do. However, had Al not, in fact, been an extremely competent taxi driver, our story would have had a very different outcome. What made a difference, and began the process of change, was not my understanding of Al's unhappy state, but my helping him to get pleasure from an achievement that he took for granted and thought of as detracting from rather than enhancing his stature.

True self-esteem, a genuine sense of one's self as worthy of nurture and protection, capable of growth and development, stems from the experience of competence, the experience of functioning appropriately. True, it can be fostered by the psychotherapist, who tries to remove obstacles to its development; but no one can give another the experience of competence: one must achieve that for oneself. Insincere or undeserved praise is at best a temporary sop to the ever present insecurity and increases the need for such reinforcement; if anything, it hinders growth and development. And so psychotherapy, like any other enterprise in the field of human development, both is based on and has as its goal helping another person to "do something" rather than "giving that person something." The psychotherapist is effective insofar as he or she has helped a person to be effective (see also Gedo 1988).

When patients, coming to see me for the first time, ask whether I have had experience in solving this or that problem that they have presented, I have sometimes startled them by saying that I have never solved any problems for anybody. I hasten to add that no one can truly solve another person's problems; solutions that might make sense to me in a particular quandary, or solutions that have made sense to others of my patients with similar difficulties, are not likely to address the nuances of another individual's situation. My job, as I see it, is to enable a patient to solve his or her own problems in the always idiosyncratic context of that person's life. In this way, I set the stage for psychotherapy as a search for competence in the patient and not a search for answers from me. The search for competence is the basic motivation for behavior (a view shared by such eminent researchers as the psychologist Robert W. White [1959] and the psychoanalyst George S. Klein [1976]), and is of fundamental importance for the theory of psychotherapy I advance in these pages. In keeping with the evolutionary imperative that each organism must both protect itself and preserve its species, in human beings competence manifests itself both in those adaptive and creative skills that further the well-being of the individual, and in the psychosexual sphere of development that prepares us during infancy and childhood for puberty and procreation (Freud 1905, 1915a).

Competence, as I use the word, manifests itself in different ways. In the behavioral sphere, it takes the form of exercising control over external events. In respect to brain functioning and the neurophysiological substrate of behavior, competence is achieved as a result of the brain's capacity to establish order among the disparate stimuli that continuously bombard the senses (see chapter 3). On the level of introspection and reflection, competence is experienced as self-esteem. In the sociological universe of discourse, competence consists of healthy adaptation; and in the world of art and esthetics, competence is akin to harmony.

In psychotherapy, competence is achieved during the final phase, that of transformation. When patients ask how they, or I, will know when they are ready to terminate treatment, I answer, "When you are competent. That is, when you are able to do for yourself what till then you have needed me to do with and/or for you—at that point it will make sense for us to think of bringing your therapy to an end."

Over the years, my search for clues to a theory of psychotherapy that is useful, and whose components can be validated by experience or experiment, has made me wary of words. Too often, terms purporting to encapsulate explanations lead nowhere but in a circle, begging the questions they are meant to answer; *mind* and *ego* are prime examples of the genre. I have come to the conclusion, made possible by the phenomenal explosion of knowledge in the field of infant research, that I would not consider seriously any explanation for mental functions whose roots cannot be inferred from observation or experimentation in the preverbal stages of life—those first two years or so that therapists agree are the most important ones for character formation. Thus, I was delighted to find that the quest for competence is experimentally demonstrable very early in infancy. In 1969, the psychologist and infant researcher Hanuš Papoušek, using milk as a reward, conditioned preverbal, four-month-old infants to turn their heads to the left when a bell sounded and to the right when a buzzer rang. The infants mastered this task readily— not surprisingly, for it was already well known that even very young babies can learn to carry out complex behavior patterns. What Papoušek found noteworthy was that these infants continued to take obvious pleasure in appropriately carrying out the assigned task long after they were satiated and had lost interest in the milk that awaited them when they performed correctly. Papoušek concluded: "So it looked as if some motivation other than hunger was involved—some demand to respond correctly or to solve a problem. And the congruence between the infant's plan or expectation and the real events seemed to please him . . . this was the basic observation" (1969, p. 255).

In order to test this hypothesis further, Papoušek designed a different experiment. Every time an infant's head happened to be turned spontaneously in accordance with a predetermined pattern—for example, two consecutive turns to the left to at least thirty degrees—a reinforcing reward, consisting of colored lights flashing for five seconds, was given. Since the lights were visible only in the midline, an infant had to turn his or her head back to the midline to see them. Soon these four-month-old babies learned what Papoušek called "switching-on movements": namely, moving the head to the side as required and then quickly returning it to the midline so as to see the display of colored lights. These babies, without any coaching, were able to figure out, learn, and repeat increasingly complex configurations—for example, alternating double turns to the left and then to the right—in order to get the lights to turn on. As the colored lights became familiar, the infants lost interest in watching them; although they did not turn their heads to the midline to watch the display they had called forth, they cheerfully and with obvious indication of pleasure continued to go through the movements necessary to turn on the lights. Here again, as Papoušek says, is the question of "what is the actual reward in these experiments: whether it is the blinking lights themselves or the congruence between expectation and its confirmation" (1969, p. 259). These, as well as T. G. R. Bower's (1977) experiment with an eight-week-old blind infant's response to an auditory mobile, discussed by Francis Broucek (1979), demonstrate that it is basically rewarding for the infant actively to establish control over events in the external world.

My emphasis here on the search for competence as fundamental for behavior marks a definite departure from a concept that underlies much of the literature in dynamic psychiatry: namely, Freud's theory that all behavior has as its goal the pleasure that attaches to the discharge of quanta of energy generated by a sexual or an aggressive instinct. That there is a more scientific explanation than the instinct theory, which Freud himself called the mythology of psychoanalysis (1933, p. 95), is buttressed by these experiments which demonstrate that even in infancy the search for competence is the prime motivator for behavior, and that its attainment is the basic source of pleasure. (See also DeCasper and Fifer 1980; Lewis and Goldberg 1969; and Watson 1985.)

Combining this fundamental concept of development with what can be learned from the manner in which a patient behaves and talks during the initial, exploratory visit(s) provides the therapist with a key to planning the most effective way of intervening in any given case.

2

The Developmental Spiral

A S ONE GROWS OLDER and matures cognitively and affectively—that is, in thought and in feeling—and as behavior becomes more complex, one continues throughout life to search for competence, much as in infancy. One makes a decision to do one thing rather than another, a decision that leads to behavior, which, if it is competent—that is, brings to closure the intention one had in making the decision—gives rise to a feeling of well-being or self-esteem. This experience then influences future decisions made in similar or related situations, and there is a progressive spiraling of development (see figure 2.1). Optimally, development continues in uninterrupted, helical fashion toward maturity, integrating innate capacities with environmental opportunities and reaching ever higher levels of competence and satisfaction. In reality, of course, things never go that smoothly. Development in one area may proceed relatively unimpeded, while in another it may be arrested, diverted, distorted, or become subject to conflict of one sort or another. The hope is that life's experiences and further maturation will ameliorate or compensate for such difficulties, but often this does not happen. The negative results of skewed developmental progress may become serious

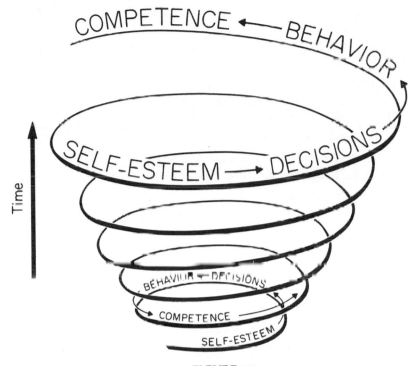

FIGURE 2.1
The Developmental Spiral

enough to impair significantly an individual's search for competence and self-esteem. A person in such psychological difficulties may then seek professional help.

Psychotherapy, as I see it, is applied developmental psychology. The therapist uses his or her knowledge of normal development to reach some conclusions about the reasons for a patient's malfunctioning and how one may enter the developmental spiral either to foster or to reinstitute a more productive, or at least less destructive, developmental process. From the clinician's viewpoint, the model of the developmental spiral provides such a framework for gauging therapeutic interventions. In an ongoing therapy, the material presented by a patient, both verbal and nonverbal, gives the therapist, at any given point in the session, information about how the patient attempts to achieve competence and protect his or her self-esteem, and about how and why the patient may have failed in efforts to do so. The therapist can then evaluate the situation and decide where the developmental spiral can best be entered so as ultimately to help the patient to repair the damage and, if possible, to permit development to resume.

In Al Gertz's case, for example, my voicing admiration for his skill was geared to entering the developmental spiral at the point of self-esteem and directly strengthening his sense of self-worth. Patients may relate to the therapist in other ways that require him or her to enter the developmental spiral by first addressing either decision making or behavior. In the following case, the behavioral segment offered the best entry.

Restoring Coping Skills: Byron Osgood

Dr. Byron Osgood was sixty-three-years old when he came for consultation. A married man, he was an orthopedic surgeon who, in addition to a successful practice, owned and operated a small hospital in a nearby town.

Dr. Osgood had been referred by his internist because he had complained for several months of increasing fatigue, loss of interest in both work and recreation, poor concentration, hypochondriacal preoccupations, anxiety, and early morning insomnia. His physical condition was reported as normal. The sedatives and tranquilizers prescribed for him had not helped him significantly; and, in spite of some mild resistance from the patient, his physician had decided that it was time to get a psychiatrist's opinion.

Dr. Osgood was tall, somewhat portly, and elegantly attired. His bearing and demeanor, in spite of a helpless, confused, and sad facial expression, signaled that he was still a person to be reckoned with. He became increasingly agitated during the interview, often running his manicured hands through a full head of white hair.

I asked him to tell me about himself, his complaints, and how he thought I might be able to help him. Dr. Osgood described himself as having been in the past a basically happy man, not a thinker but a doer. He had always congratulated himself that in his profession he would never have to retire. He liked his work, had a good relationship with his wife, and was pleased with the way his three, now adult, children had turned out. He and his wife enjoyed traveling. He had no other hobbies. "My work is my hobby," he said.

I was able to elicit no recent personal or environmental events or long-term problems that might have triggered the patient's present reaction. Although he complained that he could not think well any more, he showed no signs of thought disorder or of organic brain damage. I could elicit no evidence of past suicidal intent or present suicidal ideation (Basch 1980, pp. 128–30).

Over the three months prior to coming to see me, the patient had found himself less and less able to work. He had begun to doubt his ability, although intellectually he realized that this was a ridiculous fear. Realizing he had become too preoccupied with himself, he had given up all patient contact a month before coming to see me. He and his wife had tried going on vacation, thinking perhaps he was overworked and needed a rest; but being away from home only made him more agitated, and they interrupted their trip and returned home. He was now, uncharacteristically, spending most of his time in front of a television set that he was not really watching.

DR. OSGOOD: Now that you've heard my story, is there any other medication you can give me?

THERAPIST: Yes. Your symptoms indicate that you are suffering from a depressive episode, and there are a number of antidepressants that we can try to see their effects on you.

DR. OSGOOD: What about what I've been taking?

THERAPIST: Let's discontinue that. The anxiety and sleeplessness you're experiencing are secondary to the depression, and as that is alleviated, the other symptoms will respond also.

DR. OSGOOD: So you think the antidepressants will cure me?

THERAPIST: No, that they won't do.

DR. OSGOOD: They won't?

THERAPIST: No, they won't.

DR. OSGOOD: Why take them then?

THERAPIST: If and when they are effective, they'll make it easier for you to cooperate with me in doing what you have to do to get better.

DR. OSGOOD: What's that?

THERAPIST: You have to learn to resume your normal life. To become busy and productive again. To help people as you used to do instead of moping around the house.

DR. OSGOOD: I want to do that more than anything. But I can't! That's why I came to you. I want to resume my practice and get hold of the hospital again. [*In a pathetic voice, almost childlike*] It's a terrible mess there. As soon as I'm better, I will do everything again, I promise.

THERAPIST: Dr. Osgood, you're putting the cart before the horse. What will make you better is making the effort, with whatever help I can give you, to gradually resume your duties. Sitting around at home hasn't helped any, has it?

DR. OSGOOD: I can't possibly be responsible for patients in my condition.

THERAPIST: Of course not, but that's the endpoint of your recovery, not the beginning. There must be a lot of other things that have gone to hell in a handbasket in the last three months that you need to take care of. You said the hospital was a mess.

DR. OSGOOD: Oh, yes. There's so much to do, but I just haven't been up to doing it. My people are very understanding and are trying to carry on, but they can't do some things without me.

THERAPIST: For example? What needs to be done now?

DR. OSGOOD: There are certain checks only I can sign. There are supplies that are needed that can't be ordered without my O.K. My secretary and bookkeeper offered to bring the stuff to me for my signature, but I'm just not up to it. I don't want anyone seeing me like this.

THERAPIST: Seeing you like what?

DR. OSGOOD: Sitting around the house in my bathrobe. Some days I don't even shower or shave.

THERAPIST: Well, you look very well put together today. How
               long will it take to get home?
DR. OSGOOD: Not long, I'll be home right after lunch.
THERAPIST: I thought your home was at least three hours away?
DR. OSGOOD: We fly. My oldest son piloted me up here today.
THERAPIST: Well, that's fine. You look very professional now, and
               you'll have a chance on the way back home to stop at
               the hospital and take care of some of those urgent
               matters that you mentioned. Better call them and tell
               them to get everything ready for you.
DR. OSGOOD: Well, I don't know——
THERAPIST: I do. I've seen dozens of patients with your illness. I
               know you feel that, because you are suffering it, your
               condition must be about as bad as anything can get.
               However, I assure you that, as these illnesses go, it is
               relatively mild and will respond to proper manage-
               ment, provided you can use what willpower you have
               left to cooperate with me. You're lucky we now have
               pills to help you along. Not so many years ago, pa-
               tients like yourself also had to do just what I'm asking
               you to do in order to get better, but there was no
               medication that addressed the underlying chemical
               problem that is probably responsible for this type of
               depression.
DR. OSGOOD: Couldn't I wait till the medication helps a little and
               then go to the hospital?
THERAPIST: I can't force you to do anything, but I think it would
               be a bad idea to wait. First of all, we don't know if this
               particular antidepressant will be the one to do the job.
               Even if it is, it may not be effective for a while. And
               no pills will give you back the confidence that you lost
               sitting around worrying and sinking into this negativ-
               istic attitude. So let's get moving today; that'll give
               you a head start on your recovery. I won't ask you to
               do anything beyond your capacity. Today just go sign
               those checks and requisitions. As you said, it's only a
               formality. Then you may go home.
                    The only additional thing I'll ask you to do is to be

dressed during the waking hours, not necessarily in a suit, but in clean, presentable clothes. I won't be able to see you again until the day after tomorrow, but I want you to call me at this number tonight at eight o'clock and let me know what happened.

DR. OSGOOD: Well, I guess I have to do what you say. It would be foolish not to take your advice—you're the expert.

THERAPIST: I am as confident as I can be that, with your cooperation, we can get an excellent result.

That night I received a call from Dr. Osgood, who complained that, though he did what I asked him, he was very anxious throughout. However, in spite of his protest, his voice already sounded a bit firmer and brighter than it had. I praised him for his effort and then asked what he was wearing. Slacks and a sportshirt, he said. I praised him for that. I inquired about his dinner, what he had eaten, what he was planning to do the rest of the evening. He told me that his second son had brought his children over to visit their grandparents.

Dr. Osgood wanted to know if he should go back to the hospital tomorrow. Under no circumstances, I told him. There was to be no going back to work until I saw him. Why did he want to go back anyway? Well, there was other paperwork that had to be tended to, and sooner or later he would have to do it. "All right," I said. "We'll talk about it when I see you. Tomorrow, remember to get dressed and cleaned up, and take a walk in the morning and in the afternoon."

Had I let Dr. Osgood go back to his hospital when he was just beginning to make a recovery, it would have burdened him with too much too soon. The depressed patient should have the experience of finding that he or she can still function successfully—a task requiring that what the patient undertakes be both limited and well within the range of his or her reduced capability. Dr. Osgood was not yet in any condition to determine which of the many and complex tasks that his work required he was capable of assuming. Trying to make such decisions would have been overstimulating and anxiety provoking, and would have led him to retreat further into his depression. For the time being, I had to make those decisions for him. Furthermore, and very important, my taking temporary control over his activities gave him the necessary sense of being guided and cared for by a benign, reliable, quasi-parental authority. This reassurance would have been undermined had I agreed to let him go back to his place of work to fend for himself without my close and interested supervision of his activities.

The antidepressant proved to be beneficial, and he experienced no significant side effects. I began to increase his workload. In sessions with him, I reviewed his past life and achievements and found much about which I could be encouraging, but uncovered no hidden psychological precipitants for his depression. In four weeks he was back at work and contemplating doing surgery once more. I saw him weekly for the next few months, then bimonthly; and now he checks with me once a year or so. After continuing medication for about one year, he asked if it could be reduced gradually. We agreed to try, and he encountered no difficulties. He has been without medication for the past two years and has had no recurrence of depressive symptoms.

When Dr. Osgood came to me, he could no longer implement and use to advantage the adaptive measures he had developed to define both himself and his relationship to the world. No longer able to engage in activities that, based on his past experience, were in his best interest and on which his self-esteem depended, he was becoming increasingly helpless. I stepped in at the behavioral level of the developmental spiral, very much as a parent temporarily takes over when a child is overwhelmed by some real or imagined demand: "I'm not going to school any more!" "Really, how come?" "I'll never learn that stuff, and the teacher doesn't like me, and I have no friends. I hate it!" "What happened today, dear?" "I don't know how to do those division problems, and the teacher never explains anything right, and then she gave us so many problems I can never finish them, and nobody likes me anyway, and I had to wear this yucky dress." "You've got some homework to do?" "That's what I said, no one ever listens to me!" "Well, why don't we sit down together right now and take a look at the first problem. I know how to do long division and I can show you how it's done. Then, after supper, when you know how to do it too, we'll do the rest." "Can't we wait till after dinner?" "It's going to be a while anyway before dinner is ready, so we might as well do a little bit now. Once you see you can get the hang of it, I think you'll feel a lot better and then we'll eat."

Entering the developmental spiral through the behavioral segment makes sense when a patient with a history of satisfactory functioning is being overloaded with stress: that is, the patient's coping capacity has been overwhelmed by some demand. In Dr. Osgood's case, it happened to be a relative overload, namely, nothing more was required of him than what he had been doing every day to maintain reasonable self-esteem, but the conviction of helplessness—which is often an indicator of depression—made this too much of a burden for him to carry. He had lost the ability to function effectively; his self-esteem had suffered in the process; and that, in turn, diminished his confidence in his decision-making capacity and impaired his ability to halt his downward slide—the developmental spiral moving in reverse.

Fortunately for Dr. Osgood, his was an uncomplicated case. The sense of helplessness was of comparatively short duration, and withdrawal had not yet become a way of adapting to stress on which the patient relied; nor was his helplessness rooted in a long-standing character problem, as demonstrated by the fact that his previous psychological adjustment had been both satisfactory and satisfying. Most important, he had the readiness for an immediate positive or idealizing transference: that is, he had available in his regressive state the hopeful attitude of a child who is able to look with trust to the powerful parent for assistance and relief (Kohut 1971). His plaintive voice, his looking to me for guidance, and his willingness, in spite of superficial objections, both to acknowledge me as an expert and to follow my suggestions, demonstrated his readiness, like a distressed youngster, to find and listen to an effective parental figure who would take over and guide him, as I did. In keeping with what I said previously (pages 24–25), although I took an active role in the treatment I did not solve Dr. Osgood's problem for him but, rather, showed him what he had to do to regain his sense of competence.*

---

*I do not want to be misunderstood as advocating the technique used in Dr. Osgood's case as one to be employed in all cases of depression; nor is it applicable to all patients who feel unable to cope with life's demands. This clinical vignette is meant only to illustrate how, when it is appropriate to do so, one may institute psychotherapy by entering the developmental spiral through the behavioral segment. (See chapter 5 for a detailed discussion of depression and its treatment.)

Fostering Decision Making: Alice Senoj

While both Al Gertz and Dr. Osgood were open to letting themselves be helped psychotherapeutically, by no means is every patient ready to permit the therapist to intervene so quickly and
effectively. Mrs. Alice Senoj, in whose case the therapist was eventually able to enter the developmental spiral through the decision-
making segment, was a patient who could not be so readily helped.

Study after study has demonstrated that, in 60 percent to 80
percent of cases, the somatic complaint that initially leads a person
to consult a physician has a psychological origin. It is at the primary
level of medical intervention that the application of even minimal
psychotherapeutic skills can prevent a great deal of unnecessary
suffering for patients, to say nothing of the money and time saved
by eliminating the futile search for physiological answers to psychologically generated problems. Thus, as an example of clinical
work, the case of Mrs. Senoj has the additional advantage of taking
place in the office not of a professional psychotherapist but of a
family doctor.

Her physician consulted me about Mrs. Senoj, a forty-six-year-
old woman who had come to him complaining of daily headaches
that did not respond to the usual over-the-counter analgesics. After
a thorough general medical examination, there occurred the following interchange, which I report essentially as it was told to me, but
with interpolations for my own comments:

DOCTOR: Well, Mrs. Senoj, my examination shows that you are
basically in good physical health and that those headaches
you're having are probably due to some stress or tension.

The physician who avoids saying, "There's nothing wrong with
you" when physical examination and ancillary tests do not reveal
a somatic source for a patient's complaint, but, rather, indicates that
the pain is legitimate and that there must be another explanation for
the difficulty—implicitly inviting the patient to talk about that—
will usually hear that the patient is not only aware that his or her

aches and pains are due to psychological stress but also what may be their most likely source.

MRS. SENOJ: Wouldn't you be tense, Doctor, if your fourteen-year-old boy came home drunk most every night of the week?

If Mrs. Senoj knew, or thought she knew, the source of her headaches, why had she not spoken of it initially? We grow up believing that what is tangible and visible is real, while what is "only in the head" is not. Since they "are nothing" or "don't count," the prohibitions against acknowledging one's psychologically caused problems are so strong that in all probability, when this patient came to the doctor, she literally did not know what she knew about herself: that is, she did not have the insight into her difficulties available to her until the physician, by his attitude, gave her the opportunity to speak about and, in the process, become aware of them. Even then Mrs. Senoj responded aggressively, as if the rejection she expected for suffering from psychological problems had already come to pass: that is, she answered with a challenging question, as if her answer needed a defense.

This cultural prohibition against acknowledging emotional problems may make it necessary for the physician actively to invite the patient's confidence. For example, just asking a diabetic with an unexplained high blood sugar, "Anything else you want to tell me?" or a perfunctory, "Any problems, worries, you know?" will usually produce no response, while the same patient will probably unburden himself or herself in response to a face-saving statement: "Many of my patients find that their sugar goes out of control when they are faced with aggravation or upset. Have you perhaps been having a difficult time at home, at work, or in some other aspect of your life?"

DOCTOR: Yes, Mrs. Senoj, that sort of problem with your son could certainly bring about your headaches. Let's see now, you said your headaches began about two months ago. . . .

Here the physician demonstrated excellent technique, answering what the patient meant to ask or should have asked, rather than the actual question. In order to deal effectively with patients, one must first learn alternate ways of handling their questions: that it is not always necessary to answer a patient's question directly; or, as in the case of this doctor, that one need not answer the question as it is asked. Above all, unless it is clearly meant that way, the physician should ignore and not take personally any implicit challenge, insult, complaint, or sarcasm in a distressed patient's response. Mrs. Senoj's "Wouldn't you be tense, Doctor . . . ?" is typical. However, instead of taking umbrage at her tone or attempting to answer it on the personal level for which her question seemed to call, the physician correctly addressed her real concern: "Given my problems, I don't have to be ashamed of coming to you for help, do I, Doctor?" The physician's acceptance of her symptoms as legitimate and his wanting to hear more about them gave the patient the freedom to go further, letting herself be guided by his attempt to establish a possible connection between the onset of her headaches and her son's drinking.

(I often use this case in teaching medical students. I pause in reading the dialogue at those points where the doctor is about to speak, and ask the various participants to put themselves in the place of the physician and say what they think would be most effective and why. Once the students realize that there is no "right" answer, and that all they are being asked to do is to begin to practice and develop their respective capacities for thinking and speaking psychotherapeutically, a lively discussion usually ensues, and the students realize that they can come up with comments that are essentially as, or even more appropriate than, those made by Mrs. Senoj's physician. The student's sense of achievement is akin to that experienced when he or she first has success in tying a surgical knot, or hearing a heart murmur, and is of similar importance. Once one knows one can perform the first step in mastering a skill, one has much less fear of taking the second. This classroom experience is clearly relevant to the whole issue of competence and self-esteem.)

MRS. SENOJ: That's when Brian started drinking—at least that's when I got to know about it. Fourteen years old, and

he's already like his father. At least his father only
drinks on the weekends when he's off of work. This
boy will never get through high school the way he's
going. Up every night with these bums he calls his
friends, and then in the morning he's got a hangover
and can't get to class before lunchtime. What's wrong
with a person like that, Doctor? What gets into their
minds that they behave like that?

DOCTOR: That varies, Mrs. Senoj, but in many cases a decision
to drink, like any other decision that people make, is
seen at the moment as a way to solve some problem.

In this segment of the interchange, the patient has once again
given important information regarding her family setting, only to
end up with one of those impossible questions that, had he taken
it at face value, would have made the doctor uncomfortable, eva-
sive, and/or angry as he tried to come up with an answer that would
not leave him looking foolish. Instead, he used the opportunity to
introduce the patient to a concept that has been basic for psychotherapy ever since Freud first discovered it in work with psychoneurotic patients: namely, that unlike physical diseases, psychological
illnesses are action patterns that serve a purpose; and psychological
symptoms, no matter how bizarre, make good sense once understood in that frame of reference. What one presents as one's complaint or "problem" is the outcome of decisions made in an attempt
to deal with a situation beyond the control of available coping
mechanisms. It is for this reason that psychological symptoms, no
matter how self-defeating or destructive they may be for the sufferer, are not amenable to resolution by the dictates of common
sense and, in spite of the best efforts of the patient, usually cannot
be conquered unaided. It is as if the psychological symptom that the
patient presents for examination is not the broken leg but the
crutch, and—not surprisingly—he or she will not give it up until
there is some certainty of being able to function safely without it.
Here the doctor was beginning to convey to Mrs. Senoj that, however understandable her distress about her son's drinking, it is only
a symptom and not the primary concern. It is the problem behind
the problem, so to speak, which has to be dealt with—on the as-

sumption that the need to resort to alcohol will no longer be present when whatever necessitated her son's pathological attempt at resolution of his difficulties is either sufficiently resolved or can be dealt with in less problematic ways.

MRS. SENOJ: If he's got a problem, why doesn't he come to me? I'm his mother. I would do anything to help him. I don't know what's the matter with kids these days. We didn't behave like that.

Her son's drinking seemed to be an affront to Mrs. Senoj's self-esteem: she was afraid that it was, or would be seen as, a negative reflection on her as a mother. She tried to persuade the doctor and perhaps herself that she was not to blame, she had always been ready to help her boy. Could the times be responsible for his troubles?

DOCTOR: Has he come to you with his problems in the past, or to his father?

Neither agreeing nor disagreeing with Mrs. Senoj's face-saving maneuver, the physician uses the opportunity to question her about the manner in which problems have usually been dealt with in the family. By bringing the boy's father into the discussion, the physician indirectly acknowledges that she is, after all, not the only one involved in the boy's upbringing, anticipating her fear that she will be made to carry the burden for her son's difficulties.

What difference does it make whether the boy came to his parents with his problems in the past? One reason psychotherapists are interested in the past is that—just as a cardiologist wants to see a patient's old electrocardiograms, and a radiologist, the previous chest films—the patient's psychological history, like the physical history, provides a baseline with which the present situation can be compared, and it has implications for disposition, prognosis, and therapeutic technique.

MRS. SENOJ: Well, not really. His father doesn't talk much. He is moody. Like you say, he solves his problems with beer, and there isn't much talking when you're either boozed

up or asleep when you're home. I haven't really talked
much with Brian either. Sometimes I don't think I
know that boy at all. The one he used to talk to is his
older sister, but she got married and moved away.

Mrs. Senoj responded to the doctor's continued willingness to
listen to her without placing blame by revealing the family dynamics underlying the present difficulties in an increasingly open fashion, all of which helped to put the situation into perspective. Also,
the fact that she was adopting the physician's viewpoint and using
his words—psychological symptoms are attempts at problem solving—indicated to the therapist that what he was saying was having
an effect.

DOCTOR: How long ago did his sister get married?

Choosing to ignore the opportunity to learn more about the father, the doctor tested his hunch that Brian's resort to alcohol was
linked to the departure of the person in his family in whom he could
confide.

MRS. SENOJ: [*Resentfully*] In August, four months ago. That's why
he's so unhappy. I know that. But it's unnatural. I'm his
mother. He should come to *me* with his problems and
leave his sister to make a life of her own. I talked to her
about Brian, and she said let him move in with her and
Phil. She says he'd be O.K. with her, and Phil don't
mind, but I don't know if that's right. What do you
think, Doctor?

Psychotherapists learn to expect that, as things get clearer, they
also get more complex. Mrs. Senoj's statement does seem to confirm
the idea that her distress is, at least in great part, not related to her
son's drinking per se, but to the blow that this gives to her self-
esteem. However she may have rationalized the only too obvious
problems within her family in past years, she could no longer avoid
them when it became painfully clear to her that her son might do
better if he lived with his married sister rather than with her.

From a therapist's viewpoint, there was another shift in the situation. After it turned out that Mrs. Senoj's headaches could well be related to her son's drinking, the boy, though not present, had become the focus for concern. Now the pendulum had swung back to her. If Brian was to be helped, his mother's low self-esteem had first to be addressed. At this point, Mrs. Senoj needed to maintain the fiction that Brian's drinking was an isolated problem. Would it be possible to help her to see that the issue was not to establish who was to blame, but to understand what had gone wrong in the family interrelationship and what could still be done to ease the tension?

DOCTOR: Things haven't turned out the way you hoped, have they?

Again, correctly—rather than presuming to decide for the patient what she should do, even though she invited his opinion— the physician called attention to the underlying disappointment conveyed through Mrs. Senoj's complaint.

MRS. SENOJ: They sure haven't. I've had to be mother and father to those children, and now they can't wait to leave. It isn't fair.

Her response indicated not only concern about the possibility of her son leaving the parental home, but also a hint that she saw her daughter's marriage as a way of escaping from her and/or the family.

DOCTOR: This is a very complicated situation. Now that you've told me about it, I'm not surprised that you have tension headaches.
MRS. SENOJ: But what should I do, Doctor?
DOCTOR: As I said, it's complex, and all I'm sure about is that there are no simple answers or solutions. The way you describe it, Brian's drinking is the tip of an iceberg that involves the relationship between you and your husband; your husband's excessive drinking; Brian's relationship to you, to your husband, and to his sister; your relationship to your daughter; and—for all you and I

know—other aspects of the family situation that haven't been mentioned yet. Frankly, Mrs. Senoj, this is not my field, and I wonder whether it might not be better to turn to an expert in matters like this to evaluate what needs to be done.

The physician, feeling that he had reached the limits of his expertise, phrased the referral excellently. Too often patients are made to feel that being sent for psychiatric help is an admission of failure on the part of both patient and physician. Here the doctor reviewed and summarized his findings in such a way that the next logical and positive step would be to consult with an expert. In other words, Mrs. Senoj was not being "sent away," dismissed as unworthy and troublesome. On the contrary, the work with the doctor was successful insofar as it had uncovered the definitive problem, one that now required specialized attention.

MRS. SENOJ: I don't want to go to anybody else. Can't you help me? I trust you. You're my doctor. I'm not going to anybody else!

Yet, as happens, though the referral was made appropriately, the patient refused to accept it.

DOCTOR: Do *you* have any idea of how I might be able to help?

Instead of arguing with Mrs. Senoj, getting irritated, throwing up his hands, or dismissing her when she did not take his advice, the doctor wisely inquired whether she perhaps had a suggestion about what might be done. In psychotherapy the emphasis should be on what the patient is experiencing, rather than on dogmatically prescribing what he or she should or should not be doing.

MRS. SENOJ: You're the doctor.
DOCTOR: Yes, I'm the doctor you came to because of your headaches. Now we have established that in all probability those headaches have an emotional basis—namely, you're upset about your son's drinking. It also looks as

if behind your son's behavior a whole set of problems are begging for attention. My recommendation is that a specialist in these matters be consulted. At least at this point you have decided not to do that. I really don't have any other plan, and I'm seriously interested in hearing from you whether you do.

MRS. SENOJ: I never thought of it that way. I guess maybe there's nothing anybody can do.

DOCTOR: I wouldn't be surprised if that is what Brian thought when he started drinking—there's nothing anybody can do, so why not drink and forget, for a while at least.

MRS. SENOJ: But he's got his whole life ahead of him. He shouldn't think that way.

DOCTOR: I agree with you, but how can we help him? How can we prevent him from throwing his life away?

MRS. SENOJ: Maybe if you talk to him. Maybe he could tell you what's wrong. He won't tell me. He just says, "Throw me out if you want to, but just leave me alone."

DOCTOR: Well, I'm by no means ruling out the need for specialized help in the long run, but for the moment, if you want me to, I'll talk to Brian and see what light he can shed on the situation.

Thus Mrs. Senoj came up with a suggestion that seemed to have possibilities.

MRS. SENOJ: How do I get him to come to see you? Should I just tell him he's due for a checkup or something?

DOCTOR: No, I think it would be much better if you told him straight out that you know that his drinking is a sign of some deep unhappiness, and that because it is often difficult for a boy his age to speak freely to his parents, it might be a good idea to talk to a professional like myself who is interested in helping him and wants to hear his side of the story.

Whether at the beginning, middle, or end, trickery and evasiveness have no place in psychotherapy. One cannot hope to persuade a patient that absolute truthfulness is the quickest way to achieve results when he or she has been brought to therapy through a subterfuge.

MRS. SENOJ: And what if he won't come?

DOCTOR: Brian's behavior is a cry for help. He can't seem to discuss his unhappiness directly with you or his father but, instead, behaves in a way that shows there is something troubling him. And, sure enough, here you are, trying to figure out what's wrong and what can be done for him. I doubt very much whether he'll turn down the chance to be heard. But before you talk to him, you have to be convinced that you really want him to have outside help, and that your understandable resentment that he doesn't turn to you does not stand in the way of your wholeheartedly recommending that he come to see me.

Here the doctor, by bringing Mrs. Senoj's ambivalence into the open, tried to deal with her continued resistance regarding a psychotherapeutic approach to her son's problems.

MRS. SENOJ: [*Getting up from her chair and starting to move toward the door*] Maybe I better talk to his sister first. She knows what works with him.

DOCTOR: I think that might be a good idea. Let me know what happens so we can talk further about it then. Good-bye, Mrs. Senoj.

MRS. SENOJ: Good-bye, Doctor. Do you think we got anywhere?

DOCTOR: Let's see what you and your daughter come up with. Be sure to let me know. Good-bye, Mrs. Senoj.

As she indicated by moving toward the door, the patient had come to a closure acceptable to her. Further discussion at this point would have served no purpose, but the doctor had made clear to her that he was interested in continuing to work with her if she chose.

When Mrs. Senoj's physician first called me about his interchange with her a few days after it took place, he was upset with himself and disappointed with the outcome. He thought that perhaps he should have done or said something else to persuade her to induce Brian to enter individual or family therapy. I, on the other hand, thought that he had done a good job and achieved a perfectly acceptable psychotherapeutic result: he had engaged the therapeutic process and the developmental spiral at the decision-making level.

When Mrs. Senoj left the office, the problem underlying her somatic symptom had been identified, and she had come to what was for her a reasonable decision about what she might try to do to begin to alleviate or resolve it. She thus left prepared actively to engage the problem that confronted her rather than continuing to avoid it through somatic displacement.

I suggested to her physician that, instead of leaving it up to her to call or not call him, he should telephone her if she had not contacted him within a week. By showing an interest in the situation, he could better monitor what was happening and either buttress Mrs. Senoj's self-esteem by supporting her efforts to help her son, though this meant she had to face her own sense of failure as a mother; or perhaps exercise some influence if the family could not help Brian to deal with his difficulties in a less self-destructive way.

The only problematic note in the transaction between Mrs. Senoj and her physician occurred at the end of the session. Then, having issued a behavioral prescription to see a therapist, he was sufficiently chagrined by her refusing to accept what he felt to be the appropriate path to take as to be unable to respond to the indirect request for validation in her question, "Do you think we got anywhere, Doctor?" The necessary theoretical understanding would have offset his disappointment in what he considered his failure and might have allowed him to say something like: "We certainly did, Mrs. Senoj. We have identified the real problem behind your headaches, you have found the courage to face it, and you have made an important decision that will let you start doing something to help your son. I think your continued efforts in that direction will make a big difference in the final outcome of his problem."

The patient suffering from physical illness is in a relatively passive position vis-à-vis a physician. Given the patient's permission, the physician does all kinds of things *to* the patient's body in order to establish a diagnosis and a treatment plan so as to ultimately bring about a cure. In psychotherapy it is a matter not of doing anything *to* the patient, but of investigating *with* the patient what has gone wrong with his or her problem-solving behavior and what the patient, not the therapist, may be able to do to make things better. Although no formal arrangements were made, in a sense Mrs. Senoj's psychotherapy had already begun as the doctor helped her to realize that he alone could not provide the solution to her difficulties: that from the very beginning active participation in the decision-making process is the *sine qua non* of treatment.

As the previous examples illustrate, depending on the patient's state, a therapist can enter the developmental spiral at various points. But whether the therapist begins the therapeutic process, or any subdivision thereof, with the focus on self-esteem, decision making, or behavior, the goal is always to permit the patient to achieve the experience of competence. The antonym of competence is helplessness. Al Gertz, Dr. Osgood, and Mrs. Senoj, each in his or her particular way, were helpless to exercise the necessary control that could bring self and environment into harmony. Competence is not a state of being carefree, happy, or contented; competence refers to a state of productive, purposeful functioning that makes sense to a particular individual in light of his or her past, present circumstances, and goals.

The reason the search for competence is ubiquitous and universal is that it reflects the basic function of the brain which is, as the polymath Count Alfred Korzybski (1933) documented at length, to create order out of the myriad stimuli impinging upon it at any given moment. Since it is the psychotherapist who helps patients understand how they create order and why a particular order has failed, I shall now turn to a consideration of the ordering process and how it can be described.

3

Thinking about Thinking

WHEN FREUD first investigated neurotic symptoms and laid the groundwork for what was to become dynamic psychotherapy, not much was known about the structure of the brain or how thoughts originate. Freud and his contemporaries drew on the sciences of the day to construct models with which to illustrate how the brain might work. Newtonian physics was the paradigmatic science then, and everything that hoped to be considered scientific was cast in the framework of what had been learned about the nature of energy and its transformation. To account for the creation of thought, Freud (1900, chapter 7) postulated a mental apparatus—a model that he believed would eventually find its organic counterpart in the brain—which he saw as working essentially like a steam engine. Fueled by somatic forces or instincts that held unreleased energy, the brain or mental apparatus transformed this potential energy into thought processes that initiated behavior. The details of how all this took place Freud left to future discoveries in neurophysiology. For many years, for lack of any better theory, this unsatisfactory attempt to explain thought formation governed thinking about thinking in the psychological sciences.

Beginning in 1946 with Norbert Wiener's discovery of the error-correcting feedback cycle, many discoveries about the brain as an information-processing organ—rather than an energy-transforming one—were, and are continuing to be, made. The construction of digital and analogue computing machines, based on Wiener's discovery, provides a serviceable and operationally sound analogy for brain functioning and thought formation. One may think of the billions of functionally interconnected cells that make up the brain as an information-processing network. Messages are generated, transformed, and transmitted through the alteration of electrical potential between adjoining cells as well as through chemical changes in the space between the cells. We may think of the organic structure of the brain as the computer's hardware, and of the scripts for action generated through message-processing and pattern-matching activity as the programs or software created for the purpose of adaptation. Anything going awry in either the hardware or the software of the computing brain may generate the kind of problems that fall within the scope of psychotherapy.

Today psychotherapists are in a very different position from that of Freud and his colleagues. Even though much remains to be learned, enough is known to study in an organized way—that is, scientifically—the subject matter of psychotherapy: the experiences of thought, feeling, and volition that together constitute what is called mind or mental work. The gap between the mental and its acknowledged origin in the brain can be bridged. In the next three chapters, I summarize the discoveries by researchers in other fields which, together, constitute the scientific framework for a basic science of psychotherapy.

Pattern Matching: The Brain's Ordering Process

The experience of competence has a neurological counterpart in the brain's pattern-matching activity: that is, the brain functions here like an analogue computer.* The most frequently cited example of

*The importance of reformulating psychodynamic explanations of mental processes in keeping with advances in brain science and information theory has also been dealt with by, among

such an information-processing device is the thermostat, which controls the activity of the furnace in most modern houses. Unfortunately for a mechanical idiot like myself, that is not a helpful analogy—a difficulty in which I have a hunch I am not alone. The first time I heard this comparison made, I eagerly looked up *thermostat* in a book that claimed to make the working of all sorts of machines readily comprehensible to the layman, only to find that I understood not a word and was no closer to a meaningful knowledge of "pattern matching" than I had been before.

While trying to write this chapter, I happened to be washing my hands and thinking of how I might illustrate the brain's pattern-matching activity in a manner that would have made sense to me when I initially ran across this concept. In my frustration, I must have been lathering my palms more vigorously than I realized, for the soap slipped out of my hands and fell to the bathroom floor. I bent down to locate it, but it was not to be found. Could it have landed in the wastebasket? The tub? Behind the radiator? No, it was in none of these places—and, anyway, had it landed in any of them, it would have made a sound different from the one I heard. It had to be on the floor. In my mind's eye, I could see the soap: a green square, measuring about three by two inches; an object that should have been readily visible against the blue and white mosaic of the tile. This was ridiculous! Beginning at one end of the room and letting my eyes sweep in a straight line to the opposite wall, I systematically began to move backward, covering the area by taking in a few more rows of tile with each excursion. After having done this five or six times, I located the elusive cake of soap next to the laundry hamper. As I picked it up, I realized that I had also found the example of pattern matching I needed.

What does it mean to say that I "located" the soap? We have all had similar experiences of searching for something we "know" is there, and can verify that what seems to go on in such a situation is that we have a picture of the desired object inside our head and engage in searching behavior until something outside matches it.

---

other researchers, Leslie Brothers (1988), June Hadley (1983), Fred Levin and D. M. Vuckovich (1983), Emanuel Peterfreund (1971), Morton Reiser (1984), Allan Rosenblatt and James Thickstun (1978), and Andrew Schwartz (1987 and 1988).

At that point, searching behavior ceases; the pattern formed by signals coming in from the external world corresponds to the one that guided the searching behavior. The technicalities of the so-called error-correcting feedback cycle that make this ordering possible through pattern matching are illustrated in figure 3.1, a much-simplified diagram based on William T. Powers's computer simulation of how the brain generates its representation of reality (1973).

This diagram is not meant to be an anatomical model. It is a flow chart, a sequential listing of functions that the brain must perform to accomplish the pattern-matching task. Although the invention of analogue and digital computers has made it possible to think about thinking in a scientific way, the brain is not a computer, and none of the computers developed to date is a brain. Researchers are quick to admit that, though much has been learned about the functioning of the human brain, much still eludes our understanding. What computers and the brain—indeed, all living cells—have in common is that their output or behavior is determined by the information generated from the input: hence, the analogy between the pattern matching of the computer and the brain.

To establish order, the brain must perform a series of operations (as in figure 3.1, going in clockwise fashion beginning in the lower left-hand corner). First, the brain must transform the stimulation impinging on the system in qualitatively undifferentiated waves of electrical or chemical perturbation (sensory input 1) into signals that the brain can use. Once stimulation has been transformed, the pattern generated is compared with a pattern of expectation that is the goal or target of this particular feedback cycle. An error signal is triggered if the goal pattern and the pattern representing incoming reality differ significantly. The purpose of the error signal is to stimulate the brain's decision-making function, which, in turn, chooses among available behavioral programs, inherited or acquired, that are able to correct the discrepancy. This behavioral activity generates new sensory input (sensory input 2), which again is compared with the reference signal of the goal pattern until the error signal ceases and, with it, behavioral activity. Hence, the name *feedback cycle:* the results of behavior are fed back into the system so that there is a constant check on whether the goal has been reached

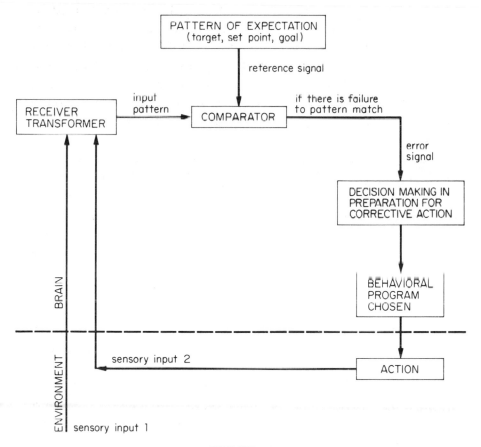

FIGURE 3.1
Error-Correcting, Deviation-Correcting, or Negative Feedback Cycle

or, if not, on how close one has come and what further needs to be done to achieve success.

Pattern-matching activity controlled by the principle of error-correcting feedback is not limited to the brain but is the basis for all life from the simplest cell to the most complex organism. Living organizations, according to the information theorist Jeremy Campbell (1982), participate—as long as they are viable—in deciding their fate by using input to gauge their output: that is, they respond to stimulation not just with simple energy transformations, as do inanimate structures, but with energy transformations that have been guided by the significance that the stimuli they receive have for their encoded goals.

The Feedback Cycle and Psychotherapy

Identification of the feedback cycle as the basis for the brain's ordering function permits unification of the three basic types of psychotherapy: the dynamic, which deals with the often-hidden or unconscious influence of development on a patient's character and motivation; the behavioral, which focuses on a patient's capacity for change in action; and the cognitive, which seeks to ameliorate or eliminate a patient's difficulties by examining and altering the manner of that patient's reasoning about his or her problems. While these approaches are often presented as disparate, even irreconcilable, in practice the seasoned therapist, whether acknowledging it or not, develops a technique that disregards the boundaries that supposedly separate one from the other—as figure 3.1 demonstrates.

Therapists tend to use a cognitive approach with a patient whose primary problem, or difficulty arising at a particular point in the therapy, is related to the inability to translate the signals he or she is receiving accurately. One can simply say to such a patient: "I don't think you heard what I said," and then repeat the statement. Or, one may say to a patient who feels continuously injured and insulted by superiors at work: "Is there another way that you could interpret what the boss told you this morning?" In some cases, such a question might be enough to set off a therapeutic process that would then let therapist and patient deal with the latter's misunderstanding in terms of patterns of expectation that have been built up over the years but now no longer apply. I had one patient who, having been left by his mother when he was eight years old, now experienced even the slightest disagreement with his wife as a threat of abandonment. His marriage was fundamentally sound, and he responded very well in a short time to my efforts to help him develop a different way of thinking about the occasions triggering his anxiety.

In many cases, of course, the problem is one not simply of the patient's misunderstanding or misinterpretation but of the patient's need to misunderstand what is happening in order to match a more powerful pattern of expectation than the one he or she consciously avows—a phenomenon often seen in patients who have work or learning inhibitions. I have seen extremely intelligent and talented women undermine what should have been rewarding careers because they received the message early in childhood that femininity and inadequacy go hand in hand: to prevail is not "womanly." A primarily cognitive technique is not effective in such cases; indicated instead is a dynamic approach, with the aim of exploring hidden assumptions that are interfering with adult fulfillment.

A third group of patients' difficulties can be addressed by devising and implementing behavioral strategies that will correct the mismatch between experience and expectation. Here the therapist often has to help a patient to develop and test new ways of behaving geared to achieving what it is he or she has set out to do. When in the navy, I frequently had to determine whether recently inducted recruits should be separated from the service as "unsuitable." Many of these young men, though eager to succeed, repeatedly found themselves in difficulties with the authorities. Often these men had never lived away from the parental farm until they enlisted, and were overwhelmed by this new and different subculture. They became increasingly depressed when their accustomed way of dealing with the environment led only to increasing evidence of incompetence and loss of self-esteem. Frequently all that was necessary was to help them learn the language of their new surroundings and how to use it: to say "deck" instead of "floor"; "bulkhead," not "wall"; "head," rather than "toilet"; and, above all, to make sure, when talking to an officer, that every second word out of their mouths was "sir." Once they began to put this behavioral strategy into action, it became self-reinforcing as they found themselves increasingly accepted. Soon they had the requisite self-confidence really to learn the skills for which they were being trained, and were on their way.

Even in the relatively uncomplicated examples I have just given, it is clear that, although one therapeutic strategy rather than another may dominate a particular therapy, by the time treatment has been completed the therapist has probably made use of a combination of dynamic, behavioral, and cognitive techniques. This is certainly what happens when, as in the extensive clinical presentations in chapters 7 to 10, during any one session the therapist may have to utilize a variety of approaches to maintain the momentum of the hour. Disputes about which method is "better" are meaningless once it is understood that all are valid in light of the manner in which the brain functions to create and maintain order.

Just as in cardiac surgery, where a patient is temporarily connected to a machine that takes over the function of the heart and lungs until those repairs can be made that will once again let the body do its job properly, so the psychotherapist lends his or her brain to the patient until such time as whatever is impairing that patient's mental functioning can be corrected. Of course, in psychotherapy this brain hook-up is functional, not anatomic; and what passes between therapist and patient is not blood, but information: more correctly, the therapist tries to provide the raw material from which information can arise.

For example, what motivated Al Gertz to change his way of behaving was information—information that conveyed in a telling manner that my picture of him was very different from his self-image. In Dr. Osgood's case, inactivity and confusion were generating information that reinforced a negative picture of himself. He improved when I was able to influence him to behave in ways that begot a different kind of information. As he found himself functioning more adequately, he was able to remobilize, step by step, the self-concept that had worked well for him throughout the years. As Mrs. Senoj was helped to reassess the significance of what was happening in her family, she also generated new information or, perhaps more accurately, was helped to observe consciously what she had already organized unconsciously but had to defend herself against acknowledging. That information makes things happen is nothing new, but it is only with the discovery of control theory— also called *cybernetics* by Norbert Wiener (1956)—that it became possible to give a scientific description of the process by which information governs behavior.

Information as used in communication science has a meaning different from its everyday usage where it is a synonym for *knowledge*. Information is defined by control theory as the effect a coded signal has in reducing uncertainty in a receiver confronted by choices. It is a collective term for what is generated by the activity of a feedback cycle (figure 3.1), and its function is to bring the decision-making process to closure. Information is quantifiable and measured in "bits," a *bit* of information being defined as that content of a message that cuts the options open to the receiver by half.

For example, a driver when approaching a traffic light that has turned red is confronted by two possibilities—going on or stopping. The reception of the light waves emanating from the traffic signal and their transformation into brain language create a pattern that is compared with appropriate goals in the brain's script or assemblage of learned programs that apply to automobile driving, including the dangers, personal and legal, inherent in disregarding our society's rules for traffic management. The signals indicative of the car's continued forward progress are incompatible with the pattern of expectation associated with the red traffic light; an error signal is triggered; one of the two alternatives open to the driver is eliminated, in effect mandating a decision to stop the car. This then triggers the appropriate muscular movements to push the brake. The sensations associated with the car's deceleration as it is brought to a stop are fed back to the brain and generate the message that the pattern of expectation associated with the red traffic light is being matched and that the expenditure of energy needed to move the muscles involved in braking the car may cease.

In ordinary talk about such events, human beings simplify by reifying the process: that is, we speak of information being generated and decisions being made as if these words referred to identifiable external events—"The red light made me stop" or "The red light told me to stop." Psychotherapists, on the other hand, being intimately and continuously involved in evaluating and trying to eliminate obstacles to information processing, must recognize this shorthand for what it is, for it is the therapist's understanding of decision making as an intrapsychic process governed by established patterns of expectation that helps the therapist to intervene effectively in a given patient's difficulties.

THE PSYCHE TODAY

For centuries, goal-directed behavior generally and human behavior particularly eluded scientific explanation. Everyone could see and feel what caused a boulder to be moved from one place to another: the rock had nothing to say about it; one got behind it and pushed. *Energy* is the name of the measure scientists devised to explain and quantify the force or power expended in accomplishing physical work, the movement of mass through distance. But what force or power moved the mover? There seemed to be an inner voice saying, "Do this." The ancient Greeks attributed motivation or action to the psyche—*psyche* being the word for "wind"—an allusion to the force behind purposeful behavior that was, like the wind, powerful yet invisible. As in the previous example, the generation of information, by mandating one sort of behavior rather than another in a system confronted by choices, represents a form of power. Information is the psychical or psychological force, the motivation behind behavior. Information is the power with which the psychotherapist—indeed, everyone dealing with human motivation—is concerned.

Thermodynamics (literally, the "movement of heat") provides the framework for understanding the fate of inanimate objects, measured by and expressed in terms of energy transformation. It is the concept of energy that Freud borrowed from physics and used, first literally and later metaphorically (Freud 1940, pp. 162–64; Basch 1981), in an attempt to quantify the intensity of thought. Indeed, in everyday language, we are accustomed to think of our thought processes as being more or less "energetic." Today, however, we need not, and should no longer, engage in this inappropriate physicalistic reductionism. The modern term *psychodynamics* can be understood as referring to the movement of goal-directed systems toward decisions. This process is measured by and expressed in terms of information. Thus is the once-mysterious psyche taken out of the realm of the supernatural to join science, the search for order in nature.

THE ILLUSION OF EXTERNAL REALITY

When I said to myself, "I've got to find that soap on the floor," the goal seemed to be located outside my brain, but actually I was trying to find sensory signals that would add up to what I already had inside my head—a previously perceived and encoded pattern of feeling, touch, and smell labeled "my soap." I was trying to match a pattern that was not an abstraction corresponding to a dictionary definition of *soap*, but an experience or experiences corresponding to "Make it look like this" and "Make it feel like that." As long as the comparison failed—"It does not look like this" and "It does not feel like that"—the brain issued an error signal, "Keep trying," which activated behavioral programs available for the promotion of such pattern matching. I engaged in a program of sweeping the floor with my eyes. Had failure to match continued, further error signals would have been sent, and I might have tried different behavioral programs. I might, for example, have called my wife or one of my children to come and help me look for the missing soap. However, the first behavioral program did work out satisfactorily—I succeeded in matching environmental reality with my goal. When that happened, behavior relating to that particular pattern of expectation stopped. At that point in the spiral of development (see figure 2.1, page 29), I experienced competence and a small increment of self-esteem ("Am I not the clever one?") and, along with it, increased confidence that when things get lost or misplaced I can probably figure out how to recover them.

Unremarkable as this example is, the point it makes generally applies: namely, that the standard by which one judges one's own competence or incompetence is always internal, not external. Thus, it is impossible to persuade psychotic patients to relinquish delusions and hallucinations that they hold in the face of contradictory external signals, sensory evidence, and common sense. So it is that the traveler lost in the desert hallucinates an oasis and dies with a smile on his face; he has found inside his head what he was looking for. Once that match is made, efforts to push on cease.

From the time one learns to speak, one is taught to accept as "natural" or self-evident the division of the world one perceives into inner and outer spheres. The external world is the "real" or "objective" world—that is, the world of things that "are there," supposedly independent of us and our observation. The "inner" or "mental" world, on the other hand, is somehow unreal, subjective, and not entirely to be trusted because it is made up of our creations—"ideas," "feelings," and the like. This dichotomy is literally built into the languages of Western civilization. Nevertheless, as the work of those who have studied the perceptual process—for example, such researchers as H. F. Brandt (1945) and Rudolf Arnheim (1969)—demonstrates, whether one projects perceptions onto the extracerebral world and calls them "objective reality"—or locates them in an imaginary, noncorporeal organ called *mind* and labels them "mental," "psychic," or "subjective"—the reality to which one responds—the only reality we know—is a construction created by the brain of the beholder. Apart from the significance that this rejection of the familiar division between mind and external reality has for psychology and for science generally (Basch 1975*a*, p. 520), it has important implications for psychotherapeutic technique.

In everyday life it may not matter much whether I say to myself, "I've got to find that soap on the floor," or think, "I must match the pattern of 'my soap' as it is registered in my brain." However, when at stake is no longer a consensually validatable physical object but, let us say, a matter of the personal values that often bring people to psychotherapy—such as feeling unloved and/or unlovable—it will do little good for the therapist to point out to a woman patient, for example, that—according to her very history—X, Y, and Z clearly do love her and see her as lovable. The therapist's job is to help the patient discover, and then to explore, the pattern that she is trying to match which the love of X, Y, and Z does not satisfy.

The corollary to recognizing that the goal guiding behavior is internal rather than external is that somebody's purpose cannot be understood by simply observing either behavior or what it achieves. Understanding another's motive or purpose requires that one somehow be made privy to that person's thoughts. For instance, anyone who had come upon me searching the bathroom floor could not have immediately known why I was so employed. Was I looking for cracks in the bathroom tiles? Searching for a coin I had dropped? Exercising my eye muscles in this peculiar way on orders from my opththalmologist? Even someone observing my behavior who had then seen me pick up the bar of soap could not know whether that was my intent or merely an incidental by-product unrelated to the goal. Only someone who asked me what I was doing—and if I volunteered to tell—could know (assuming I was not lying) that I was indeed in search of a piece of soap I had accidentally dropped. In other words, behavior is not, or at least not necessarily, self-explanatory.

For another example, Al Gertz, the taxi driver, behaved in a very angry, off-putting fashion with me. While the initial effect was first to frighten and then to antagonize me, that was, of course, not his primary purpose. What he was trying to do, albeit in counterproductive fashion, was to shore himself up, to maintain his self-esteem in the face of what he experienced as an unempathic world, one only too ready to sneer at rather than help him in his distress.

An additional and important complication is that, unlike what happened in my search for the elusive soap when I could tell anyone interested why I was doing what I was doing, Al Gertz could not articulate the purpose of his behavior. At best, when questioned, he might give an unconvincing rationalization, referring to external circumstances to justify his anger—"Doctors have it too good, etc." The same unsatisfactory attempts at explanation are routinely heard in psychotherapy; patients are, by and large, unable to tell the therapist why they behave in one or another sort of problematic fashion. This problem was considered by Freud, who postulated a *System Unconscious* as being responsible for generating—and, in many instances, concealing from consciousness and reflective consideration—the purpose of a person's behavior (1900, 1915c). The emphasis on unconscious motivation is one of Freud's most important contributions and is the basis for dynamic psychotherapy.

THE OPERATION OF UNCONSCIOUS THOUGHT

Unconscious, applied as an adjective to *thought,* refers to Freud's clinical observation that one's brain arrives at decisions, initiates behavior, and resolves problems without one's being conscious (subjectively aware) of that process; indeed, one may be at times precluded from becoming conscious either of what is happening to one, or of why it is happening.*

One is ordinarily not aware of the operation of one's digestive tract or respiratory system. But should one eat some spoiled food

*I use the terms *conscious* and *consciousness,* as did Freud (1940), in the everyday sense of self-awareness or knowing that one knows—what the philosopher Leibnitz (1646–1716) called "apperception." *Conscious,* as used in psychotherapy, should *not* be confused with such terms as *attentive* or *awake.* By the same token, *unconscious,* as it was used by Freud and continues to be used in the literature of psychoanalysis and dynamic psychiatry, does *not* mean "asleep," "comatose," "unaware," or "inattentive." *Unconscious,* used as an adjective, refers to a situation in which one is not subjectively aware of the activities of one's brain.

or suddenly run short of a supply of air, one quickly becomes conscious of the fact that something has gone wrong, that something unexpected has happened. In this respect, the brain functions no differently from all the other organs of the body: it does not call attention to itself and its activity as long as pattern matching is going well.

Precisely because one is not directly cognizant of the brain's activity, one finds it hard to accept that the problem-solving activities of reasoning and thought are proceeding apart from consciousness (self-awareness). Or, as Karl Lashley, a pioneer in the field, put it, no mental process is ever conscious (1958): that is, consciousness always occurs after the fact and should, correctly speaking, be called *conscious reflection* because it always deals with perceptions or ideas that have already been formulated by the brain's activity. This concept is now supported not only by the clinical evidence of psychoanalysis but by discoveries in neurophysiology as well. Experiments have established that there is a measurable gap of ⅕ to ½ second between the cortical registration of a stimulus and its becoming conscious (Eccles 1970; Libet et al. 1979). This interval, minimal as it may seem on our everyday scale of events, acquires a great significance when applied to brain physiology. There are more than 10 billion neurones in the brain, with possibly 60,000 to 100,000 functional connections being made between each nerve cell and its fellows; since transmission of impulses between nerve cells takes only about ⅟₁,₀₀₀ of a second in the ⅕ to ½ second interval between stimulus registration and the possibility for consciousness, the brain makes literally trillions of decisions regarding the significance and implications of what it has registered as the transformed stimulus is compared with established programs, scripts, or other patterns that serve to orient and adapt the organism to its environment. Furthermore, because the brain can process thousands of bits of information per second, whereas the individual can entertain about twenty bits of information per second in self-conscious awareness, the vast majority of decisions made through mental work never can become conscious. These findings corroborate J. Winson's (1985) suggestion that the brain's pattern-matching function provides a neurophysiological basis for Freud's *System Unconscious.*

As long as problem-solving or pattern-matching activity proceeds unimpaired, there is no need for the brain to call upon conscious reflection for assistance in carrying out mental work. As early as 1890, William James pointed out that consciousness seems to arise only in response to a problem. This idea applied to our current understanding of the operation of the brain allows us to say that, when the pattern-matching activity we call thought is unsuccessful, the phenomenon of consciousness permits the brain to re present what does not fit so that the brain may re-examine it as often as necessary until either it does match established expectations, or a decision is made to disregard it, or a new pattern or a variation of an old pattern is created (Basch 1975*a*).

For example, when driving home on a familiar route, the fact that one is not usually conscious of the landmarks along the way does not mean that one is not paying attention to where one is going. The pattern of the route is so well established that one need not become conscious of it, for what one is experiencing unconsciously from moment to moment is sufficiently correlated with what the brain has been led to expect. However, let something be amiss or unfamiliar—a sign announcing structural repairs on the road, let us say— and one immediately becomes conscious of the new, unexpected event just registered and readjusts one's patterns of expectation accordingly. What has been difficult to accept is that the aforementioned sign was not first conscious and then thought about, but, rather, was first thought about and only then made conscious so as to make sure that it really had been dealt with appropriately. Furthermore, since we are accustomed to equate consciousness not only with thought but also with attention, one may say, "Oh, I was driving along the expressway not paying attention until I saw that sign about repairs having started, and then I decided to get off and come home on Sheridan Road instead." But that is not what happens. If one had not been paying attention, an accident would very quickly have occurred. Consciousness is only brought into play when what one is attending to does not make sense—that is, does not correspond to what past experience has led one to expect.

Most patients come to psychotherapy feeling that something unaccounted for is interfering with their ability both to solve certain problems and to continue their accustomed adaptation to life. It is as if—to continue my analogy—one were unable to recognize and hence to heed the road signs meant to alert drivers to alter their customary behavior appropriately, and continued to drive as if the situation had not changed. Eventually this failure to use the signs will impair the driver's progress and bring the journey to a halt. Just so with patients: when a new situation contradicts particular patterns of expectation unconsciously regarded by the patient as necessary for his or her psychological survival, the patient is prevented from becoming conscious of either the discrepancy or its significance, and from developing appropriate patterns to fit the new circumstances. Instead, the old order is maintained, often at great cost to a person's overall adaptation.

Interruption or hampering of the cycle—from decision to behavior to competence to self-esteem—leads to maladaptive decision making and behavior that may need to be addressed in psychotherapy. In the treatment situation, the therapist has to determine, from what a patient says, feels, and does in particular situations, how to enter the developmental spiral effectively. It is the therapist's task to help the patient to undo self-defeating cycles so as to be able to receive and appropriately utilize new input.

In summary, mental work is a product of a pattern-matching function, whose goal or purpose is to establish meaningful order among the many stimuli impinging upon the brain. This ordering or pattern-matching activity is essentially, and at least initially, always unconscious. Optimally, a failure to achieve correspondence between what one expects and what one seems to perceive activates consciousness and permits a reconsideration of perceptions or ideas until either a pattern match has been achieved, the perturbation that gave rise to the problem has been dismissed, or learning has taken place: that is, correspondence has been achieved through modification of an old pattern or the creation of a new one. Thus, in terms of experience, optimal ordering leads to competent behavior and self-esteem and serves as the basis for effective adaptation in the future.

Having dealt with the basic manner in which the brain functions, I can now consider the most important signals that the human brain has to organize—the stimulation afforded by our affective responses to the environment.

4

Affect: The Gateway
to Action

EVERYDAY EXPERIENCE as well as the clinical evidence from psychotherapy attest to the fact that the most important source of information guiding human decision making and behavior comes not simply from the things we see, hear, smell, touch, and taste. It is the nature and intensity of the affect generated by or in connection with a particular event that determines one's behavioral reaction: affect is the gateway to action (Basch 1976c).* (Here, for the moment, I use the term *affect* in its generic sense, subsuming both certain basic physiological reactions to stimulation that are already present in infancy as well as their later transformations into feelings, moods, and emotions.) The importance of affect for psychotherapy is acknowledged in everyday language where such terms as *emotional disorder* or *emotional illness* are used as synonyms for *psychological disturbance* or *mental disease.*

Freud (1915c) acknowledged the centrality of emotional life for psychotherapy when he said that defense is always directed against affect. That is to say, whatever a patient may be struggling with in

*Concerning behavior, there is a contradiction in Freud's explanatory theory: although he made it clear in "The Unconscious" (1915c) that everything attributed to consciousness can be accomplished without its participation, he had already committed himself—both in the *Project for a Scientific Psychology* (1895) and in chapter 7 of *The Interpretation of Dreams* (1900)—to consciousness as the trigger for behavior (Basch 1975a, 1976a). The recognition of affect, not the experience of consciousness, as motivating behavior corrects this paradox.

therapy, at bottom is always an affective experience that he or she cannot deal with effectively. Freud emphasized, and dynamic psychiatry still operates on that principle today, that a patient's intellectual knowledge of his or her problems is of little use if the affect attached to those problems has not also come into and been worked on in the treatment.

It is affect that gives meaning or a sense of force to our thoughts and behavior. Thus, Freud, in an evocative analogy, equated affect with what he called *psychic energy* (Basch 1976*a*). However, he never dealt theoretically with the complexity of affective experience, but reduced it simply to pleasure and unpleasure. The sense of drivenness stemming from affect, especially at times when one is passionately involved in thought or action, was for Freud the pressure for instinctual discharge. He considered affect as only the conscious expression of sexuality and aggression, the instincts he had postulated as basically responsible for all psychologically determined behavior.

And, until recently, that is pretty much where matters stood. However, today we can take into account theoretically what has always been known experientially, namely, that it is the quality and degree of affect that accounts for the nuances of behavior.

Affect as the Motivator of Behavior: Joe Herman, Sr.

Joe Herman, bored by television, has left his house to take a leisurely stroll through the neighborhood. After walking a few blocks, a siren makes him aware of an approaching fire engine. His first reaction is of mild interest in what might be happening somewhere to bring out the firemen. When he realizes that the siren's sound is continuing with unabated intensity instead of fading into the distance, his curiosity gives way to vague apprehension—a tightening of his chest muscles and a discomfort in the pit of his stomach. He begins to calculate from which block the sound might be coming. He pauses in midstride and turns back toward his home with quickened steps. The siren's unrelenting wail stimulates feelings of guilt and a morbid fantasy: he knew he should have replaced that frayed lamp cord in the basement; in his imagination, he sees his family in the upstairs window trapped by flames. His wife is holding the baby, Joe, Jr.; she is going to drop him into a safety net. What if she misses? At this point in his fantasy, he breaks out in a sweat and starts first to trot and then to run. In the minute or so that it takes him to get back to his house, he is aware of the clammy feeling of nausea that encapsulates his fear; and of the hope that maybe nothing catastrophic has happened after all, in which case he will be embarrassed to have the neighbors see him tearing like a madman down the street. He is also aware of a combination both of guilt and fury directed at himself for having neglected the electrical repair; and—though he recognizes it as irrational and unjustified—of anger at his wife and the thought. "It's all her fault. She should have made me fix the cord. She knows how dangerous exposed wires can be."

Attracted by the sound of the siren, a couple looking out of their window see Joe running down the street. "Isn't that Joe Herman?" the wife says to her husband. "I hope it's not his house. Maybe you'd better go and see if you can help."

As Joe rounds the corner, he sees that the firemen are merely putting out a blaze in a pile of leaves near the curb. A feeling of relief and gratitude flows through his body as the tension in his muscles eases. He slows down to a walk and finds himself smiling and whistling. Instead of resuming his stroll, he goes into his home and repairs the light fixture. Afterward, he makes an effort to be particularly nice to each of his children and welcomes their noisy play.

The next day, Joe Herman tells a friend at the office, "I had a bad scare yesterday. I was out for a walk when I heard the fire engines coming to our block. Boy! I didn't think I could run that fast!" "I can imagine," his friend replies, looking concerned. "That must have been very frightening."

Going home on the train after work, Joe takes the opportunity to tell the conductor on the 5:30, with whom he usually exchanges brief pleasantries, about the events of the previous evening. Having launched into his recital, he notices that the man is looking down the aisle, his face expressionless. Joe finishes his story as quickly as he can and receives the conductor's noncommittal smile and unfeeling, "Yeah, well, I guess those things can happen." Ashamed, warm with embarrassment, Joe lowers his head into his newspaper, hoping that he is not blushing noticeably and feeling like a fool for having presumed interest where none existed.

That night Joe's friend reports Joe's story at the dinner table: "He heard the fire engines coming to his block, but he didn't know if it was his house or not. Boy, was he scared! He's got that little baby, you know. I bet he could see the whole family go up in smoke without his being able to do anything about it. Like what happened back in Michigan when we lived there—I'll never forget that as long as I live—you remember, to those people who had the Doberman pinscher." Joe had by no means told his friend the whole story, only reporting his feelings and barely mentioning what had precipitated them. But that is enough to allow his friend to believe that he has heard the details, and to pass on to his wife, as Joe's story, the images he himself conjured up while Joe was talking to him. And, indeed, the scenario that his friend paints is quite close to Joe's experience.

As I have said, the reason for particular behavior can be found in the affect that has motivated it: so, Joe Herman left his home because he was *bored,* paused when a siren attracted his *interest,* interrupted his walk when he became *worried,* ran back when he became *frightened,* relaxed in response to the *joy* he felt when the tragedy he had imagined did not materialize.

The affect attached to a particular perceptual goal moves a person to engage in behavior that will fulfill or reach it; and only if the affective context is clear can one make an educated guess about why someone is behaving in a particular way. Joe Herman decided to go for a walk not because he wanted to move his legs, but because he already anticipated the affective (emotional) reward of being in the quiet of the open air, busy but not taxed as he strolled along, perhaps meeting and talking to a neighbor, doing something interesting. The purpose of taking a walk was not to walk but to achieve certain affectively tinged goals. When being away from home was colored by fear instead of the anticipation of pleasure, Joe's behavior changed drastically. Similarly, when his neighbors saw him running, they could guess that he feared his house was on fire because they also heard the siren and empathically supplied the affect he was experiencing.

Affect is, indeed, the gateway to behavior, and there is no action and no thought that is not affectively motivated, including such mundane activities as going to the shoemaker to pick up a pair of shoes. Even a pair of shoes has affective significance. If it is my favorite pair of shoes, I might walk a little faster, anticipating the pleasure of being able to wear them again. If I dislike them, but it is the only pair of brown shoes I own, I might not go so soon to pick them up, until it dawns on me that I have to wear my brown suit and will need them. The affective motive for picking them up then would be to avoid the shame I anticipate experiencing were I to show up at a party with shoes that do not match my suit.

While affect does not have to be dramatic or in the forefront of consciousness to engender behavior, it is always present. Unlike the chicken in the ancient joke, we do not cross the street just to get to the other side: there is always an affective reason that takes us there.

Baby Talk: Joe Herman, Jr.

Just about the time Joe Herman, Sr., leaves to take his walk, five-year-old Jennifer Herman runs to her mother and says, "Joey woke up, he's crying. I bet he's wet. Can I help you change him?" Her mother turns off the water in the kitchen sink and listens a moment. "I think you're right, Jenny. Sounds like he's finished with his nap and is bored up there all alone. Why don't you go up and give me a few minutes to finish here."

When Mrs. Herman comes into the baby's room, she sees that twelve-month-old Joey has pulled himself up in his crib. Jenny, standing on a footstool that brings her even with his face, explains something to him about a teddy bear she is holding. Joey listens intently, his eyes following her every movement; and periodically he babbles right back to his sister as if he understands every word she is saying. Smiling to herself, Mrs. Herman waits, not wanting to interrupt the cheerful scene. Suddenly, she sees Joey's eyebrows go up. His eyes begin to blink, and he turns his head in the direction of the window. For a moment she cannot figure out what has startled him, but then she too hears the siren.

The smile on the baby's face fades as the noise continues without letup. Now the corners of his mouth turn down, his eyebrows arch, and tears begin to form in his eyes. Mrs. Herman, noting his fear, quickly calls to her daughter, "Hold him, Jenny," and runs to the window to locate the fire. All she can see is a pile of burning leaves at the curb two houses away. She feels annoyed at the thoughtlessness that keeps up a racket worthy of a five-alarm fire for something so insignificant. As she turns back to the room, she realizes that her daughter is not comforting the baby but has joined her at the window. Mrs. Herman instantly notices that the baby has stopped crying and is standing paralyzed with fear as the earsplitting sound of the siren continues to fill the room. His eyes are open wide and staring; his face, beaded with sweat, is pale; and his whole body is seized with a fine trembling. She scoops him up in her arms and hugs him to her, at the same time turning to Jenny: "What's the matter with you? Is this what you call helping me? Leaving that baby——" Rocking Joey and cooing to him, she says, "Come on Joey, we're going to get out of this noisy room and down to the basement where it's quiet and we can play, and maybe we'll forget all about the nasty noise that frightened the poor little boy."

As she reaches the door, she turns back and sees that her daughter is not following her but still standing at the window. Jennifer is not looking out but standing with her head bowed, her face flushed, her eyes cast down, shuffling her feet awkwardly. "You're ashamed of yourself, aren't you? And you should be, young lady! Poor Joey." Then, softening, "Well, maybe it isn't all your fault. I suppose you got scared too by that idiotic racket and wanted to see what was going on. I guess I shouldn't expect so much of you. Sometimes I forget you're only five years old. Come on, Jenny, I'm sorry I lost my temper. It's those stupid firemen I'm really mad at. Why don't you get Joey a nice bottle from the refrigerator and bring it downstairs." Jenny raises her head, and her face resumes its normal color as she skips, with obvious relief, out of the room.

Once away from the noise, the baby no longer looks terrified but is still restless and won't let himself be comforted. Suddenly his face turns red, his brow wrinkles in a frown, he clenches his fists and his jaw and begins to hit his mother. "You're angry, aren't you, baby? Get it all out. The bad mommy let the nasty noises upset you, didn't she? Well, it's all over now. Here comes your good sister with a nice bottle. Thank you, Jenny, you're a big help. Would baby like a bottle? Shh, shh, quiet down now. It's all over, everything is fine. This good little baby is going to have some milk. There, there."

As the soothing, rhythmic voice of his mother envelops him, the baby soon ceases to flail his arms and kick his legs. He is at first hesitant to drink the milk and mouths the nipple in desultory fashion. Soon, however, he is drawing in long draughts. An expression of joy comes over his face, he smiles, his lips part and widen, and his breathing becomes regular, slow, and deep. Mother and daughter smile at each other with relief. "He's all right now, isn't he, Mom?" "He's fine now, honey, thank you. Was that the door closing? Run upstairs and see if Daddy came back."

COMMUNICATION FROM INFANT TO ADULT

What is striking in this story is that Joe Herman and his one-year-old baby run much the same gamut of affects: boredom, interest, fear, anger, and joy. Joe, Jr., showing only the rudiments of the adaptive skills he will later develop, nevertheless already displays a range of facial expressions that remain essentially unchanged throughout life. Photographs of Joe, Jr., and his father would show, for example, that the latter's facial expressions when he is variously angry, interested, and happy look exactly like those of his angry, interested, or happy infant son.

Equally intriguing is the question of how Joey knows which facial expression to use. How can a Joe, Jr., go through the complex evaluations required to produce the affective responses that also motivate his father's behavior? Joe, Jr., does not have either the cognitive wherewithal or the experience to say to himself, "That siren sounds like the fire engine is at my house. This could spell catastrophe." Why, then, does Junior panic at the same time as his father? We can understand Joe, Sr., taking a stroll in response to his boredom, anticipating all sorts of pleasant things happening to him as he walks along, but why does Joey cry out for company when he wakes up, and why is he so interested in his sister's discourse about the teddy bear when he probably does not understand most, if anything, of what she is saying? Why instead of just drinking his milk and going to sleep does little Joey smile and look happy? His mother would probably not be puzzled, but would—we now believe correctly—attribute the baby's upset to the earsplitting intensity of the siren's continuing blast, and his joyful expression upon being soothed and fed to a decrease in tension.

Joey Herman's display of affective expressions is essentially identical with his father's because, according to the psychologist Silvan Tomkins, the founder of modern affect theory, human beings are born with that capacity. Affective experience is initially a genetically encoded reflex phenomenon. Although the affective response is a total bodily response involving body temperature, skin, hair, glands, muscles, and viscera, in humans the face has become the prime communicator of affective states, with each specific affect reflex expressing itself by temporarily taking over the group of voluntary muscles that together give rise to the prototypical expression associated with it. Tomkins (1962–63, p. 337) identified and systematically described the facial features of the following eight basic affects, each with a range from mild to intense expression, present either at birth or shortly thereafter:

> Surprise-startle: eyebrows up, eyes blink.
> Interest-excitement: eyebrows down, tracking behavior, attitude of looking and listening.
> Enjoyment-joy: smile, lips widened and out, slow deep breathing.
> Distress-anguish: crying, arched eyebrows, corners of the mouth turned down, tears and rhythmic sobbing.
> Contempt-disgust: sneer, upper lip lifted.
> Anger-rage: frown, jaw clenched, face red.
> Fear-terror: eyes frozen open, pale, cold, sweaty, facial trembling with hair erect.
> Shame-humiliation: eyes cast down, head down.

(Sadness, which Tomkins considered a variant of distress, seems also to qualify as a separate, basic affect. My colleague Douglas Detrick suggests, and I agree, that understimulation/boredom should be added to the list of primary affective reactions.*)

*Personal communication, 1986.

A baby, of course, cannot think logically about what is happening to him or her and draw a reasoned conclusion that then recruits an affective reaction, nor is that necessary. According to Tomkins (1962–63, 1970, 1980, 1981), the affective reaction to stimulation is, initially, not a response to the quality or nature of the stimulus as such, but is, rather, selectively triggered by the intensity, the duration, and the shape formed by the rise and fall of the stimulus as it impinges on the nervous system. It does not matter whether the stimulus is sound, light, or touch; practically from the first day of life, if the number and frequency of nerve impulses set up by the excitation fall within the infant's optimal range for stimulation, the baby's face will assume an expression that everyone everywhere will recognize as one of interest. If the excitation is above the optimal level, there will first be a reaction of surprise; and then, if stimulus intensity is maintained steadily at a higher than optimal rate for a length of time, first distress, then fear, and finally anger make their appearance. Joy is registered whenever a sharp rise in stimulation is followed by a sudden drop (figure 4.1). (Father, having playfully tossed his baby daughter in the air, catches her; and the baby laughs—not because she knows she is safe after having been in danger, but because there has been a sudden decrease in the stimulus input produced by the act of tossing her up and letting her fall.) Somewhat later, at about seven months of age, when interpersonal validation of the infant's behavior assumes great importance (Stern 1985), the absence of a confirming response leads to inadequate reduction of excitement and results in a shame reaction (Nathanson 1987).*

The only exception to the quantitative determination of affect is the qualitatively triggered protective withdrawal reaction of disgust. This primary affect is based on an inherited avoidance response triggered chemically by tastes or odors that register as noxious: for example, the smell of rancid butter (butyric acid) invariably produces a curling of the lip and a flattening of the nose in newborn humans (Tomkins 1962–63).

*The subcortically triggered affect programs described by Tomkins are a good example of what is understood by *instinct* in biology today. Human beings inherit a "blueprint," a set of transformation rules (Campbell 1982) that program one to respond to stimulation in such a way as to make more likely individual survival and, ultimately, the survival of the species (Gould and Gould 1981; Gould and Marler 1987).

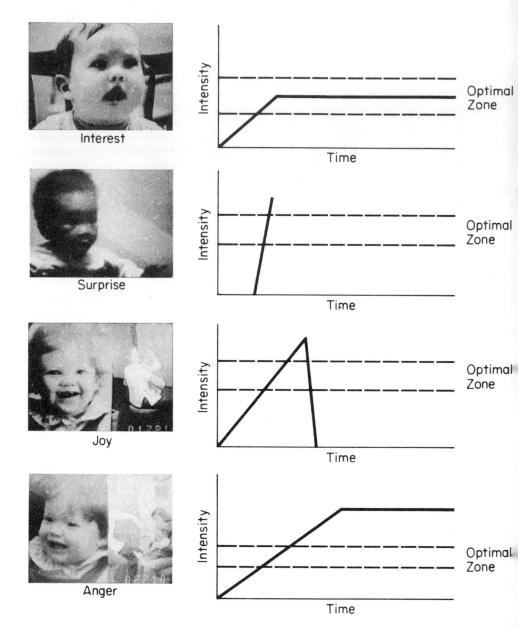

FIGURE 4.1

The Shape of Stimulation and Subsequent Affective Reaction (Not Drawn to Scale)

To illustrate the point that affect in infancy is the product of the intensity and shape of stimulation, I have supplied schematic drawings next to the pictures illustrating four of the basic affects. The vertical axis represents stimulus intensity; the horizontal one, the fate of the stimulus over time.

COMMUNICATION FROM ADULT TO INFANT

Therapists have long been convinced that many patients' difficulties can be implicitly traced back to traumatic experiences and
deprivations suffered in early infancy. It is now taken as essentially
self-evident, for example, that a depression in the mother will in all
likelihood have a negative effect on the personality development of
her baby. How, then, does a mother's dysphoria, or any other affect,
communicate itself to the infant? Clearly, a baby's affective expression serves to communicate his or her state of being to surrounding
adults, but how can that baby know how those adults feel and be
influenced by their moods? Recent work by the infant researcher
Tiffany Field and her colleagues has dramatically illustrated the way
in which the communication from adult to infant may take place
(Field et al. 1982; Field 1985). In Field's experiment, infants—on an
average of thirty-six hours after birth and long before they could
have learned anything from experience—looked at various facial
expressions, made by a model trained for that purpose. The infants
responded in kind, making a joyful face when the model looked
happy, looking surprised when she expressed astonishment, and sad
when she looked unhappy (figure 4.2). Although Field calls the
newborn infants' behavior an "imitation" of the model's face, this
is not an acceptable explanation. The skills necessary for imitation
are developed later and require a more mature central nervous system and greater muscular control than newborns possess. As Tomkins's theory would predict, the model's face serves to release the
infant's affective response and is not an object to be aped (Haviland
and Lelwica 1987). These newborns were responding to the model's
face with a reflex action, thereby attaining what Stern has called
affect attunement: that is, they were sharing the adult's inner affect
state (Stern et al. 1985).

CHARACTER FORMATION IN INFANCY

The mirroring of another's affective state by the infant's nervous
system explains how, long before sophisticated reasoning is a possibility, the infant is able to resonate accurately with the affective

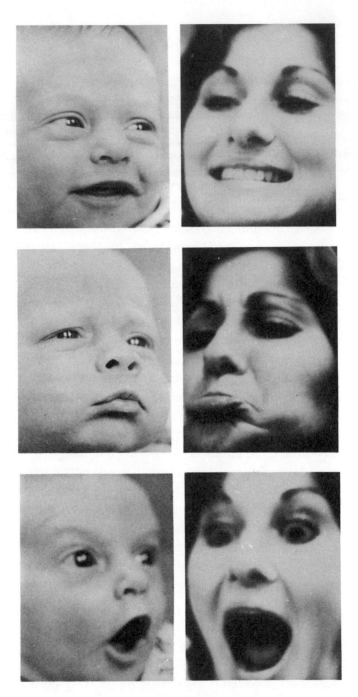

FIGURE 4.2
Adult Affective Communication and an Infant's Response

messages being sent by the adults with whom he or she interacts. The infant lays down memory traces of such experiences, which then influence future behavior. These encoded memories constitute the patterns of expectation that are remobilized when sufficiently similar circumstances arise in the infant's life. (Neither recall nor imagery is involved in this process. What is reactivated is the sensorimotor complex which has become associated with the autonomic response to stimulation that constitutes affect.)

How a baby will react, whether to welcome or withdraw from a potential re-experience, depends a great deal on the nature of the affect that has come to be attached to the memory of similar previous occasions. In other words, the baby does not react essentially differently from the way he will when he gets older. One is much more likely to anticipate with interest, and to explore further, those situations that have given pleasure and enhanced self-esteem rather than those that leave one tense with fear, anger, or shame. Through such affective ordering the immature infant is able to lay down an accurate, permanent record of his or her transactions with the world, which then forms the basis for what will become the adult's character or personality.

THE MATURATION OF AFFECT

Words like *joy, shame,* and *fear* are so connected to adult self-conscious reflection that it may seem uncomfortably adultomorphic to attribute such experiences to infants. This is no longer a problem if affect, like cognition, is thought of in terms of a maturational line. Then, though the words may be the same, what they are meant to describe is not.

Elsewhere (Basch 1983a) I have postulated a distinction among affect, feeling, and emotion. I reserve the term *affect* for the group of biological responses to stimulation described by Tomkins. Like any other reflex reaction—the knee jerk when the patellar tendon is tapped, or the blinking of the eyelid when a dust particle flies into the eye—this response, because it is stimulated by the limbic system (part of the subcortical or nonvoluntary part of the brain), involves no reflective evaluation of the precipitating stimulus: it "just happens." Furthermore, the message generating the physiological response that constitutes affect is carried not by the nervous pathways for voluntary behavior, but by the autonomic nervous system, which is faster and recruits a more total response (Ekman 1973; Ekman, Levenson, and Friesen 1983). For these reasons, affect often seems to come unbidden from within, so that as an adult one may experience an affective reaction before becoming consciously aware of the nature of the stimulus and the reason for one's response. It is this visceral and vascular reaction that I call *affect*. So in referring to the baby as "joyous," I attribute to it no thought about why he is happy or even that he *is* happy, but only that he is experiencing the same bodily sensations that adults have when in that state. Nevertheless, the baby is happy: that is, he is experiencing what he would call "joy" or "happiness" were he cognitively mature enough to reflect on his state and describe it.

Similarly, when the infant, who has been reprimanded in a harsh tone of voice, breaks eye contact and, with his face suffused by a rush of blood, drops his chin to his chest, he does not just look *as if* he were ashamed; he is experiencing the sensations of that affect. That does not mean, in my vocabulary, that the infant *feels* ashamed or is experiencing the *emotion* of shame.

Feeling, as I use the term, comes into being only later, around eighteen to twenty-four months, when the involuntary basic affective reaction begins to be related to a concept of the self. To be able to say, "I am angry," is to have already abstracted and objectified the affective reaction. *Emotion,* a further step in affective maturation, results when feeling states are joined with experience to give personal meaning to complex concepts such as love, hate, and happiness. The final maturational step in affective development is the capacity for *empathic understanding*—that is, affective communication that goes beyond the self-referential (see pages 145–53).

The distinction made here among affect, feeling, and emotion serves to resolve a contradiction that has existed since Freud's day. Because, as I mentioned previously, Freud (1915c) thought of affect as being simply the conscious aspect of instinctual discharge, *unconscious affect* was a contradiction in terms. However, in the same paper he acknowledged that he had many clinical experiences that necessitated attributing to his patients unconscious affect—anger and guilt especially. That affect is an unconscious, physiological, automatic response to stimulation which may then become conscious in the form of a feeling or an emotion resolves Freud's dilemma. For example, a particular patient may behave in a very angry fashion and yet be unaware of that experience until, with the therapist's help, it is transformed and brought to the patient's consciousness as a feeling.

Because the infant is not independent, either motorically or in thought (that is, cannot distance himself physically or in imagination from his state of being), much depends on whether his messages are understood and responded to appropriately. Fortunately, there is a wide margin of safety, and perfection is not called for. For example, what is important about little Joey Herman's experience is not that he always received an optimal response but that, for the most part, his messages were noticed and understood, and that his mother attempted to correct any failures of communication she noted.

There are, however, limits. Parents who—probably because of the lack of response to their own early attempts to communicate affectively—have become frightened of their feelings may well respond to their children so as to make them ashamed and/or frightened of their own affect, or expressions of affect. The children, in turn, have difficulty maturing affectively as they grow up. (For such a case, see chapter 7.)

The reality of what a patient recovers in the way of memories during psychotherapy and psychoanalysis is often called into question. It is well known that memory of past events is altered by time, cognitive maturation, and the overlayering of other experiences. Nevertheless, I do not agree with the argument that therapist and patient are engaged in a hermeneutic exercise in the sense that whatever they agree upon regarding the patient's past history is their shared reality, and that no further validation is possible or necessary. What remains immutable are the patient's basic affect patterns which, however they may be adapted by the patient to present circumstances and to the therapist's personality, play themselves out, when the treatment is successful, in the transference to the therapist. Or, to put it another way, the affects transferred to, or reactivated with, the therapist are expressions both of the patient's problematic or otherwise disappointing past attempts at affective communication and of the effects of these on the patient's character. So, for example, when I talk about a patient's "father transference," I do not mean I have become the patient's father in some total sense; rather, I am alluding to the idea that some significant affective communication or miscommunication between the patient and his father is there to be understood as it emerges in treatment.

This discussion of affect adds a new dimension to the brain's ordering process and the generation of information, on which learning—the linking of signals to form or modify patterns of expectation—is based. Every stimulus is organized on both cognitive and affective levels. Accordingly, I have amended the diagram of the basic feedback cycle by indicating that there is an affective anticipation attached to every goal-seeking behavior cycle (figure 4.3).

Let me stress again that what I portray schematically here is extremely complex. All the aspects of the feedback cycle—reception, transformation, comparison, decision making, and behavior—have an affective component that influences the desirability of pursuing a particular goal. Nor are affects always singular; several different and contradictory ones often coexist. A feeding experience that is pleasurable one time may be marred by a baby's illness another time, and affected adversely by a mother's dysphoric mood on still a different occasion. The resulting composite or adaptive script is geared to coping with reasonable variations of affect without undue consequences. Still, it is also true that there are limits to adaptability, and that one can develop aversions to activities that in and of themselves could otherwise be pleasurable. So, for instance, if angry reproaches routinely meet one's self-assertion, one may well come to avoid exploratory behavior and other forms of initiative. Fortunately, as the following example demonstrates, minimal intervention by properly informed professionals can, especially during the early years, make a dramatic difference when a child's development seems to be going awry.

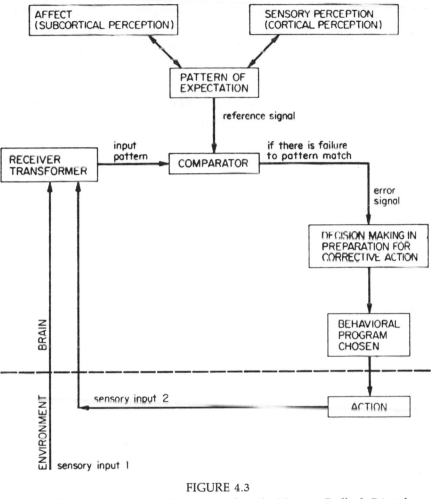

FIGURE 4.3

A Model for the Process of Thought Based on the Negative Feedback Principle

Preventive Psychotherapy: Billy Kruger

One of my greatest gratifications as a psychotherapist is to see how my treatment of one person can have a salutary effect on the other members of his or her family, especially when this occurs with young people who have just or are about to become parents for the first time. The new parent never fails to comment on how he or she can already observe directly in the baby some of the same vicissitudes of affective communication—as reconstructed in therapy—which the parent had experienced in childhood. This knowledge of one's own affective development and of how much parental understanding and communication means to a child is very helpful to new parents. Far from making them overconcerned or excessively cautious, their own affective freedom makes them more sure of themselves with their child and lets them enjoy parenthood more than they otherwise might have done.

This felicitous process need not wait to be exercised by the specialist in psychoanalysis and psychotherapy, who sees patients after they have developed significant problems. The primary physician has a unique opportunity to detect potential difficulties and to nip them in the bud. Once physicians practicing pediatrics and family medicine have been alerted to the nature and significance of affective development in early life, they are usually able to use that information advantageously in what can truly be called preventive or prophylactic psychotherapy. The following is an example of just such an experience.

Mrs. Gladys Kruger brought her eight-month-old infant to her family doctor for an examination. In the office, in addition to the physician, was his nurse and a medical student on a family practice preceptorship. The mother reported that the baby had been eating poorly for two weeks, was spitting up quite a bit, and appeared to be losing weight. He had no fever and did not seem to be in pain. As the doctor was examining the child's lungs and heart, the infant smiled and reached for the stethoscope.

MRS. KRUGER: [*Anxiously, while reaching to restrain the boy's hands*] Billy Kruger! Stop bothering the nice doctor this minute. [*In a softer voice*] Behave yourself now, be a good boy. [*When he first heard his mother's voice, the boy started, looked searchingly at her face, back at the stethoscope, and then began to cry.*] I just don't know what to do with him lately, he's so irritable, I guess I've spoiled him too much.

DOCTOR: Nothing of the sort. Billy is being a very good boy and developing beautifully. Did you notice how, when you brought him into the office, an unfamiliar place where he's surrounded by strangers who do all kinds of things to and with him, he didn't get all upset, but has been smiling, "talking" to me, and showing curiosity about all that's going on? That tells me he is a bright boy who has a very good mother, one who talks and plays with him and makes him feel very secure. I would be much more concerned if he just lay there and showed no interest in what was going on.

When Mrs. Kruger became upset with her son, the doctor might have said, "Oh, that's all right. I'm used to it. Billy isn't bothering me at all"—a perfectly polite response, but he would have been missing the significance of the exchange between Billy and his mother. Instead, in attending to the irritation and tension in Mrs. Kruger's voice, this physician inferred that her reaction was due not to the boy's behavior per se, but to her loss of self-esteem as she judged herself to be an incompetent mother and expected that the doctor would share this invidious opinion of herself—a mother who was raising an ill-mannered child. The physician's grasp of affective development enabled him to respond to what he believed were Mrs. Kruger's fears with a definitive statement that gave her son's behavior an evaluation quite different from her own. The doctor was able to underscore the competence of both mother and son and, in so doing, to reinforce Mrs. Kruger's developmental spiral in the area of self-esteem. Not only did this mother think better of herself, but she might come to look more positively at Billy's attempt at phase-appropriate competence—that is, exploring his surroundings and making things happen—and not simply regard his show of interest as a potential source of annoyance.

MRS. KRUGER: [*Smiling*] I'm glad to hear you say that his behavior is normal. We do have a good time together, or did——

DOCTOR: [*Continuing with his examination*] And now you don't?

MRS. KRUGER: My husband's mother is staying with us, and I just don't have the time for the baby that I had when we were alone during the day.

DOCTOR: Another person in the house makes a difference. Usually, though, when it's a baby's grandmother, the mother will complain that the child is being played with too much and can't be quieted down at bedtime.

Patients often say things that just do not fit in with what the therapist has learned is more or less average, expected behavior. It usually pays to explore, rather than to ignore, such seeming non sequiturs as Mrs. Kruger's equating Billy's grandmother's presence with not having enough time for the baby.

MRS. KRUGER: She's from the old country and her ideas are different. She tells me I'm spoiling him——

DOCTOR: I was wondering where you got that idea——

MRS. KRUGER: When Billy gets excited, squeals, laughs, and pulls himself up in his crib, she says he's becoming a nervous child, that he'll be a discipline problem unless I put my foot down and make him behave. She wants him to have a regular schedule, and tells us to let him cry it out instead of going to him at all hours when he wakes up. She says he should have been sleeping through the night by three months—all her babies did.

DOCTOR: What do you think about that?

MRS. KRUGER: I don't know any more.

DOCTOR: How do you mean?

MRS. KRUGER: I mean he isn't doing anything bad. I won't let him break or hurt anything. The other day he was playing with the dog and was getting rough, and I told him to stop it. It doesn't bother me if he gets upset then, he's got to learn how to get along. I'm not one of those parents who thinks her child is perfect—if he's wrong, he's wrong—but just letting him cry out his heart at night——

DOCTOR: In other words, every time a baby makes a noise, it doesn't mean he's on the road to reform school. You sort of have to figure out first what the noise means and go from there.

MRS. KRUGER: That's what I thought.

Here Mrs. Kruger shed light on a legitimate question. Was grandmother right? Was Billy being permitted to grow up without discipline and without respect for others? The doctor found out that this was not the case, that Mrs. Kruger was setting reasonable standards and enforcing them.

DOCTOR: And your husband? What does Hank say about all this?

MRS. KRUGER: Well, it's *his* mother. It upsets him if I say anything about her. He wants us to get along. Whatever I say, he says she's an old lady and she won't be here long.

DOCTOR: She won't be staying with you long?

MRS. KRUGER: No, he means she won't live much longer. She's seventy-five and healthy as a horse, but she's had all her sons convinced for the last twenty years that she's on her deathbed.

DOCTOR: How long will she be staying with you?

MRS. KRUGER: She's here for three months. It's another two months before she flies back. I don't mind that, it'd be silly to come across the ocean for a weekend. She means well and tries not to be a bother, and she's always willing to help.

DOCTOR: She tries not to be a bother?

MRS. KRUGER: She goes to her room after dinner so that Hank and I have a chance to talk. She's careful not to intrude, usually, you know.

It seemed clear that Mrs. Kruger did not have a vendetta against her mother-in-law, and that her report of what went on between them was not colored by some long-standing antipathy totally unrelated to Billy's situation.

DOCTOR: [*Finishing the examination and washing his hands*] Well, he's a healthy little boy. No infections. All the parts seem to be meshing O.K. Looks like you're doing a good job with him.

MRS. KRUGER: But he has lost weight, hasn't he? And he's so fussy.

DOCTOR: Couple of pounds, but that's nothing to worry about. He can get those back in no time. And he's not fussy—at least he wasn't here with me until you got upset with him when he was just being playful. I guess he's not used to his mother behaving like that.

MRS. KRUGER: I guess I have been on pins and needles. . . . Nothing I do with him seems right any more.

DOCTOR: I think we've got a case here of too many cooks spoiling the broth. Billy is getting mixed signals: he senses the inconsistency in your behavior with him and doesn't know what to do. Put yourself in his place. After all, what kind of an appetite would you have if your world was turned upside down—if the people you depended on treated you differently all of a sudden and what used to get a smile is now frowned on?

MRS. KRUGER: She tells me to prop his bottle at bedtime. He's used to me or his Dad holding him. It's terrible to hear him cry, it tears my heart out. Hank's, too. That's probably why he spits up so much, he's so upset he can't hold anything down.

DOCTOR: I don't like what I'm hearing one bit. Billy is still capable of bouncing back, we saw that here. Probably when you're alone with him, you're your old self and he responds nicely. However, I'm afraid that if this continues, there may be a point where he will no longer take a chance on getting his hopes up only to have them disappointed. Then you might very well have a quiet baby who won't be a bother to anyone. He'll eat well again—as a matter of fact, that's all he will want to do—and he'll sleep through the night and most of the day as well. The technical term for that is "depression."

MRS. KRUGER: Oh, that would be terrible. Maybe things will get back to normal when she leaves.

DOCTOR: You've seen what happened in one month. Three months is a long time in a baby's life. This is the time when Billy is laying down the basic attitudes that will shape his personality. I wouldn't want to take a chance on these next few months.

MRS. KRUGER: You make it all sound so complicated. How do I know when I'm doing the right thing?

DOCTOR: You've been doing fine so far. Billy is a happy, smiling, curious, responsive, sweet kid. That tells me you have a good feel for the boy and can trust yourself to do what is right for him.

MRS. KRUGER: I suppose my sensitivity about Greta's—my mother-in-law's criticism doesn't help matters. I know Hank is uptight. He walks around the house as if he's on eggshells so I won't have any excuse for flaring up at him. I've been so irritable.

DOCTOR: The baby gets the same signals and is responding to them in his own way.

MRS. KRUGER: His way of saying, "Come on, Mom, when are you going to be yourself again?"

DOCTOR: Exactly.

MRS. KRUGER: I guess I better get busy and do something about this. What do you think I should do, Doctor? What would you do if you were me?

DOCTOR: I think it would make sense to think through your priorities. What bothers you most? What do you want to see changed first?

MRS. KRUGER: [*Angrily*] The crying at night. I'm not going to tolerate it. That's that. When Billy wakes up and cries, he's going to be held, and if he wants a bottle, he'll get it. I don't care what other people do. If he needs it, that's enough for me.

DOCTOR: And then?

MRS. KRUGER: Oh, I know exactly what will happen. Greta will be grim at breakfast the next morning, and once Hank has gone to work, she'll start in on me: "Now Gladys,

> I know you are the baby's mother, and I don't mean
> to interfere, but——"
>
> DOCTOR: And then?
>
> MRS. KRUGER: I'm just going to have it out with her, I can see that.
> She's welcome, but it's my house and my child, and
> she's going to have to learn that. If I'm making a big
> mistake with the boy, then it's my mistake. I'm enti-
> tled to raise him my way. Billy is more important
> than peace in the house. Not that it's so peaceful
> anyway. It's quiet but very tense.

I have found that physicians who are not psychiatrists are often afraid to broach psychological issues with their patients because of the inevitable question, "Now that we understand what's wrong, what should I do, Doctor?" In the case of somatic illnesses, the physician is prepared to give specific advice, surgical or pharmacological, once the diagnosis has been made. In psychotherapy, with the exception of patients like Dr. Osgood (see pages 30–36) where one intervenes directly to mobilize a patient who would otherwise regress further to no purpose, one need feel under no compulsion to give advice or specific directions. In this case, Mrs. Kruger's sense of competence as a mother was shaken by the pattern of expectation imposed by her mother-in-law. Having brought out this conflict, the physician was able to use his authority and knowledge to reinforce the mother's self-esteem and confidence in her ability. Now, as was done here, it is much more productive, once the patient has identified the problem and seems ready to do something about it, to see what solution seems possible to her, and then to play out the possible scenarios involved in implementing it, both to see if the ideas will hold up, in fantasy at least, and to help the patient anticipate and prepare to deal with difficulties that might arise in carrying out the plan—in other words, to help the patient with the decision-making part of the developmental spiral.

> MRS. KRUGER: Well, Doctor, I'm afraid I've kept you too long al-
> ready. I'd better let you get to your other patients.
>
> DOCTOR: Not at all. Billy's future is important to me, too. What

you say makes good sense to me. I think it's worth a try.

MRS. KRUGER: I really feel I can handle it now. Thank you. Thanks a lot.

DOCTOR: Call me in a week for sure, sooner if you wish, and let me know how things are going.

Late that afternoon, as they always did when there were evening hours, the doctor and his student broke for dinner and to discuss the day's experiences.

DOCTOR: Well, what do you think of today, George? Anything you want to talk about?

STUDENT: That baby with the weight loss——

DOCTOR: Ah yes, Billy Kruger. I was wondering if you'd pick up on that one.

STUDENT: It was a lucky break that she started talking. We might never have figured out what was wrong with the kid otherwise. I mean, weight loss of unknown origin, that can make you think of all kinds of things.

DOCTOR: And order all kinds of tests and studies that are not only very expensive but subject the child to unnecessary trauma and the parents to unnecessary anxiety wondering what could possibly be wrong. But it wasn't luck.

STUDENT: What wasn't luck?

DOCTOR: That Gladys Kruger started talking about her problem with her mother-in-law.

STUDENT: I didn't hear you ask her about her home situation or any possible upsets. You were just talking, and she opened up.

DOCTOR: I was just talking the same way I just happened to be palpating Herb Jones's abdomen yesterday, when we just happened to find an enlarged liver.

STUDENT: Come on now! I could see that the guy had yellow eyeballs, and that, combined with a complaint of fatigue and loss of appetite, is certainly going to make you mighty interested in his liver.

DOCTOR: True. But Billy's mother was also sending out signs by her unaccustomed tenseness and the frown on her face. I noticed that before she ever told me about the boy.

STUDENT: I suppose if I had noticed that she was tense and worried, I would have attributed that to her concern over the child's symptoms.

DOCTOR: A good point! Of course, I've the advantage of knowing her and her family for a number of years. That's one of the things I like so much about family practice, you have the opportunity of getting to know your patients as people. I've seen her when the baby was sick before, and though she's a concerned mother she's not an anxious one. The minute I saw her I wondered what was troubling her personally. Then it was a matter of finding the opportunity to explore what stress, if any, she was under. I got my chance when she snapped at the boy for being a little playful. Very uncharacteristic of her, I might say.

STUDENT: What if she hadn't said anything and just waited for the examination to be completed?

DOCTOR: Then I would have had to seize the initiative by saying something like: "Well now, Billy is in basically good physical condition, but I wonder what's going on with you? You seem nervous and tense to me, which may account for the baby's not eating well. If something's troubling you, I'd like to hear about it and help if I can. Perhaps we can go into my private office and talk there alone and undisturbed."

STUDENT: Maybe that would work with her, but I wonder if other people might not take offense at your asking them about their personal business?

DOCTOR: They might, but if they do, I would just explain that I consider the psychological stress and strain my patients are under as much my business as their physical aches and pains. Actually, I can't remember that problem ever coming up. People are hungry for understanding, and you seldom run into any objections when you show an interest in a patient's emotional life. Quite the contrary, they usually welcome it. If patients have any complaint in that department, it's that we don't show enough interest in them as people.

STUDENT: I suppose one reason for that is probably that we don't have time to get involved that way. If you had to spend half an hour or an hour with every patient, you wouldn't have time for anything else, then you'd be running a psychiatric practice.

DOCTOR: How much extra time did I spend with Billy and his mother? I'm not talking about doing psychotherapy with people who need the services of a specialist. What I am talking about is what you saw today. We talk to our patients anyway. I only mean that we should pay attention to what they say and use it productively and not just think of it as mere pleasantry and idle chitchat. As a matter of fact, instead of losing it, I probably saved myself and Gladys Kruger quite a bit of time, to say nothing of anxiety on both our parts regarding Billy's welfare, by establishing a reasonable explanation for the boy's problems.

STUDENT: It sounds plausible all right, but what if you're wrong?

DOCTOR: What if I am? Sometimes, in spite of our best effort and the most refined tests, we are mistaken, but that ought not to stop us from making decisions and acting on them if we feel it's in the best interest of our patients. Like any diagnosis, this is a hypothesis that will be put to the test, and we'll see what happens.

The doctor received a phone call from Gladys Kruger a week after the appointment.

MRS. KRUGER: [*Bright and cheerful*] Just thought I'd call you, Doctor, like you asked me.

DOCTOR: Good. I was wondering how things were going with you and Billy.

MRS. KRUGER: Billy is fine. I think we're on the right track.

DOCTOR: Glad to hear it. He's eating nicely again, being his normal, cheerful self?

MRS. KRUGER: Yes, everything is fine.

DOCTOR: And your mother-in-law? Big problems?

MRS. KRUGER: That's what was so funny. The big blowup never came.

DOCTOR: You gave Billy a bottle at night, and she didn't make a federal case out of it?

MRS. KRUGER: Actually, things came to a head sooner than that. When I got home from your office, Billy wanted to play. Greta said I looked tired and it was time for the baby's nap anyway, so he should go to bed and she would make me some coffee and we'd sit and talk. I just decided right then and there to have it out with her. I told her that I was going out in the yard with Billy. It was a nice day and he'd been cooped up inside and needed fresh air—he'd slept in the car anyway and wasn't about to take any nap. I told her we'd be out back, and if she wanted to bring her coffee and sit with us and keep us company she was welcome to do so.

DOCTOR: Wow! What happened then?

MRS. KRUGER: I was so surprised. I got no argument at all. As a matter of fact, she sort of apologized, said she didn't mean to interfere, she was only trying to be helpful. I guess my voice must have sounded pretty angry. So I did tell her that I knew she meant well and that she was very helpful, but that times change, and we raise kids differently now from when hers were little. She seemed to accept that.

DOCTOR: Good. And everything has been O.K. since then?

MRS. KRUGER: I think so. It's easier to be nicer to her now that we've settled things. We're both trying. She does have some very good ideas about the house, so I ask her advice about that—decorating and things—and that pleases her. She just wants to be useful.

DOCTOR: I think you've hit on the right formula. She doesn't want to be put on the shelf just because she's older. She wants her ideas to count, as we all do, so it's great that there's an area where she can make a difference that doesn't step on your toes. So, unless anything out of the ordinary happens, I'll see you when Billy is due for his next checkup.

Like Gladys Kruger, patients often come to therapy seeing a host of obstacles in the way of any solution to the interpersonal aspect of their particular problem; but, like her, too, when they succeed in resolving the intrapsychic aspect of their difficulty, they usually find that they are not blocked in their efforts to improve their lot. I have seen this happen repeatedly with adolescents and young adults who come in all upset because parents object to their choice of career, or friends, or clothes, or what-have-you. Once one works through one's own ambivalence about, let us say, not following one's father's profession, and confronts one's parents in a determined, but nonantagonistic way, and makes a case for one's decision, suddenly there are no objections: instead, offers of help and good wishes are forthcoming. In Mrs. Kruger's situation, her mother-in-law's criticism may well have stirred up some latent doubts about her own efficacy as a mother—and what parent does not have those lurking somewhere in the background? When Mrs. Kruger was helped to think matters through, she came to the conclusion that perfection was not required of her, and that she could trust herself sufficiently to take the chance that whatever mistakes she made with her son would not be irremediable. Once she came to that point, she was able to interact with her mother-in-law in a different fashion, paradoxically reassuring the latter that she did not have to worry about her grandson, that she (the mother) was handling matters, and that Billy's welfare was not her (the grandmother's) direct responsibility.

Billy Kruger's case exemplifies the importance of preventive psychotherapy. Among children in the classroom and on hospital wards, I have observed that depression—the retreat from age-appropriate, goal-directed behavior—seems to be the norm rather than the exception—an impression generally confirmed by my colleagues trained in child psychiatry and psychoanalysis. Much of this depression is, I think, unnecessary, and is brought about by a lack of adequate information regarding the significance of children's affective development and the importance of fostering affective communication from the beginning of life. (See pages 113–21 for a discussion of depression.)

Educational efforts by physicians, visiting nurses, and caseworkers to help parents understand something of the importance of affective development in infancy and childhood, and to foster affective communication between them and their youngsters, is especially important in families that the sociologists are now categorizing as belonging to the "underclass." Parents in this group of economically and educationally disadvantaged people are often significantly depressed and, as a result, withdraw from their offspring as they do from the rest of society. Understimulated and affectively deprived during the first and most important formative years of life, these children are then seldom able to take advantage of the opportunity for development that the educational system offers, in spite of programs designed to help them do so. When at age three or four, they come to the so-called head-start programs in the public schools, it is already too late to remedy the affective deficiencies that many of them have suffered in infancy. These children, who as adolescents and adults often are underachievers and not infrequently turn to delinquent behavior to achieve some sense of competence and self-esteem, are routinely found to have grown up in an emotionally uncomprehending and unresponsive environment. Such children are not prepared to benefit from what they are offered by a school system where success is based on the expected transfer of a positive affective bond between child and parent to the person of the teacher (Basch 1988a).

Physicians and other health-care workers are in a unique position to remedy this grave deficiency by working, in prenatal and postnatal clinics, to teach parents the rudiments of affective communication and to demonstrate its importance for the well-being of child and parents alike. This unparalleled opportunity to practice preventive psychiatry could spare future generations immense suffering and society enormous economic and civic loss.

The Regulation of Affect in Infancy

THE FUNCTION OF COGNITION

As I have already mentioned, Freud (1915c) emphasized that psychological defense, and therefore the work of the psychotherapist, is always concerned with affect. Basically, whatever diagnostic label is given to their difficulties, patients who come to a psychotherapist are suffering the consequences of inadequate or skewed affective development or from the effects of poor emotional control. In some ways, insofar as they are ill, patients display the kinds of affective extremes observed in infants—from affective storms that reason cannot influence, to dramatic total withdrawal from affective experience. An examination of the optimal development of control over affective life, of how affective responses come to be modulated and chosen, rather than simply precipitated or evoked, allows the therapist better to judge what has gone awry in the affective life of a given patient, and then serves as a guide to correcting the problem.

As figure 4.3 indicates, the generally accepted separation of mental life into cognition and affect is misleading. Cognition means "coming to know"; and, as we have seen, much of what we know comes to us through affective communication. *Cognition* or *thought,* as these terms are traditionally used (and as I, in this case bowing to custom, shall also use them), refer to what is roughly subsumed under the heading of *reason* or *logic,* and represents the contribution made to experience by the cerebrum or neocortex. As its name indicates, the neocortex is the most recent portion of the brain to evolve and fits as if it were pulled down, like a stocking cap in winter, over and around the older midbrain, the seat of affect. Here anatomy mirrors function, for, as I conceptualize it, the primary purpose of cognition is to protect the affective system against unnecessary stimulation and guard it from overreacting.

LEARNING THROUGH EXPERIENCE

If affect were to remain an unmediated modality around which the brain organized its decision making, the results would be far from adaptive. The infant's total involvement in the affect of the moment would soon exhaust his or her resources. It would also make the infant oblivious to the environmental signals that called for modification of response. This is where the neocortex and learning come into play.

I would define learning as the linking and encoding of signals to form patterns of expectation whose function is to control tension (see also pages 64 and 80). We can readily observe that a newborn infant who is awakened by hunger in the night will cry until he has the sensation of a nipple between his lips. And we can also observe that, before many days pass, the same baby ceases wailing as soon as the parent enters the room, turns on the light, and prepares for the midnight feeding. The infant has linked signals to form a pattern that stands for or signifies feeding; the parent's footsteps, the turning on the light, and the sleepy but calm voice, all match the baby's expectation sufficiently to halt the stress and initiate interest: the baby has learned something and modulated his affective response to hunger pangs accordingly.

This process involves neither reflection nor recall on the baby's part. For the first eighteen months or so of life, the brain functions according to what Jean Piaget, the world-renowned developmental psychologist, has called the sensorimotor mode (Piaget and Inhelder 1969). What is not operational during this time is the capacity for imaging. Hence, the baby, although learning a great deal during this year and a half—perhaps proportionately more than during the rest of life—cannot use imagination to reify his actions and reflect upon them. Until he reaches the next stage of maturation, he is locked into the reality of the moment.

We have all heard the heart-rending cry of distress when a baby tries to master a challenge by applying the skills he has developed, but does not succeed. If motoric activity does not produce the desired result and decrease the tension generated by interest/excitement in a toy that is out of reach, the infant cannot soothe himself by reflecting that perhaps it would be just as well to wait until his mother comes to help him, and meantime watch the overhanging mobile instead. The tension of frustration mounts until it generates the cry of distress. However, if mother is right there, past experience may have created an adaptive sensorimotor pattern that forestalls unbearable tension by changing reaching behavior to pointing behavior. To this the mother may respond by handing the infant the toy, thus reinforcing a new and less frustrating way of getting what he wants. One should take care not to attribute to the baby the thought, "I can't reach it, but Mom will get it for me." Thoughts of "I," "Mom," "get it," are not yet possible. The pointing behavior is an action schema that under other circumstances has brought about tension-relieving results and is available now to be used as a way of getting things.[*]

ORGANIZATION THROUGH COMMUNICATION

The infant's incapacity to soothe himself by reflecting on his experiences during the sensorimotor phase of cortical development underscores the importance of having reasonably good communication between infant and caregivers. For the first year and a half or so, the adult has to supply the reflective component to the child's sensorimotor behavior in order to maintain optimal tension levels and keep open the channels for learning (Beebe and Sloate 1982; Beebe and Stern 1977; Demos and Kaplan 1985; Stechler and Kaplan 1980; Stern 1984).

If an infant's affective signals are not responded to appropriately—and what is appropriate will vary with the infant and the circumstances—then the increasingly unmanageable tension created by mounting affect could lead to the infant's isolating himself so as to avoid all tension by eliminating occasions for frustration. This outcome has been demonstrated by Virginia Demos and Samuel Kaplan (1985), who based an experiment on the fact that

---

[*]The noted infant researcher and psychoanalyst Daniel Stern (1985) calls these infantile adaptive generalizations in action "RIGs" (Representations of Interactions that have been Generalized).

infants are instinctively programmed to pay particular attention to things human and will often look long and searchingly at the mother's face so as to organize their (the infants') behavior. These researchers have, over a period of months, recorded on film how two mothers' reactions to their respective infants' searching gaze resulted in very different personality development. One mother understood her baby's gaze to be an invitation for facial communion, held the baby's eyes with her own steady but animated gaze, combining touch with talking and cooing until the infant girl turned her attention elsewhere. This sort of experience taught the baby that interest and activity were rewarding. Further films showed her developing into a self-assured infant, confident in initiating activity. She could play independently but also welcomed interpersonal contact and eagerly shared her interest with whatever parent, sibling, or visitor happened to be present.

Another mother, who misunderstood her infant's steady gaze as a sign of boredom, would quickly avert her head in a move to find some toy or other distraction to entertain the baby. It did not take long for this infant to give up trying to enlist her mother in activities. At first she just lay and stared into space. Eventually she learned to play by herself, but languidly and without much interest. She did not readily respond to her mother's voice or attempts to engage her in play. Her father and brother could divert her from her solitary occupations, but only by raising their voices and persisting in efforts to reach her.

Clinicians have long had the impression that the first two years of life are in many respects the most important ones for psychological development. Experiments like this one validate that belief. Long before she can reflect on the nature of her environment and the people in it, the vicissitudes and consequences of affective communication between infant and caregiving adults provide a preverbal sense of what the infant may expect of the world. With the patterns of expectation laid down during the sensorimotor phase of development, the infant brings to childhood a character structure already complex and definite, one that will color all future experience. Optimally, of course, this set is influenced and modified by continued maturation. Since patients in therapy, however cognitively mature, tend to transfer to the therapist the seemingly unaltered affective expectations laid down during this preverbal period, the therapist's knowledge of the findings of infant researchers is invaluable. Current knowledge about early development can guide the therapist as he or she lives with a patient through the reactivation of these primitive, once adaptive, but now self-defeating patterns of behavior in order to help the latter to understand, and eventually gain control of, the past by raising those early experiences to a verbal, reflective level. While I deal with the issue of transference in chapter 6, I shall now turn to the development of the self system: that is, to the system that allows one to make this change.

5

The Self System

PSYCHOTHERAPY has long been a method in search of a truly explanatory theory. As long as the target of psychotherapeutic effort is a mythological and inexplicable entity called *mind,* no verifiable, cohesive, and organized explanation for psychotherapy's successes—and, more important, for its failures—is possible. On the other hand, it is also unsatisfactory simply to reduce the complex decision making usually denoted by the term *mind* to the neurological activity of the brain that gives rise to this decision-making activity.

The invention of general systems theory by Ludwig von Bertalanffy (1968) offered a way out of this dilemma. A system is an entity identified by its function, rather than its physical attributes; it is a stable, information-processing collective made up of a hierarchy of interacting feedback cycles. A system has continuity in time, resists deformation, and expands its influence when conditions are favorable (Paul Weiss 1973). Together, the affective and cognitive information-processing activities of the brain form such a system—here called the *self system*—which governs adaptation to the environment. *Learning, creativity, free will* are all terms that describe the effects of self-system functioning. By the same token, various forms of psychological difficulty are reflections of the unsatisfactory compromises the self system has had to make in the process of adaptation as a result of its limitations, environmental stress, or problems with the neurological substrate in which the self system exists.

The Power of Choice: Early Control of Decision Making

Human beings learn during infancy essentially as do other mammals. We combine inherent perceptual/ordering capacities with experience—especially the experience derived from affective communication—so as to adapt to the world around us. But between eighteen and twenty-four months of age, the capacity for imaginary recall, for perception independent of external experience, matures. This marks the dividing line between infancy and childhood; and it is this function, and not reasoning per se, that makes human beings unique.

IMAGINATION AND RECALL

Recall by means of imagination permits the child to abstract and deal with previously encoded perceptions as objects in themselves, which can then be examined and manipulated. Now the child not only plays with the mother but can later, by abstracting the image of mother from the total experience, deal with her image, and the affect it recruits, separately from the games that they play together (Basch 1981). This capacity for *objectification* is also called *symbolization* because the abstracted recollection stands for or symbolizes an actual event that has taken place earlier.* At this point the child can begin to create immaterial "things"—imaginary entities that exist only in the brain. "Mother" and "Father," for example, do not exist out there—they are designations for relationships attached to the physical person. (With the exception of proper nouns, the names we use for people are indicators of relationships: among others, *doctor* and *teacher*.) The child can go further and invent ghosts, dragons, and the like, which *only* have intracerebral existence. Thinking can now proceed in terms of pure categorization using nominal entities—like subject and object; part and whole; and past, present, and future. Imaging can be carried out on what has been imaged; and that can, in turn, serve as the basis for further imaging ad infinitum. The

*Symbol, as I use the word here and throughout the book, should not be confused with Freud's (1900, 1933) use of the term for certain dream images that, frequently at least, lend themselves to standard interpretation. Such fixed representations are called *signs* in communication theory and linguistics.

dissection and manipulation of events made possible by symbolic representation frees human beings from the immediacy of experience that governs all other animals.

CREATIVITY

Symbolic representation through imagination or fantasy is the basis for creativity. Imagination makes it possible to introduce into a pattern-matching feedback cycle a goal that has only psychic reality—some hope for the future, let us say—and then initiate the decision making that one believes will best transform the virtual into an actual achievement.

Somewhat confusingly, a feedback cycle with a future-directed goal is called a *feed-forward cycle.* The latter's operation is, in fact, no different from the usual goal-directed feedback mechanism, but it is given a different name because the goal exists for the moment in fantasy only and remains to be realized in external experience. Feed-forward cycles make possible both planning for the future and creativity. So, for example, I was in fantasy a physician and then a psychotherapist—long before I received the credentials certifying my status as such.

FREE WILL

Imagination allows for a delay between impulse and action. In everyday usage, this ability to delay action, using consciousness to replay a situation and picture alternative outcomes before coming to a conclusion about what to do, is often equated with "thinking." At first this control of behavior by imagining the future is confined to problem solving in the physical world. When it comes to affect and the impact one's behavior can have on the emotional life of other people, children, especially young children, are notoriously inconsiderate. With further maturation, however, one comes to imagine the affective consequences of planned actions on oneself and on others; and, indeed, affect can be generated in the process. No longer is affect mobilized only by external stimuli; it is now also possible for signals originating from within the cortex to stimulate the limbic system of the subcortical brain as one recalls past experiences or imagines new ones. By thus being able to generate affect and join it to fantasied action without necessarily initiating muscular behavior, a person has an opportunity to reflect on the consequences of actually engaging in such behavior. This reflection, in turn, mobilizes affective responses that either strengthen the initial affect and tip the balance in favor of the planned activity or else modify the affect in such a way that the person changes the plan or abandons it. When such evaluative activity is conscious, it is experienced as the exercise of free will: that is, one is subjectively aware of how one retains control of both the decision-making process and subsequent behavior by managing one's affects instead of being managed by them (Basch 1978).

The interaction of affect, cognition, imaginative representation, and the experience of exercising free will generates the superordinate structure whose functioning is synonymous with psychological life* and which is the focus of psychotherapeutic activity: that is, what I call the *self system* (see also Basch 1988*b*).†

The Self System

SYSTEMS: OPEN AND CLOSED

Life on any level—vegetative, psychological, or social—depends on the ability of the organism to adapt to the environment that makes possible existence, or some aspect of it. This adaptation necessitates the continuous processing of signals by interrelated, error-correcting feedback cycles. Together these feedback mechanisms form hierarchical organizations or systems that monitor the

*I call "psychological" whatever takes place at the interface of the environment and an affectively responsive brain whose patterns of expectation are potentially capable of modification. (I am much obliged to George Klumpner for first suggesting to me that psychology, in its broadest sense, can be thought of in terms of the interface of physiology and experience; and to my discussions with Douglas Detrick, which narrowed the focus of the psychological to those activities between the brain and its environment involving the generation and/or communication of affect.)
†The term *self system* was, to the best of my knowledge, coined by the founder of the school of interpersonal psychiatry, Harry Stack Sullivan (1940), although he gave it a different meaning from the one I use here.

environment and adjust themselves to it. Since the pioneer work of Norbert Wiener (1948, 1956), who first described the feedback concept and its significance, there has grown up a whole group of sciences—information theory, control theory, cybernetics, communication theory, systems theory, structuralism, computer science—to delineate the nature of such organizations and the laws governing their operation (see Buckley 1968; Campbell 1982; Fields and Abbott 1963).

Systems whose manner of functioning can change as the surrounding conditions change are called *open systems.* In other words, open systems are organizations that can learn from experience. Systems that operate through programs that are relatively inflexible and cannot change with the circumstances are called *closed systems.* For example, the biologist Dean E. Wooldridge (1963, 1968), in studying the habits of the digger wasp, *Sphex ichneumoneus,* observed that at egg-laying time the female prepares a burrow, flies off to find a cricket which it stings and paralyzes, brings that cricket to the burrow, puts it down on the threshold, enters to make sure that all is still well, and only then brings the cricket inside, lays its eggs next to it, seals the burrow, flies off, and does not return. Though the young are left to hatch alone, they are well provided for, feeding off the cricket until they are ready to leave the burrow and fend for themselves. If, while the wasp was inspecting the burrow, Wooldridge moved the cricket a few inches from the threshold, the wasp would not simply relocate its prey and bring it into the previously inspected nest, but, instead, would place the cricket on the threshold again, enter the burrow to inspect it once more, return, and only then drag its victim inside. Wooldridge moved the cricket as many as forty times; and never did the wasp simply come out, refind the cricket, and bring it inside. Each time the entire ritual had to be repeated. Thus, though clever and complex, the system responsible for this performance is nevertheless closed—incapable of generating new information on the basis of experience, incapable of learning. (Similarly, the problems that patients bring to psychotherapy exemplify the operation of closed systems. While a patient may think he or she has and is making all sorts of choices, observation of the outcome of a given patient's behavior, time and time again, shows that in the area of pathology a fixed pattern is repeating itself, unaltered by experience. Precisely because of the closed-system nature of a patient's problems, the therapist can confidently anticipate being able, in the transference, to observe a faithful replica of the behavior responsible for the patient's difficulties.)

As in other animals, the management of the human visceral or vegetative milieu is controlled by relatively closed systems. So, for example, we cannot live without air for more than a few minutes: our respiratory system cannot use the information that air is not available to adapt itself to extracting oxygen from water, or to substitute another gas for oxygen. In other respects, however, we are the most flexible of creatures—a flexibility made possible by the self system. The programs that comprise the self system are the guardians of order, the ensurers of competence and, ultimately, of self-esteem.

THE EVOLUTION OF THE SELF SYSTEM

Below the mammalian level of evolution, adaptation to the environment is accomplished through essentially fixed, inherited programs—like that of the digger wasp—that determine how an animal is to behave in response to a limited number of specific stimuli. These animals, because they are not subject to uncertainty, cannot generate new information from environmental stimulation; they function as essentially predictable or closed systems. Mammals acquired superior adaptive flexibility when rigid instinctual programs for interaction with the environment evolved into increasingly open systems that confronted the animal with uncertainty, choice, and the possibility of learning. So a frog, instinctually programmed to respond to the patterns created by a moving black dot, will starve to death surrounded by freshly killed but immobile flies. A mammal, deprived of its usual manner of stilling its hunger, can, however, adapt itself to an unfamiliar situation through trial and error.

In mammals, instead of response being inextricably coupled to stimulus, the genetically inherited instinctual blueprint that governs development operates more as a guideline for adaptation, ensuring the preservation of the species while leaving the individual animal room to develop a variety of behaviors in response to its immediate environment (Arnold 1960). Once an animal no longer functions as a preprogrammed automaton, and is faced with making significant adaptive choices, it needs to develop some sense of functioning as an entity distinguished from its surroundings. The self system is the mediating structure between instinctual drive—the inherited blueprint for generating information in a given species—and the demands and opportunities of the environment. Through the aegis of the self system the mammalian brain functions, so to speak, as a self-programming computer.

SELF SYSTEM AND PERSON

Self system is not interchangeable with *person*. *Person* refers to a social being; *self system* is a collective term encompassing the hierarchy of neurologically encoded, goal-directed feedback cycles whose activity constitutes character and governs behavior. Since these terminologic distinctions have practical (clinical) implications, when the nonspecific term *self* is used it is important to establish whether it is meant to refer to the *person* in the general sense or to the underlying *self system*—the biological entity whose activity supports the former's sense of identity.

Since the self system is never conscious as such, our ideas about its functioning or malfunctioning must be inferred. The person, on the other hand, is available to inspection. Thus, what one learns about each does not necessarily coincide. For example, the woman sitting across from me is supremely self-confident: nothing is beyond her. Indeed, she has been brought in by her relatives because she has just signed contracts and promissory notes far exceeding her means. Judging from her behavior and history, I come to the conclusion that in fact this confident *person* has a *self system* that is defending itself with a manic psychotic episode against overwhelming anxiety and insecurity about its ability to continue functioning.

Again, the neurotic believes that his hand-washing compulsion makes no sense: as Freud (1916–17) said, he views his symptom as a foreign body and disowns it. However, with the analytic investigation of the formation of this person's self system, the symptom takes on greater significance and appears, for example, to reflect a need to absolve a sense of guilt related to unconscious patricidal impulses.

As these examples show, the use of *person* and *self system* reflects the distinction between the interpersonal and the intrapsychic; between what is consciously available and what remains unconscious and, to a greater or lesser degree, beyond one's reach.

THE SYMBOLIC WORLD

A brain capable of imagination and recall can generate its own environment, what Bertalanffy (1967) called the symbolic world. Consequently, our self system has, in its decision-making function, to mediate at two interfaces: one between itself and the outer world; the other between itself and the world of symbolic experience that is, patterns created through imaginative manipulation of previously registered perceptions.* The self system, initially a creation of the brain, comes, through its mediating function, to control and guide the brain in its relation to the world. In establishing a balance between the symbolic activity of thought and the constraints and opportunities of the external world, the self system gives rise to what I have called the developmental spiral (see chapter 2).

MIND

While the term *mind* has often been used collectively to subsume thought, feeling, and volition (see pages 57–64), it has always had another meaning: that of a mysterious guiding or direction-giving entity, which, like Descartes's "soul," through its decision-making capacity controls behavior. The concept of a self system as I elaborate it fills this latter function, thereby eliminating the need to postulate *mind* as a supernatural or further unknowable entity.

*I do not employ the term *ego*, which was used by Freud (1923) and, later, by the psychoanalyst Heinz Hartmann (1939), to describe the adaptive agency because it is inextricably linked with the instinct theory of development, psychic determinism, and the belief that the basic needs of infancy—the id—are nonadaptive and in conflict with the ego. I reject these three propositions on the basis of recent findings in the field of infant research, as summarized by myself (1977), John Bowlby (1969, 1980), Joseph Lichtenberg (1983), and Daniel Stern (1985).

THE CLOSED SELF SYSTEM: PSYCHOPATHOLOGY

The human capacity to symbolize allows for creativity and potentially frees us to a significant extent from the tyranny of both instinct and environment. More often than not, however, the long and indeterminate developmental history of the self system (which is experienced phenomenologically as character formation) is so dependent on constitution, chance, and the recruitment of appropriate input from the environment as to be vulnerable to threats of deformation or annihilation, which it is not always prepared to deal with effectively. To protect itself against such dangers, the system may close itself to stimuli, thereby inhibiting the generation of information necessary for continued growth. These attempts at self-protection, necessary as they may be when they occur, become part of the self system and affect its future course. Psychopathology in varying degrees of severity may be the end result of such distortions.

When a portion of one's self system lacks necessary creativity and adaptability, one loses freedom of will: that is, one no longer has any choice about what one does, but, rather, finds oneself repeating a preordained pattern. (Freud called this the *repetition compulsion* [1920].) In other words, the patient who comes for treatment presents the therapist with a self system that has been closed in some significant respect. It is, as I shall elaborate in chapter 6, the psychotherapist's task to help such a distressed patient to open up the system—that is, to overcome resistance to altering the patterns in the patient's nervous system that govern how he or she interprets relevant signals. The aim is not simply to remove symptoms but, by reworking the self system's information-processing mode, to restore the patient's creative capacity and freedom of choice.

As do all systems of the body, the self system has available mechanisms designed to protect its integrity and its functions when those are in danger. These protective mechanisms are much like coughing and shortness of breath in the respiratory system, or nausea and vomiting in the gastrointestinal system, in that they are nonspecific: that is, they signal only that something is wrong, but do not identify that something. Consciousness of self as perceiving or acting promotes reflection and is the first of these protective mechanisms. If this fails to restore order, varying degrees of anxiety supervene. By focusing all the resources of the self system on whatever may be disturbing its ability to function effectively, anxiety may eliminate the problem. If that does not happen, various defenses such as withdrawal, repression, or disavowal may be called into play to sequester the difficulty. Alternately, the self system may retreat into depression and finally apathy to escape what cannot be dealt with.

The Vicious Circle of Anxiety

In the self system, the first manifestation of disorganization is consciousness. As I discussed in respect to the driver on a familiar route who is suddenly alerted by a road-repair sign (page 63), consciousness comes into being only when there is a need to replay perceptions so that they may find their proper place in the aggregate of experience, or lead to the revision of some aspect of the relevant patterns of expectation, or be dismissed as inconsequential. If consciousness fails in its task, the continued disorder creates a state of overstimulation. In the prereflective infant, overstimulation leads to the emission of distress signals, such as crying and thrashing about. Ideally, that behavior will attract the attention of caregiving adults, who can enter the system and restore order, either through specific interventions (changing a diaper, bringing a toy within reach) or through generally soothing behavior, such as rocking and holding the baby. In adults, if reflection—that is, conscious replay of problematic perceptions and ideas—fails to reduce overstimulation and to restore order, anxiety results.

Anxiety is usually defined as an uncomfortable feeling of apprehension generated by inner and unknown, rather than external and observed, danger. In my scheme of things, however, anxiety is not a feeling but an emotion because the affect of fear involves the person as both subject and object; it is as if the person were to say, "I feel endangered by a disorder that seems to be coming from me."

Very much as Freud (1926a) described, anxiety serves as a signal. I think of it as an internal distress signal originating in the self system, but rather than being directed at others—as is the case with a distressed infant—it is a message to the self system itself to mobilize all its resources and restore a threatened state of order.

THE PSYCHOLOGICAL ORIGIN OF ANXIETY

In the therapy situation there is frequently a period of anxiety just before a patient's heretofore unconscious or unformulated memories of traumatic past experiences become available for conscious examination. At that point, neither the patient nor I may have any inkling of what is precipitating the anxiety. In that case, I often find it useful to give the patient a general explanation of the process, pretty much as I have just described it here. This explanation is often enough to give the patient a feeling of control over what is happening to him or her, and this then allows the specific thoughts behind the anxiety to surface and be talked about.

Anxiety can be mild, or it can mount to a sense of nameless, impending doom or panic which the sufferer will make a great effort to escape. Severe anxiety is often accompanied by discharge from the nervous system resulting in sweating, rapid breathing, and increased heart rate. These bodily signals, in turn, feed one's sense that things are out of control, and increase the anxiety, thus intensifying the bodily response and setting up a vicious circle.

THE PHYSIOLOGICAL ORIGINS OF ANXIETY

This situation can be reversed, with nervous system activity triggered by other causes actually generating anxiety. Some years ago, for example, I was sitting in a seemingly interminable committee meeting, bored beyond belief, when all of a sudden I found myself in the throes of what I identified as an anxiety attack. I wondered whether something that was being talked about might have triggered some tender or conflicted spot, threatened my self-esteem, or made me insecure; but all I had heard so far had provoked nothing in me but somnolence. Nor was I ambivalent about the chairperson: I would gladly have shot him if I thought I could get away with it, so unconscious hostility was not agitating me. As I quickly reviewed them, neither the experiences of the previous day nor any dreams of the night before gave me the slightest clue why I should be having this increasingly painful and by now quite frightening experience. I was in a sweat, my pulse was more than two times my normal heart rate, and I felt a great urge to get up and run out of the room and out of my skin. It finally occurred to me that this was my third meeting in as many hours; and that for want of anything better to do, I had been drinking several cups of coffee in each of these torture sessions. The excessive amounts of caffeine I had consumed were responsible for my anxiety symptoms. By making a mistaken association based on past experience, I had, as Donald L. Nathanson (1987) puts it, formed an emotion out of a chemically triggered affective reaction.

I observed how similar my response was to that of a patient to whom I have satisfactorily explained what he or she is experiencing during an anxiety attack: my escalating fear of what was happening within me, my anxiety about my anxiety, disappeared as soon as I understood what had occurred. Even though my symptoms persisted for at least an hour and I remained uncomfortable, my sense of panic subsided.

More seriously, hormonal difficulties—thyroid storms, for example, or tumors of the adrenal glands or of the brain—are able to bring about such autonomic crises. The therapist may not, therefore, assume that the origin of a patient's anxiety is necessarily psychological, but must also consider the possibility that the malfunction of a system other than the self system has precipitated it. This issue becomes more important with a patient the therapist is seeing for the first time. With a patient the therapist knows well, it is usually much easier to establish whether a symptom's origins are psychological or due to disturbances in the functioning of another system. I once treated an elderly woman for a depression severe enough to require hospitalization. She responded well to psychotherapy, and I subsequently saw her in the office on a weekly basis. A short time after her discharge, she called me one evening complaining of anxiety and expressing the fear that she was getting depressed again and might have to re-enter the hospital. Having just seen her that day, I knew she had been managing her life very well and that her past problems were not interfering with her functioning. She replied in the negative when I asked her whether, since our visit, her circumstances had changed. The feeling that something bad was going to happen to her had descended upon her out of the blue. Although she had recently had a physical examination that had uncovered nothing untoward, I nevertheless told her to contact her internist immediately and said I, too, would talk to him. On my advice, she was hospitalized, and it was found that she had had a sudden, severe elevation of what had been mild hypertension. Unfortunately, her physical condition deteriorated; she suffered a stroke and died a few days later (see also Beigler 1957).

THE CONSEQUENCES OF ANXIETY

Anxiety serves a useful purpose insofar as it calls attention to the presence of an unresolved issue and brings one's cognitive resources to bear on this threat to inner order. But, as with any other pain signal, when anxiety is prolonged and intense, it itself becomes the problem; and in the immediate need to relieve the discomfort of the moment, re-establishment of order at any cost becomes paramount, while the more basic difficulty that gave rise to the anxiety in the first place may well be set aside.

I have equated anxiety with other forms of pain that tell us something is going wrong somewhere in the body's organization. There is, however, a significant difference between the self system and the rest of the body, one to which I have already alluded— namely, the adaptability of the former. While the pain of appendicitis can be eliminated with morphine, the odds are high that the underlying disease, unless surgically cured, will in a short time end the patient's life. So it is for most serious somatic ailments because a basically closed system has relatively little tolerance for prolonged distortion of function. However, where the self system is concerned, even if conscious replay of the disorganizing factor does not resolve the discrepancy between expectations and the disturbing traumatic element, order can still be restored, albeit at a sacrifice.

When no help is forthcoming and the self system has no better way to deal with an anxiety-provoking situation, it compromises its own functioning so as to forestall the threat of overwhelming disorganization. One's self system may compromise itself through a retreat into depression, or avoid further traumatization through a developmental arrest, or cope with or compensate for the trauma through symptom formation or other distortions of normal character development.* Eventually, more often than not, the attempt to deal with anxiety in a pathological fashion fails. One then consults a therapist because of the secondary difficulties—for example, neurotic symptoms or characterologic problems—that this creates. The therapist must take care not to mistake the symptom for the disease itself. Initial temporizing with anxiety through pathological compromise formations, leaving unresolved the underlying threat to order, often makes for a lengthy and tortuous course of insight therapy. Here the therapist must help such a patient retrace the steps of his or her development with the goal of gaining understanding of and control over whatever psychological circumstances precipitated anxiety so severe as to distort the self system in the first place.

Depression

Anxiety is a communication to the self system to mobilize its available resources to cope with some stress. The failure of that effort may result in depression, which I think of as a general protective mechanism open to a self system unable to restore order (Basch 1975a). Depression indicates that the self system has had to retreat to a lower level of functioning in the face of its inability to meet higher goals. Depression also serves as a communication, a message to the world at large that the self system can no longer be counted upon, that it has ceased to function in some significant degree, that one

*Psychosis may also represent a general protective retreat of an endangered self system in people predisposed, probably by heredity, to such illnesses. Painful as it often is, the idiosyncratic world the schizophrenic or the manic patient constructs for himself or herself is still a form of functioning—a way of holding the self system together. The therapeutic approach to such patients is a field in itself, not to be dealt with here.

has lost hope, and that help must come from the outside.* Within limits, depression, like anxiety, is a useful communication. A depressed face, whether that of an understimulated infant in a crib or of an elderly person abandoned in an old-age home, is a pathetic sight. It is an expression that ordinarily evokes pity or tenderness and a wish to help.

Not many of us are strangers to feelings of depression. For myself, I have while writing this book become frustrated and balked more times than I can count about what I was trying to express, and then retreated into a depression, thinking to hell with the whole enterprise; suffered the miseries of thinking what my life would be like if I did not finish the job or did it in slapdash fashion; tried to soothe myself by going to the refrigerator for a snack, hating myself for knowing how much I would hate myself when I stepped on the scale the next morning; complained to my wife about the impossibility of continuing my existence, only to be (1) reassured that, as had happened innumerable times before, I could and would overcome the problem, and (2) ordered to get busy; saw no way out but to do just that; got anxious again, but sat down and tackled the problem once more, finding that, whether or not I was successful in resolving it, the gloom dissipated as I found myself once again creatively employed in the ordering process.

Alternatively, when there has been no one around to complain to, and I have suffered enough to convince myself that the misery of being miserable outweighs the misery of frustration with my writing, I have done with myself what I did with Dr. Osgood—namely, put aside the task whose contemplation is making me anxious and substituted a more achievable one. Usually I straightened out my desk, went through the mail that was piling up, paid bills, answered a letter or two, and, as I demonstrated to myself that I was capable of creating order, found myself thinking about whatever had been puzzling me when I temporarily gave up. And—lo and behold!—the creative power of the unconscious began to operate, and an idea

*My point of view contrasts with that proposed in *Mourning and Melancholia,* where Freud saw depression as a sign of aggression turned inward (1917). I do not mean to say that there are not depressive retreats in the face of conflicts around unconscious anger, but the two are not inevitably linked. It is a therapeutic and technical mistake to assume, as is still often done, that where there is depression there is hidden aggression; and that if such feelings do not appear in the clinical material, the patient is of necessity concealing them from the therapist.

suggested itself that might get me out of the mess I was in; and so on.

Depressed feelings are not the same as clinical depression. The obvious differences between my experience and Dr. Osgood's were, of course, that, first of all, my retreat from my goal-directed functioning was not as global and deep as his; and, second, I was still able to help myself, or could readily use the help offered me by another. A clinically depressed state is less easily reversed and usually requires professional intervention.

Clinical depression takes two forms, endogenous and exogenous. Differential diagnosis is very important because the nature of the depression plays a large role in determining what form of therapy to use for a particular patient. Reverting to a computer analogy, we may say that the endogenous depression is brought about by a problem in the functioning of the brain's hardware—the neuronal network itself and/or the chemical exchanges that make nerve impulse transmission possible; while an exogenous or reactive depression reflects the failure of the software—that is, the inability of one's inherited and learned programs for adaptation to cope adequately with stress bearing on the system from without. Endogenous depressions are typically accompanied by such vegetative, or organic, signs as insomnia, dysphoria that is worse in the morning and clearing toward evening, inability to concentrate, loss of appetite with accompanying weight loss, constipation, and amenorrhea. However, these signs do not in themselves rule out reactive, or exogenous, depressions, which are precipitated by an event in the outside world that creates demands that the self system cannot cope with adequately. Only a careful examination of the patient's past and present dynamics can establish the likely source of the depressive syndrome.

PRIMARY REACTIVE DEPRESSION

Exogenous or reactive depressions may be primary or secondary. For example, as might have happened with Billy Kruger, an understimulated infant may come to suffer from a primary reactive depression. Similarly, in retirement and old age, one may experience a lack of challenge and stimulation, with no opportunity to demonstrate competence, a subsequent loss of self-esteem, and a retreat into primary exogenous depression. The depression of both child and old person may be treated by appropriate stimulation. While it is easy to provide this for the infant and the child, it is harder to do so for the older man or woman who feels cast aside and views his or her life as a failure.

Rather than adopt the all-too-frequent attitude in our society that the superannuated worker or housewife is uninteresting and without a future—an embarrassment to be kept out of sight or shut up in an old-age home—I treat these older patients as I would any patient, and invite them—insist if necessary—to tell me about their past and present lives in detail. The very idea that a person they respect is interested in listening to them and wants to learn not only about them but *from* them, often lets these patients re-evaluate their lives. What they have thought to be uneventful and trite turns out not to be so at all; what they think of as a failed life often hides real heroism and achievement. This new-found perspective often brings dramatic change, permitting such patients to renegotiate their relationships and, in some cases, to make their last years their happiest. The therapist's conviction that the developmental spiral need not end until life does is perhaps the most important ingredient in the treatment of the older patient with an otherwise uncomplicated depressive reaction. Thus, the young or middle-aged therapist must guard against identifying with the patient, and letting his or her own fear of failure, growing older, and dying prejudice the clinical situation.

SECONDARY REACTIVE DEPRESSION

In a great number of the patients with reactive depressions who come for treatment, depressive symptoms are secondary to an earlier disturbance. When pathological constellations fail to control anxiety, there is a secondary retreat to the helpless depressive state. The therapist must then work from the surface down: first, dealing with the depressive symptoms; and, when the patient has sufficiently recovered from these, pursuing a therapeutic investigation of the origin of the underlying problem that precipitated the patient's depression. The case of Roger Flynn (see chapter 8) elaborates on the treatment of just such a patient. Al Gertz and Mrs. Senoj also were likely candidates for secondary reactive depressions.

ENDOGENOUS DEPRESSION

While the endogenous depressions of the milder sort—Dr. Osgood's illness is a typical example—may resemble the reactive depressions, they differ, as I have suggested, in origin and, therefore, in treatment. In diagnosing a patient's depression for which no external precipitating situation can be discovered, the therapist must assume, until evidence to the contrary turns up, that it has a significant organic component. It may be that the brain's activity is being interfered with electrochemically or mechanically; the latter may be due to the presence of tumors or other space-occupying lesions. Multiple sclerosis and other degenerative diseases of the central nervous system, malignant tumors in other parts of the body (especially carcinoma of the pancreas), infections, and circulatory problems may also be responsible for depressive regression. Usually, in mechanical or infectious interferences with the brain's normal functioning, neurological signs and symptoms in addition to the depression are also in evidence. It is possible that depression may be the only sign of a brain tumor, for example, although I have not seen such a case in over thirty years of clinical practice.

Since the early 1950s, medications have been discovered that, though their mode of action and the nature of their salutary effect is not exactly known, have proved helpful in alleviating the symptoms of endogenous depression. Before these psychotropic drugs were available, as I told Dr. Osgood, psychotherapists successfully treated simple endogenous depressions with psychotherapy alone, helping the patient to do what I described as doing for myself, gradually getting him or her back into the routine of maintaining self-esteem.

With the advent of psychotropic drugs it became important to consider the possibility of there being an organic component even in those depressive retreats that seemed to be clearly related to developmental and/or immediate environmental difficulties. I have had cases in analysis or intensive psychotherapy where intractable depression responded to medication. Several such patients have reported that once on antidepressants they knew for the first time in their lives what it felt like not to be dysphoric. Their improvement in mood did not, however, do away with the problems that brought them for treatment originally. These patients felt better, but they did not feel well.

While the advertisements of pharmaceutical companies report such medicated patients suddenly making great strides in psychotherapy, in my experience the lifting of the endogenous undercurrent of depression does not make it any easier for a patient in therapy to deal with his or her psychological—or "software"—problems. I have a hunch that the people who are reported as responding so dramatically to medication, having been impervious to psychotherapeutic efforts, are patients who had a primary endogenous problem and should have been medicated all along; whereas the patients I am talking about are suffering from two types of depression concurrently: one endogenous; the other, a reactive secondary depression linked to characterological difficulties.

Because of the nonspecific origin of depressive illness, psychotherapists who are not also physicians must have appropriate consultation during the diagnostic period with depressed patients to determine whether identifiable organic causes for the depressive episode are present and/or whether treatment other than psychotherapy should be prescribed for the patient. In the latter case, joint therapy is indicated. In cases where the recommendation for medication is not made at the time that the initial treatment plan is laid out, but the patient does not subsequently respond to psychotherapy as expected, the patient's status should be reviewed periodically with a psychiatrist consultant to consider other forms of treatment.

As a psychiatrist who almost exclusively practices psychotherapy and psychoanalysis, I have found that psychopharmacology has become so complex as to constitute a subspecialty beyond my ken. With patients like Dr. Osgood, for whom both psychotherapy and medication are indicated, I still prescribe simple antidepressant medication to accompany my psychotherapeutic efforts. If, however, satisfactory results are not forthcoming, I refer that person, after discussing the situation with him or her, to a colleague skilled in such matters while I continue to conduct the psychotherapy.

In cases where the formation, management, and resolution of the therapeutic transference is the main goal—that is, in psychoanalysis or insight psychotherapy—but where medication is also deemed necessary, I always refer the patients elsewhere for that aspect of the treatment. In my opinion, any prescribing of medication on my part would constitute an unnecessary interference with my primary therapeutic role. Of course, colleagues practicing in other than urban environments may not have the option of readily referring patients to skilled psychopharmacologists and thus may have to medicate these patients and then deal psychotherapeutically with any incidental psychological problems precipitated by this dual role.

Deeper endogenous depressions, including the state of profound apathy called *melancholia,* usually do not respond to psychotherapy and require medication or electroconvulsive therapy. Why the latter treatment works, no one knows; but in selected cases, it dramatically reverses the symptoms of the illness.

My first patient as a resident was a middle-aged woman who had been in the hospital for eight years, passed from one resident to the next as each finished his rotation on the in-patient service. She was treated psychotherapeutically in groups and individually, three and four times a week, and family sessions were held on weekends—all to no avail. Occasionally she would seem somewhat improved, return to her home, only to relapse after a few days or weeks and be rehospitalized. I read the lengthy history in her chart and tried to talk to her on several occasions. She was typically uncooperative and monosyllabic, but her face and demeanor spoke eloquently of the terrible pain she was experiencing. Common sense told me that the likelihood was great that I, a callow beginner, would not accomplish more with psychotherapy than my more experienced predecessors had been able to do. I had read about electroconvulsive therapy, and it seemed to me that nothing would be lost by trying it here. I was working in a psychotherapeutically oriented milieu at a time when physical therapies were considered to be second rate and their use equated with giving up on a patient. Nevertheless, my unit chief accepted my suggestion, albeit reluctantly. I think he probably wanted to teach me a lesson about the futility of such treatment.

We planned a series of convulsions and began to administer them. Nothing much changed in the patient's symptomatology after three treatments, and I began to wonder whether indeed this, too, would fail to help her. I had other patients on this unit and was coming to see one of them when a patient whom I did not know came up to me and, in an animated, friendly way, began to talk to me. I had that uncomfortable feeling I often get at parties when someone I have obviously met, and should but do not recognize, engages me familiarly, leaving me trying to cover my ignorance while desperately reaching for some clue to the speaker's identity and where we had previously connected. She must have understood what was troubling me for, with a big smile, she said, "Dr. Basch, don't you recognize your patient?" and then of course I did. I had just never seen her with life in her face. She was a different person after the fourth convulsive treatment. Her improvement held, and she was soon discharged. I was able to follow her for several years thereafter, and she remained well.

As I said, no one knows why electroconvulsive therapy works. My guess would be that the disorganizing effect of the electric current passing through the brain stimulates some total reorganizational effort of that organ, which has a salutary effect—much as, before the discovery of antibiotics, artificially high fevers were induced in patients with certain intractable infections in a sometimes successful attempt to stimulate the immune system. Unfortunately, electroconvulsive therapy acquired a bad name because it was used indiscriminately—much as is now often done with psychotropic medications—and given to patients who required psychotherapy. Not surprisingly, these patients did not get well—indeed, grew worse—not because they had electroconvulsive therapy, but because they did not get the treatment that might have helped them. Electroconvulsive therapy should not be forgotten, especially when pharmacotherapy is not effective in patients with disabling endogenous or vegetative depressions.

The argument that electroconvulsive therapy should not be used because it is followed by memory loss does not, in my opinion, hold up. My experience, admittedly not recent, has been that the permanent memory loss in patients receiving electroconvulsive treatment was only for the details of the illness and the treatment itself. Any confusion about and forgetting of details of the patient's life predating the illness cleared up within a few weeks, leaving him or her able to function as usual. In any case, to forbid the treatment because of the possibility of such sequelae makes no sense to me, considering the dreadful suffering that has been alleviated by electroconvulsive therapy when it is appropriately used. I would compare withholding this treatment when needed to an interdict on lifesaving surgery because a patient's skin may be scarred in the process.

Just as the therapist must be alert to patients who need medication in addition to psychotherapy, so one should never neglect the importance of psychotherapy for patients who are on psychotropic medication or receiving electroconvulsive treatment. Medication and electroconvulsive treatment are not substitutes for psychotherapy. My rule of thumb is that any patient sick enough to require psychotropic medication deserves concomitant psychotherapy and follow-up. However, patients who have had endogenous depressions seldom welcome attempts to conduct insight psychotherapy, even after they have recovered. They are usually uncomfortably and unproductively stressed by any attempt to get them to introspect with a view to exploring their personality structure. What they do need, however, is support in dealing with the shame that they often associate with having been ill and unable to function. Also, an understanding relationship with the therapist is usually helpful in preparing the hospitalized patient to reenter his or her normal milieu. Periodic follow-up is reassuring for these patients, who are often understandably fearful of getting sick again and may become anxious under psychological stress. Furthermore, recurrent episodes may be forestalled or minimized if detected in their early stages, often before the patient is aware of what is happening to him or her.

Defense Mechanisms

If an insult threatening the integrity of the self system and giving rise to anxiety is not appropriately resolved, one may, as I have said, suffer a depressive retreat and a potentially severe and global regression of functioning. The self system may, however, try to avoid this outcome through activation of so-called defense mechanisms.

The brain is constantly generating more information than is needed for adaptation. It makes no difference that, as you drive down the highway, coming toward you is a green Chevrolet with three passengers in the front seat. What is important is that that car is straddling the midline, and you must veer slightly to the right so as to avoid an accident as you pass it. The brain, however, notes it all and then filters out what is not necessary. If your fellow passenger were to ask you, "What kind of a car did we just pass?" you might well answer, "I don't know. I wasn't paying attention to that. Whatever it was, though, it came mighty close." If, however, later in the day you hear on the radio that three bank robbers fled the scene of their crime in a green Chevrolet, that information suddenly becomes important and enters consciousness: there is a "flash" of memory. These sorting and filtering mechanisms of the brain can be used pathologically: that is, information is blocked not because it is unimportant, but rather because the self system has evaluated it as threatening to arouse unmanageable affect. These gatekeeping maneuvers are called *defenses.* The continued use of defense mechanisms interferes with maturation. When an affect is blocked from expression around some set of experiences, that prevents affective maturation in that area. This, in turn, has an effect on character formation and/or functioning. I suspect that any thoughts Al Gertz, the taxi driver, might have had of wanting to be held, comforted, and understood had to be eliminated—that is, defended against—because somewhere along the line—probably very early in his development—he learned that such needs did not elicit a desired or satisfying response. Why continue to experience such pain when there is no relief? Ergo, instead of his learning more about such feelings and how to cope with them successfully, they were automatically replaced by an amorphous anger.

The earlier in development the trauma necessitating defensive action occurs, the more global the inhibition of affect tends to be. With further maturation, defenses can act more selectively so that affective maturation may seem to be quite satisfactory until one touches on the problematic aspects of the patient's mental life. A knowledge of the patient's primary defense provides a telling clue to the developmental problems that need to be addressed in the treatment and to the manner in which the therapist can most productively approach the patient. Freud identified three basic defenses against painful affect: primal repression, disavowal, and secondary repression or repression proper (Freud 1915b, 1927). To these, I add withdrawal, the first defense available to ward off overstimulation.

WITHDRAWAL

Withdrawal is the earliest defense available to the human being. The infant, in turning her head away, falling asleep, or focusing attention elsewhere, is employing necessary healthy maneuvers to avoid unnecessary overstimulation. As the Demos and Kaplan (1985) study indicated (pages 97–98), this initially protective mechanism becomes pathological and interferes with normal development when communicative failure makes human contact itself so frustrating that the baby isolates herself.

PRIMAL REPRESSION

I find it clinically useful to see what Freud called *primal repression* as a form of arrested development in which the infant's sensorimotor patterns for coping are not transformed into *ideas*—higher-level symbolic concepts that can let one think about what one is doing or experiencing rather than just acting in response to stimulation (Basch 1977). Without symbolic representation one can experience but not manipulate events: that is, one cannot recall them or reflect on them. Through primal repression, one can, at a cost, protect oneself against painful affective experiences by not raising them to the level of feeling. Alternatively, such arrests in development can, and often do, occur through default. Lack of affective stimulation, whether global or circumscribed, impoverishes mental life and offers no base for symbolization when the child has reached that stage of cognition (see also Stern 1985, pp. 209–11).

SECONDARY REPRESSION, OR REPRESSION PROPER

The capacity for verbal representation and logical reasoning makes possible two complex defenses: *secondary repression,* also called *repression proper* (Freud 1895, 1915*b*), and *disavowal* (Freud 1927). Secondary repression disrupts the bond between affective memory and words; disavowal blocks the formation of a bond between perception and affect.

To psychotherapists, secondary repression is perhaps the most familiar and most thoroughly studied of the defenses. Freud taught that the seemingly forgotten memories of early childhood sexual fantasies and/or experiences are not forgotten, nor do they just disappear. Instead, they are secondarily repressed: that is, the bond to verbal language that these affect-laden experiences at one time had has been destroyed, so that one can no longer deal logically with these memories. Freud called this repression secondary because, unlike the exclusion from representation that occurs in primal repression, in this case the verbal symbolic link to experience has been established at one time only to be destroyed when a once exciting and/or pleasurable memory has become transformed into a forbidden one, the threat of its emergence into consciousness arousing sufficient anxiety to bring repression into play.*

DISAVOWAL

Even though Freud considered disavowal to be the counterpart of secondary repression and on a par with it in importance, disavowal is probably the least familiar, most often misunderstood, and therefore most neglected of the defenses (Basch 1983*b*).† Whereas secondary repression is directed at the danger from within—that is, at recalling and striving to fulfill forbidden sexual and aggressive wishes—disavowal is directed toward danger from the external

---

*See pages 267–69 for a further discussion of secondary repression.
†Anna Freud, in her widely cited *The Ego and the Mechanisms of Defense* (1937), conflated denial, a psychotic defense in adults, with disavowal, probably the most common defense encountered in the practice of insight psychotherapy with narcissistically vulnerable patients. As a result, much that has been written clinically about disavowal is called *denial* with the qualification that the patient is not psychotic (Basch 1983*b*).

world. Disavowal, by preventing the formation of an affective link between a potentially traumatic experience and the affect it would ordinarily be expected to arouse, minimizes that experience's importance for the self system, for, though acknowledged, what is not affectively charged can be disregarded. As Freud's term *Verleugnung* makes clear (in a way unfortunately lost in translation), disavowal is a way of unconsciously deceiving oneself regarding the true—that is, the affective/emotional—significance of an event.

Freud (1927) first became aware of disavowal in patients who had lost a parent in childhood, but did not talk about it in analysis, and, when this omission was called to their attention, dealt with the parental death in a matter-of-fact, unemotional manner. They had not denied the reality of their loss, nor had they repressed the memory of its occurrence; they had just remained seemingly unaffected by it. In my own practice, I treated such a man. Eight years old when his father died, he came to see me in his middle thirties. To my question about what he remembered about the time of his father's death, and what it meant to him then and now, he had essentially nothing to say. His rationalization was that his childhood circumstances were not much affected by his father's death. The family remained in the same house in which he had been raised, there was plenty of money, and life went on as before. His indifference became more understandable as it became clear that he had been actively prevented from talking about his reaction to his father's demise by his mother's and grandparents' anxiety around the subject of death. He had not been taken to the funeral; and afterward, his father's name was seldom if ever mentioned, and all photographs and memorabilia of the father were removed from sight.

This man had been encouraged to disavow the traumatic impact of his father's death by the anxiety of those who should have been able to help him to talk about what had happened, and reassure him that he would continue to be loved and cared for. Had they behaved in this positive way, the event of his father's death would have become integrated into his life in a phase-appropriate way, rather than being a blow that disorganized and precluded affective reaction. In his treatment, this man, with great difficulty and for the first time, permitted himself to become aware of and then deal emotionally with loss in relationships. This working through began with his reactions to my vacations; then, in retrospect, connected with his father's death; and, finally, and most highly affectively charged, with the termination of his therapy with me.*

This case brings out a common feature in patients whose main defense is disavowal: namely, that in childhood this defense has been fostered by an environment that did not encourage, or positively discouraged, discussion of anxiety-provoking issues. A child in such a milieu soon learns that attempts to speak about such concerns lead the adults to withdraw; and his or her discomfort and anxiety thereby increase. It is only a short step to adopting the attitude that, as long as one does not talk, or think, about painful events, one can escape their emotional consequences.†

The neglect of the defense of disavowal, and of its effect on character formation, is probably responsible for a large percentage of therapeutic failures in both psychoanalysis and psychotherapy. Usually disavowal is confused with repression and treated as such: that is, the therapist remains relatively silent and uninvolved, waiting expectantly for the transference of the patient's underlying affect so as to interpret it and, in so doing, give the patient the appropriate words with which to describe what he or she is experiencing. This is exactly the wrong approach to a patient who contains anxiety through the defense of disavowal—and, indeed, plays into that defense instead of resolving it. Whereas in the treatment of neurotic patients, where secondary repression is the main defense, the therapist's relative silence builds up useful anxiety and permits heretofore hidden memories to emerge, in the cases of disavowal patients have no loss of memories: the memories of trauma are available to consciousness, but they do not seem to matter. The patient who utilizes disavowal needs the therapist's permission and help in finding and expressing the affect that needs to be attached

*I am often asked, when I describe the defense of disavowal, how it differs from isolation of affect. This so-called mechanism of defense (A. Freud 1937) is usually associated with obsessive-compulsive patients. However—in keeping with Freud's (1915c) observation that all defense is a defense against affect—all defense is, operationally speaking, a form of isolation of affect. It then becomes a question of determining with obsessive or any other form of psychopathology what basic defense a particular patient employs to isolate affect so as to prevent anxiety: withdrawal, primal repression, repression proper, or disavowal.
†Further descriptions of the operation and consequences of disavowal will be found in Theodore L. Dorpat (1985, 1987) and Robert Jay Lifton (1986); while the case of Esther Romberg (chapter 9) provides a further clinical illustration of the effects of this defense.

to the conscious but disavowed memories—a process that, as in the case of Esther Romberg (chapter 9), requires a different technique from that used to treat secondary repression, as will be illustrated by the case of Otto Neubach (chapter 10).

THE FAILURE OF DEFENSE

If a patient's defense cannot contain the anxiety, or later breaks down under increased stress, further symptoms develop. For example, a psychoneurosis is the result of the failure of repression; attacks of narcissistic rage represent the failure of disavowal; and a secondary reactive depression may develop when primal repression is no longer effective.

Let me emphasize, however, that neither the effect that defenses have on character development, nor the secondary symptoms that develop if defenses fail, identify a patient's basic problem. The symptoms provide us with only a glimpse of how the self system has attempted to defend and adapt itself; further, and often lengthy, investigation is required to determine the nature and etiology of the patient's difficulties. For that reason, I think of the initial diagnostic evaluation of a patient as serving primarily to tell me, in the case of long-standing character pathology, at what level of maturation the basic trauma occurred; or, if the trauma is identifiable and occurred later in life (a divorce, a career reversal, a life-threatening accident), where there are vulnerable areas in the maturation of that patient.

I should clarify that, developmentally speaking, *trauma* does not necessarily mean that either the patient's parents or anyone else are to blame for what happened. *Trauma,* or what is now often called *empathic failure* (Kohut 1977) or *selfobject failure* (Stolorow and Brandchaft 1987), refers to the *patient's* perception and registration of events seemingly instrumental in generating a pathological outcome. For example, the infant born prematurely or with congenital hyperirritability, somatic illness, sensory deficit, or cognitive handicaps may experience even loving care and attention as traumatic. Also, the embellishment and/or misinterpretation of events through and by the patient's conscious and unconscious *fantasy life,* both at the time of their occurrence and later, can and do often create situations that call for defensive maneuvers.

My assessment of the patient's capacity for affective integration and communication guides me in thinking about a treatment plan and in determining the technical approach I will use. Since the primary defense in a patient's pathology depends to a great extent on when the self system suffered the significant trauma that established a person's basic vulnerability, the nature of that defense often determines the phenomenological picture of a patient's difficulty. That is, whether a patient is suffering from a borderline state, a personality disorder, or a neurosis, for example, depends to a great extent on when the damage to his or her affective development occurred. Defenses may well coexist, however, and, in the more mature patient, earlier, more primitive defenses may come to the fore during periods of stress. It is not uncommon for patients for short periods in a given therapeutic session, sometimes for longer intervals, to experience such defensive regressions. When that happens, I gauge my interventions accordingly, taking into account the extant earlier level of development that such regression indicates.

The study of the self system—its nature, its significance, and the manner in which it maintains its integrity under adverse conditions—prepares the way for establishing a comprehensive approach to the process of therapy: how the replay of the past in the ongoing patient-therapist relationship can be used to advantage in reversing the effects of earlier developmental difficulties in a person's life.

6

The Heart of
Treatment:
The Therapist and the
Transference

THE THERAPEUTIC TRANSFERENCE lies at the heart of dynamic psychotherapy. The patient fails to achieve competence and lacks self-esteem because his or her decision-making process is in significant respects hampered by traumatically induced patterns of expectation. These patterns usually involve the patient's relationships with other people and preclude the patient's making the most of either abilities or opportunities. These counterproductive programs for relationships are unconscious and cannot be dealt with directly by either the patient or the therapist. Sooner or later, however, these pathological patterns find their way into the relationship to the therapist, giving the therapist the opportunity to help the patient to recognize and to resolve, or, in those cases where that is not possible, ameliorate and work around them. This repetition of these characteristic but self-defeating patterns with the therapist constitutes the therapeutic transference.

Freud's identification of the transference phenomenon (Breuer and Freud 1893–95) and his discovery of the psychoanalytic method for working with it therapeutically are the basis for modern-day psychotherapy. However, Freud considered only psychoneurotic patients as capable of forming a therapeutic transference, a so-called transference neurosis (1915c, p. 196; 1916–17, p. 445; 1920, p. 18; 1926b, p. 268). For many years that dictum severely limited the application of Freud's method to other than neurotic patients, and led to the fragmentation of the field of psychotherapy as practitioners seeking to help non-neurotic patients cast about for other ways of dealing with those patients' problems (Basch 1985). This limitation of the psychoanalytic method to patients with psychoneuroses—that is, to patients whose primary problem lies in the area of psychosexual development and the oedipal conflict (see chapter 10)—was shown to be false by the psychoanalyst Heinz Kohut (1971). Kohut demonstrated clinically that there was no justification for restricting therapeutic transference formation to those unconscious patterns of expectation that were related to infantile sexuality and the oedipal conflict: patients with other types of problems, specifically narcississtic personality disorders, also formed transferences to the therapist that enabled Freud's method to be applied successfully to their difficulties. Eventually Kohut (1977, 1984) developed a general classification of transferences that narrowed the gap between less intensive forms of psychotherapy and formal psychoanalysis (Basch 1983c).

Potentially, Kohut's extension of Freud's basic contribution, together with what has been learned about normal development and the self system, opens the way toward formulating a universally useful technique for psychotherapy. This potential is made actual through the therapist's capacity for empathy: the ability to hear, understand, and use appropriately the affective message behind a patient's words. The therapist's empathic understanding permits him or her to introduce into the therapeutic relationship interventions that address the patient's difficulties in a manner that is phase appropriate—that is, interventions that take into account the cognitive and affective level of development that the patient is displaying in relation to the therapist at any given time. That, in turn, enables the patient to integrate what the therapist communicates into his or her self system and use it to advantage in attaining competence and self-esteem—a process that Kohut (1971) called *transmuting internalization.*

The Affective Bond

For practical purposes, I think of four broad categories into which my patients sort themselves, regardless of specific symptoms. These are: patients who have experienced failure of affective bonding in the first few months of infancy; those who have learned to be ashamed of their affective responses; patients who have had problems with affect attunement; and, lastly, those whose difficulties stem from affective trauma during the oedipal phase of psychosexual development. Only outlined here, each of these categories will receive detailed attention in the case reports to follow.

FAILURE OF THE AFFECTIVE BOND

Failure to establish a viable affective bond between mother and child in the first months of infancy can interfere with basic tension control—the development of the regulatory functions needed to titrate affective input and prevent both understimulation and overstimulation. This makes later attempts to relate to other people in a productive, meaningful way very difficult. Patients who seem to have suffered such damage usually herald their problems immediately by the way they relate to the therapist—displaying irascibility, mistrust, and an inability to postpone or compromise gratification, which, combined with a seeming total disregard of the needs of others, is the hallmark of what is usually called the *borderline personality.* * The cases of Jim Zurf and Tina Pearl will serve as examples of the treatment of this disorder (chapters 7 and 9, respectively).

*The diagnosis of the borderline disorder is also used to describe patients who are in danger— or on the borderline—of a psychosis. The patients I am describing, however—although functioning primitively—show no evidence of thought disorder and, unlike many prepsychotic patients, have relationships that, generally destructive and unsatisfying as they may be, are often of a surprisingly long duration.

SHAME OF AFFECT

A large group of patients are ashamed of affect and overcontrol their affective responsiveness. This condition commonly stems either from affective understimulation in infancy and/or from a parent's intolerance for the baby's affective expression—an intolerance that results in an arrest in development which later interferes with the transition from affect to feeling (affect is experienced but cannot be talked about or recognized readily or effectively). Unable to deal competently with this transition, these patients defend themselves by withdrawing from affect or its stimulation. Consequently, their inner life is impoverished, and their relative inability to identify and express their affective reactions makes it difficult for them to relate to others in meaningful depth. Usually in good control of themselves, these are responsible, hard-working, productive people. However, there seems to be little joy or satisfaction in their lives; they seem chronically bored and sad. They are slaves to duty and lost without it. Challenged by circumstances requiring emotional flexibility, they are ready to retreat into a secondary, reactive depression, which may be accompanied not so much by vegetative signs as by hypochondriasis and somatization. When the therapist can help these patients to overcome their shame and/or fear of affective responsiveness by helping them consciously to experience and then to articulate their affective reactions, the results are usually gratifying for both patient and therapist. Roger Flynn (chapter 8) belongs to this group; probably so do Al Gertz and Mrs. Senoj, though since I did not study the problems of these two in depth, I cannot be sure of the diagnosis.

PROBLEMS RELATED TO AFFECT ATTUNEMENT

There is a phase in infancy when the baby develops a subjective sense of self—a time between seven and eighteen months of age, when the infant demonstrates awareness of the interpersonal dimension of relationships and requires a response that Daniel Stern has called *affect attunement* (Stern 1984, 1985; Stern et al. 1985). At this time the infant needs his mother to let him know through her voice, gesture, facial expression, and other behavior that she is participating affectively with what he is doing—that she, too, feels what he is experiencing, that the person in whom he is most interested at the moment shares his affective experience, thereby validating his competence: he is understood and what he does makes a difference. This sort of interaction sets the stage for a healthy concept of self when that becomes a cognitive possibility. Significant failure to receive appropriate responses at this level of development may lead to an increasing sense of shame about such needs and a subsequent disavowal of one's longing for other people's interest and participation in one's psychological life. Having gone unsatisfied too long, such needs become too painful to acknowledge—though, far from disappearing, covertly they govern all relationships. Also, this developmental deficit often leads to a compensatory, achievement-oriented, self-reliance that, though it may be socially adaptive and economically rewarding, remains subjectively unsatisfying.

I find that so-called narcissistic personality disorders commonly struggle with these issues. In recent years, significant strides have been made in the psychotherapeutic treatment of such patients, of whom Esther Romberg is an example (see chapter 9).

EMPATHIC FAILURE DURING THE OEDIPAL PHASE

In the fourth category are patients who first attracted Freud's attention: people with psychoneuroses and psychoneurotic character disorders. Unlike those described so far, these patients have had a healthy affective development in infancy and formed a basically sound character structure, but then, during early childhood, around three to five years of age, experienced an empathic failure—that is, an absolute or a relative failure of affect attunement vis-à-vis their competitive strivings, especially in the area of childhood sexuality. Such a child may then be unable to progress from feelings of global sexual excitement centered on parental figures to the variety of loving emotions that include, but are not limited to, genital sexuality and permit appropriate transformation and redirection of childhood sexual impulses. The cases of Otto Neubach, Irma Waller, and

Norma Newton illustrate therapeutic treatment of the possible consequences of such trauma (see chapter 10).

Although, for the sake of convenience, I have separated out these pathological types or syndromes, they are by no means always discrete, simple, and easily identifiable entities. One may mimic the other; one or more may combine; and any patient, even in any single session, may regress from a higher developmental level of pathology to an earlier one. By and large, however, I have found these categories useful. By following the sequence of the patient's affective communication and/or affective deficit, a therapist can maintain an intrapsychic stance, one focused on the unconscious decision-making process that governs the patient's behavior. In this way, a therapist can avoid being confused by or caught up in either the nature of a patient's symptoms per se or in the always complicated details of his or her life, past and present (see also Socarides and Stolorow 1984–85).

The Development of the Transference

The two key words in dynamic psychotherapy are *unconscious* and *transference.* And, like *unconscious,* the term *transference,* far from being arcane, has its roots in readily available everyday experience. Parents spend a great deal of time teaching their children to have good manners: that is, to observe certain rules of conduct in social situations. Rules are, of course, one way of designating patterns of expectation. Having learned the conduct appropriate to the various rooms of a house—foyer, living room, dining room, bathroom, and bedroom—children are considered ready to enter society. Mother says, "Now I can take him anywhere," by which she means that her child will not disgrace the family by behaving inappropriately, but can be counted upon to apply, reactivate, or repeat—that is, to *transfer*—what he or she has learned at home to comparable new situations. So, strictly speaking, transference is ubiquitous. That is, one always begins by bringing or transferring old patterns of expectation to new situations so as to organize the experience of the moment.

Sometimes, however, the rules or patterns of expectation one has learned are no longer applicable. Stationed in Japan while in the navy, I had occasion to be the guest of a Japanese physician and his family. I could not even enter their house properly: How and where was I to take off my shoes? Before stepping over the threshold? In the entrance hall? Once they were off, what to do with them? And so on. To transfer my acquired script for social conduct to this new environment would have been totally inappropriate. Like a child, I had to ask for the most basic instructions and, haltingly, learn what was expected of me in a Japanese household.

It is this step of recognizing when old rules no longer hold, and that new ones can and must be searched out and mastered, that a therapist's patients, insofar as they are in the grips of their pathology, cannot perform. As used by therapists, ever since Breuer and Freud (1893–95) first used the term in its technical sense, transference refers to the inappropriate sphex-like, or closed-system, application of patterns for perception and behavior, as described in chapter 5. Thus, following an early childhood situation to which one responded with defensive behavior, one evaluates and responds to similar situations as though they were the same: that is, under these circumstances what one expects from people and the roles one assigns to them may have little to do with what they are actually trying to communicate (see also Basch 1980, pp. 35–69).

In therapy, the patient adapts to the therapist according to these old patterns of expectation; and it is from their repetition or reactivation that the therapist can learn about a patient's unconscious expectations, disappointments, hopes, wishes, and fears. In the transference, a patient relives in more or less disguised form the effects of trauma on his or her maturation—a trauma that has prematurely closed the system to further development because protection of the self system took precedence over learning.

THE DEFENSE AGAINST THE TRANSFERENCE

The course of psychotherapy can, in terms of the patient's repetition of unmet basic affective needs, be roughly divided into two periods: the defense against the transference, and the work within the transference. In the first, defense against or fear of the transference, the patient unconsciously resists bringing thwarted affective needs into the therapeutic relationship and, instead, redoubles his or her characteristic defensive maneuvers against re-experiencing those needs whose past disappointment forms the core of his or her difficulties. One may, for example, focus on one's symptoms per se and insist that, instead of exploring their meaning, the therapist address them directly. So, for example, a hypochondriacal patient may deny that his or her fear of catching the therapist's cold and dying needs to be understood and instead may insist that the therapist either wear a surgical mask, or else cancel the appointment when the therapist has even the mildest viral infection. The patient may also adapt his or her characteristic defensive posture to the therapeutic situation. Thus, an obsessive patient may go into such detail about peripheral matters that what he or she has begun to speak about never becomes clear. But, if the therapist points this out, the patient is likely honestly and reproachfully to say that he or she was only doing as asked: that is, saying *everything* he or she was thinking and feeling. (When this not uncommon defense against the transference creates an impasse, I have found it useful to ask, "Here you have tried to do what I asked you to do, and I am not satisfied. What are you feeling and thinking right now about that?" and then to focus on the patient's affective reaction to my question.)

SHAME

In my clinical experience, the patient's shame is the most likely and most important affect that occupies the therapist in trying to work through the defense against the transference. Not that shame is in itself pathogenic; far from it. Shame is such a painful emotion in adulthood that it is strange to think of it as a basically protective maneuver; that it is so is clearer in infancy.

Once an infant requires affect attunement, a failure to validate that pattern of expectation leaves the child in a state of frustration and mounting tension, a state of incompetence with which she must now cope. Take, for example, a baby whose creative play has generally met with approval and who, instead of napping, has busied herself with tearing up a book accidentally left in her crib and scattering small pieces of paper all around her. When the child's father comes into the room, instead of responding to his daughter's excited, proud smile with facial and vocal expressions of admiration and praise for the girl's innovative productions, he scowls angrily and in exasperated tones complains of the mess that now has to be picked up. The little girl has lost contact with her father, has failed to elicit affect attunement: that is, the father gives every evidence that they are not on the same wavelength, and that he has no intention of participating in his daughter's excitement and pride. Unable to sustain eye contact with her parent, the child averts her gaze and hangs her head, displaying the basic shame reaction. Though the baby cannot conceptualize her experience as adults would, physiologically she is subject to the same inner turmoil an adult would suffer under similar circumstances. The child is victim to the unpleasant tension of an anticipation and excitement that now, with nowhere to go, results in rushes of heat throughout the body, especially the face. But how much worse it would be for the child if, heedless of the angry parent's message, she just continued to babble excitedly, continuing to expect her father to be pleased. The child would, in all probability, be subjected to more of father's anger, the subsequent increased internal disorganization that attends continued disappointment, and ever higher levels of distress. Shame, by putting an end to the child's unrealistic expectation that this particular performance will meet with happiness and appreciation on the parent's part, has protected her.

In chapter 4, a similar situation played itself out in adulthood when Joe Herman became aware that the train conductor to whom he was recounting the occurrence of the night before had no interest in the tale. Joe's excitement at sharing his experience instantly turned into shame; and, though he controlled its outward bodily expression, he experienced the inner discomfort that is the hallmark of that affect, and as quickly as possible ended the attempt to engage the conductor in his story.

Shame is the counterpart of surprise; both are ancillary affects connected with interest/excitement (Tomkins 1962–63). Whereas surprise signals "stop everything else and pay attention to this," shame signals the self system that it should protect itself by terminating interest in whatever has come to its attention (Nathanson

1987). Secondarily, the shame reaction has come, with evolution, to signal surrender, the need for forgiveness, and the wish to re-establish contact (Lewis 1981). Thus, Mrs. Herman, having given a tongue-lashing to her daughter, responded to Jenny's shame reaction by restoring her to grace.

The utility of the shame reaction in protecting the self system by modifying patterns of expectation in the interest of social maturation is perverted when the child's need for the parents' validating affective response or mirroring is consistently ignored, misunderstood, or punished. Such treatment may precipitate a chronic shame-producing tension directed at the child's own affective signaling activity. Now the shame reaction ceases to be useful and instead compounds the damage already done. When one becomes ashamed of one's affective life generally, rather than of specific behavior, one retreats defensively from the mobilization of affect. In psychotherapy, this retreat often manifests itself in the aforementioned defense against the transference (see also Broucek 1982).

RESOLUTION OF THE DEFENSE AGAINST THE TRANSFERENCE

Usually the earlier in development that significant damage has occurred, the longer it takes to overcome the defenses built into the patient's character that protect him or her from re-experiencing in the transference the trauma that threatened the self system originally. So, in the case of borderline patients, it may sometimes take years before such a transference forms; indeed, as the case of Tina Pearl (chapter 10) will illustrate, the treatment not infrequently either does not progress, or even founders, because of the seeming impossibility of promoting a transference. On the other hand, patients with either narcissistic personality disorders or psychoneuroses tend to be transference-ready—some giving unmistakable evidence that transference material is present in the first session.

If the therapist finds that the transference either cannot be or, because of the limited nature of the patient's problem, need not be promoted and explored, he or she may employ basically cognitive and behavioral techniques to help the patient (pages 54–56). Behavioral strategies can sometimes be used to circumvent the defenses, and cognitive techniques can help some patients to alter the manner in which they employ their defenses so that they become more effective and/or less disruptive of a patient's life style. However, in insight or dynamic therapy, though the therapist continues to employ cognitive and behavioral techniques as ancillary maneuvers when indicated, the primary focus is on the overt and covert goals of behavior, especially when these are in conflict. These dynamics can be most effectively studied and resolved within the therapeutic transference.

EVALUATING THE MATURATIONAL LEVEL OF THE TRANSFERENCE

Once any defense against the transference which is present starts to be worked through, the therapist begins to see evidence that the patient is mobilizing and reliving in the therapeutic situation the fixed patterns of affective communication that indicate both when and how the anxiety arose that interfered with healthy maturation. The period in development when the basic problems occurred is indicated by the maturational level of the affective communication. Is the patient unable to tolerate any affective pressure? Is the patient responding affectively, but unable to put his or her experience into words? Does the patient evince shame of his or her own needs by being desperately eager to please the therapist who, the patient seems to be sure, will find him or her wanting? Or, alternatively, does the patient indicate the same problem by trying to dominate the therapeutic situation and the therapist with his or her intelligence, achievements, wit, or what-have-you? Is the patient aware of his or her own feelings but seemingly unable to recognize or take into account the feelings of others? The answers to such questions can indicate to the therapist on what level of affective transformation—from control of affective tension, to feeling, to emotion, and then to empathy—a given patient's difficulties occurred.

The level of affective maturity on which a patient is functioning indicates to the therapist both what that patient is ready to hear, and the manner in which the therapist can intervene most effectively. There is, for example, no point in talking to a man about his need for empathic understanding when it is clear that he is barely aware of his own feelings. The therapist must approach him much more concretely: "Now we know how you felt when your boss said nothing to you about your working all week on that project. I think that it is quite likely that your reaction today is related to what happened to you when you were little and your dad never acknowledged how helpful you tried to be—washed his car, mowed the lawn, and so on. All you remember are the stomachaches and the headaches you'd often get, but I think that that was anger and disappointment coming out. Since you knew you would only be punished if you showed any anger, this was your way of saying, 'I hurt.' " With an affectively more mature patient, the therapist might only have to say, "Just like your father"—a statement whose meaning the patient would immediately grasp.

The Form of the Transference

The therapist learns *when* in development a patient was adversely affected by establishing the level of affective maturation displayed in that patient's pathology. The indicators of *how* a patient was affectively traumatized appear in the form the transference takes. The form of the transference guides the therapist in searching for the nature of the need that was thwarted in the patient's development. Here the psychoanalyst Heinz Kohut's concept of what he called the *selfobject* transferences has proved essential.

During the long period of human extrauterine maturation, it is the adult who, guided by the baby's affective communication, must function at times as an adjunctive self system protecting the infant's self system from being overwhelmed by demands made upon it. Kohut (1971, 1977) called this the *selfobject experience.* That is to say, the caregiving adult exists for and is experienced by the baby as an extension of that infant's self, available to perform as needed to stabilize the infant's self system whenever that system is endangered (see also Marian Tolpin 1971).

Kohut distilled three basic needs from early development: to have one's competent performance validated and approved; to be protected and supported at times of stress or tension that are beyond the competence of the infant or child to manage satisfactorily; and to be acknowledged by one's kin as a fellow being. When these needs go significantly unmet or are otherwise misunderstood, they may be eventually transferred to the therapist in the therapeutic relationship. Kohut referred to these repetitions, respectively, as the *mirror,* the *idealizing,* and the *alter ego* transference. In the mirror transference, the patient seeks to be validated by the therapist's approval; in the idealizing transference, one looks upon the therapist as an admired and powerful helper who will protect one and from whom one can gain strength; in the alter ego transference, the patient seeks the comfort that kinship, "being like," has to offer.

THE MIRROR TRANSFERENCE

As the experiments of Papoušek (1969) and other infant research ers have shown, nothing is as reinforcing for a baby as to establish a contingent relationship between his or her behavior and what is happening in the environment (pages 26–27). It is especially important for infants and children—as they seek to establish competence in communication and in autonomous behavior—to be able to recruit an appropriate, validating, affective response from their parents. The mirror transference demonstrates the patient's need or wish for such validation from the therapist.

THE IDEALIZING TRANSFERENCE

One's unrequited longing to be strengthened and protected when necessary by an alliance with an admired, powerful figure gives rise to the idealizing transference. The contentment, safety, and reassurance conveyed to the infant and small child when he is tenderly but firmly enveloped by or carried in his parents' arms forms the basis for this reaction. It is a need to be united with someone one looks up to, and who can lend one the inspiration, the strength, and whatever else it takes to maintain the stability of the self system when one is endangered, frustrated, or in search of meaning.

THE ALTER EGO TRANSFERENCE

The need for a response acknowledging a bond of sameness or kinship between the participants in a therapeutic relationship is expressed in the alter ego transference. This phenomenon was at first seen as a part of the mirroring process; but Kohut (1984) later drew a distinction between the two, because he concluded that the alter ego transference answers a basic human need: the need to have one's humanness, one's kinship or sameness with others of the species, quietly acknowledged. It is understandable why the alter ego transference was initially subsumed under the mirror transference, since the validation of an infant's or a child's worth, the pleased and proud recognition of his accomplishments, also happens to meet the youngster's need to have his belonging to the group affirmed. There are, however, situations in everyday life when the strengthening of the self comes about, not through the calming effect of joining with the greater power of the ideal, or through the mirroring that attests to competence and achievement, but through being quietly sustained by another in whose presence one feels accepted. The little boy who decides to move his play table into father's study, so that he too may do his "work" alongside father, illustrates the search for this sort of selfobject experience. Perhaps the most dramatic and telling example of the need for alter ego selfobject experiences is Kohut's suggestion that even when dying the self can remain cohesive and functioning if only there is someone to hold one's hand and, in this way, affirm the self by literally, physically, maintaining the connection to humanity, even as one departs from life (see also Detrick 1986).

Kohut stressed that, although seen clearly and in the most dramatic form in infancy and early childhood, the need for appropriate selfobject experiences is present throughout life whenever the self system is in danger of fragmentation, devitalization, or disorganization (Kohut and Wolf 1978). Maturation consists not of leaving behind one's selfobject needs but, rather, of developing the capacity to recruit strengthening selfobject experiences in an age- and situation-appropriate manner when the self system is endangered. One may draw at such times on the strength of others, or rely for suste-

nance on one's memories of previous mirroring, alter ego, or idealizing selfobject experiences (see also Goldberg 1988).

I have already demonstrated how these basic needs were manifested in an uncomplicated form in the manner in which Al Gertz, the
taxi driver, related to me. Al's anger, though ostensibly directed at
me, indicated a vulnerable self system and had nothing to do with
myself as a person. When I could minimize the painful contrast he
saw between our life styles by emphasizing instead our similarities
in both having been in the service, I met his need for the acknowledgment of kinship. We were not so different after all, and he could
then forgive me for my fur-collared coat. And then he let his idealizing needs emerge: perhaps he could go to school, as I had, and
prepare himself to leave behind what he considered to be demean-
ing work. When I then disagreed with his self-deprecating view of
himself, I met his need to be validated in his competence in a
manner he had never thought possible. Together, my interventions
led to what Kohut called *transmuting internalization* (1971, 1977, 1984,
1987): that is, a change in how one thinks about and copes with
problematic situations based on one's assimilation of the therapeutic transaction.

TRANSMUTING INTERNALIZATION

By *transmuting internalization,* Kohut meant that the patient is able
to take the function of understanding that is initially the therapist's,
and, bit by bit, make it his or her own. Transmuting internalization
is not identification with the therapist but a selective process geared
to the needs of the patient by the patient. The famous psychologist
Lev S. Vygotsky (1934) described how one teaches a child mathe-
matics. First, one exposes the child to the formula and teaches him
how to use it. Then one poses problems so the child can use the
formula over and over with increasing skill and flexibility. One day,
seemingly all of a sudden, the child "catches on" to the meaning of
what he is doing, and then what has been done by rote has now
become a usable mathematical concept, a part of what Vygotsky
called "inner speech." The process described by Vygotsky is similar
to what Kohut subsumed by *transmuting internalization*: what once
belonged to the therapist has now become the patient's.

To clarify this point, Kohut (1984) would make a humorous analogy to the manner in which the body assimilates food stuff: the patient eats a beef steak, but what he ingests undergoes transformation and becomes part of *his* body—he does not turn into a cow.

There is, however, one very important difference between ordinary learning and therapeutically induced transmuting internalization: that is, the promotion of insight through psychotherapy takes place in the face of the unconscious resistances offered by the patient's defenses—patterns of expectation that have formed a closed system. The patient—prevented by the threat of overwhelming anxiety from opening himself or herself up to new experiences—can entertain the possibility that things could be other than they are only when the therapist's empathic attunement to the patient's situation reduces that fear. For that reason, intellectual insights imparted by the therapist—as Freud (1912, 1913) pointed out long ago—are effective only with patients affectively prepared to hear them.

The Content of the Transference

In addition to a patient's level of affective development and the form his or her transference takes, a third factor guides the therapist's intervention—the content of the transference. Does the need for mirroring arise in the context of psychosexual issues—the oral, anal, and phallic tensions that Freud (1905) investigated and described so thoroughly? In other words, is the patient saying that he or she needs to be acknowledged as a sexual person without being made to feel guilty or ashamed? Alternatively, is this a need for acknowledgment of autonomy and creativity, praise for being a center of initiative? Or is it a question of what Bowlby (1969, 1980) called *attachment needs*: the validation of one's right to support when the occasion calls for it? Here, the patient's words and behavior, how he or she expresses transference needs, guide the therapist.

Altogether, the information gathered about the patient's affective maturity, the form of the transference, and the nature of the patient's need form a three-dimensional grid that orients the therapist and prepares him or her to enter the developmental spiral in a way that will ultimately be most productive.

Empathic Understanding: Clarence Albright

The therapist's empathic understanding of a patient's communication forms the bridge between the theoretical knowledge of the developmental process and its therapeutic application. Empathy comes from the German *Einfühlen*—to "feel" or, more accurately, to "find" one's way into another's experience. Practically speaking, empathy means that the therapist does not simply take a patient's words at face value but looks for the deeper meaning of what the patient is saying, or not saying, in the affective signals that the patient is, often unwittingly, transmitting—as in the case of Clarence Albright.

MR. ALBRIGHT: Oh, what's there to say? Nothing has changed since yesterday.

THERAPIST: Yet your mood seems different. You left yesterday feeling good about yourself, but seem quite down in the mouth now.

MR. ALBRIGHT: Maybe it's the weather.

THERAPIST: Maybe. Did it start when you looked out the window this morning?

MR. ALBRIGHT: Nah. As a matter of fact, I was feeling really good till I got here. I was even whistling on the way over.

THERAPIST: But your mood changed. When did that happen? When you stepped into the office?

MR. ALBRIGHT: In the waiting room, I guess.

THERAPIST: As soon as you hung up your coat? As soon as you sat down?

MR. ALBRIGHT: When you were late. But it was only a couple of minutes, I don't know why that should bother me. Anyway, yesterday you must have given me extra time; they charged me an extra buck in the garage, so I must have gone into the next hour. So it evens out.

THERAPIST: You mentioned you were whistling on the way over.

MR. ALBRIGHT: So?

THERAPIST: What tune was it?

MR. ALBRIGHT: Oh, I don't know. I can't remember what it's called.

THERAPIST: Whistle it for me.

MR. ALBRIGHT: Can I just hum it?

THERAPIST: Sure. [*Mr. Albright hums.*] That's from *South Pacific.*

MR. ALBRIGHT: Oh, yeah. Isn't it called, "Never Let Me Go"?

THERAPIST: Actually, I think, the song title is "Some Enchanted Evening," but maybe what's important is that last line, "Never let me go."

MR. ALBRIGHT: You mean you and me?

THERAPIST: Yes. The feeling in yesterday's session of being understood, of feeling good that we were on the same wavelength, of anticipating how glad we'd be to see each other today—and then I'm late coming out for you. That hurts.

MR. ALBRIGHT: That could be right. I'm sort of not so mad now. Why couldn't I have figured that out? It's kind of like the way I feel when I come home from work and Shirley's making dinner, or she's on the phone, and she doesn't stop everything to say hello to me.

Beginning with Freud (1921), who called empathy the *sine qua non* for understanding another person's mental state, therapists have had difficulty describing what exactly happens to bring about empathic understanding. For lack of a better definition, empathy has often been spoken about as if it were a quality or talent inherent in the therapist: one is either "empathic" or "unempathic," as one may be said to be "musical" or "not musical." I do not think this is the case. I believe that coming to an empathic understanding is a process that can be dissected, described, taught, and learned. Much of the

time, in the hands of an experienced therapist, empathic understanding may be arrived at quickly and unconsciously, as if through
some instantaneous, mysterious process of intuition. But this result
shows only that the therapist, like the person who drives over a
familiar route without needing to be consciously aware of every
twist and turn, has learned to perform a complicated task expertly.
However, when one teaches psychotherapy to students, one can see
clearly how laboriously and often painfully this skill is acquired.
Often enough, the expert, too, will become frustrated and unable
to make empathic contact with the patient. In such instances, it
helps to identify the steps involved in reaching empathic understanding and think about each in an effort to identify the problem
preventing such contact.

While I did not consciously attune myself to what was playing
itself out behind the shame that Mr. Albright's need aroused in him,
I could, in retrospect, trace the steps involved:

1. I became aware of the affect awakened in me by the patient.
2. I stepped back and viewed my affective reaction objectively.
3. I identified the patient's affective state.
4. I established the significance of the patient's message.
5. I decided how most effectively to use what I had learned.

THE THERAPIST'S AFFECTIVE RESPONSE TO THE PATIENT

As I have previously discussed (pages 71–75), one's initial response to the intensity and shape of stimulation is not under cortical
control: that is, it is a matter not of reflection but of becoming aware
that what has happened has produced an effect upon which we can
then elaborate in terms of feelings and emotions. Before Mr. Albright even began to speak, I found myself reacting to the washed-
out way in which he returned my greeting and to how downcast he
seemed to be as he walked from the waiting room into the office.
I started to feel sorry for myself—it had not been a great day
so far, but I had thought that with this patient I would at least
garner the fruits of our last, very productive session. But I felt worse
when he began to speak, and further weighed down by the dull tone

of his voice and his general lack of animation. I began to feel guilty: Mr. Albright was making me feel as if I had failed him. And now I began to get angry. I had done such a terrific job the last time we were together. "Oh, what's the use? I'm just trying to write on water," was the self-pitying thought that summed up my disappointment in the first minute or so of our session.

DECENTERING THE THERAPIST'S AFFECTIVE REACTION

To decenter one's affective experience is to be able to step back from what one is feeling and think about it dispassionately. Instead of simply reacting to how I felt as a result of Mr. Albright's demeanor and tone, I was able to take into account the fact that what was happening in me was being triggered by the patient for reasons of his own. It was an intrapsychic, not an interpersonal, issue: that is, he was not making me miserable because he wanted to attack me per se. In making me unhappy with him, he was unconsciously trying to tell me something; and it was my job to find out what that message was, and, if possible, help him put it into words. My own psychoanalysis had taught me enough about myself to know why my sense of competence and my self-esteem had been threatened by Mr. Albright's words and demeanor; and, once I understood them, I could put aside those concerns of mine in favor of investigating with the patient his reasons for feeling so poorly. Having reached that point, my dysphoria and anger dissipated and were replaced by interest. I was now once again in charge of myself and in a position to focus on the patient: I no longer needed to struggle with the reaction Mr. Albright had set off within me when his behavior made me feel momentarily helpless and ineffectual.

Optimally, a person's potential for affective responsiveness is maximized by appropriate parental/infant interactions, so that affective development can proceed unimpeded into adulthood. In practice, such an outcome is the exception rather than the rule. In later life, the consequences of having been significantly, often traumatically, misunderstood in infancy and childhood may lead some people into psychotherapy, others into becoming psychotherapists. In the latter case, the fear of committing oneself affectively lest one be again hurt or disappointed creates a barrier to the therapist's effective functioning. That is, a therapist may, without realizing it, guard against fully experiencing and acknowledging the feelings, both positive and negative, that patients stir up within him or her. For that reason, it has been accepted, almost from the beginning of the Freudian era of depth psychology, that a therapist must be treated before he or she can treat others. Two of the principal functions of a therapist's therapy are: firstly, to help one understand the negative vicissitudes of one's affective development so as to restore sufficiently one's capacity for affective resonance; and secondly, to permit one to gain control over one's affective experience instead of being controlled by one's affective response to the patient.

Decentering permits the therapist to think about what the patient is feeling; not about what he or she is feeling about the patient. Not that the latter is immaterial and useless. On the contrary, what the therapist feels about the patient often gives a clue to what goes awry between the patient and other people. I do not hesitate, especially with patients who have early impairment in affective development, to use, when I think it appropriate, the feelings they have engendered in me to explain the difficulties that they have been telling me about. For example, I might say, "What the boss [wife, friend] is reacting to in such an angry manner is the kind of feeling that I, too, experienced when you presented yourself as you did today. You thought you were being factual when instead I felt you were putting me down."

Therapists sometimes make the mistake of thinking that an affective reaction, especially an intense one, to a patient is "countertransference" and therapeutically inimical. I think, instead, that the therapist's affective reaction to what a patient is saying or doing is—properly used—invaluable in coming to understand the patient. It is the therapist's inability, because of unconscious problems of his or her own, to decenter affective reaction to the patient that Freud (1910) called *countertransference.* And, indeed, in the grip of his or her own unrecognized and unconscious problems, the therapist is often helpless to know what has gone wrong in the therapy, much less to do something about it. A therapist in such a dilemma requires self-analysis, supervision, and/or further personal treatment.

The therapist is now in a position to compare the content of what the patient is saying with the affective message that he or she is conveying. When I thought about Mr. Albright's opening comment, "Oh, what's there to say, nothing has changed since yesterday," I said to myself, in effect, "If that were so, he should sound calm or bored, but he doesn't. When I sound as this man does, I feel helpless, lost, put upon, misunderstood, and abandoned. Indeed, that is exactly how he made me feel with his unhappy face and voice." I had a momentary flash of memory to the time I saw an older boy go bicycling with his friends, telling his younger brother that he was too little to come along, leaving behind an eight-year-old, who only moments before had been so proud of his new two-wheeler, crying desperately at the injustice of it all. I now decided to call attention to the seeming discrepancy between what Mr. Albright was saying and the mood he was signaling with both the tone of his voice and his dragging behavior. And, as I recounted, we were then able to establish that, indeed, he did feel bad, and that his dysphoria was precipitated by having to wait and start his session with me a few minutes later than the appointed time.

Strictly speaking, one can achieve empathy with another person's communication, what Kohut (1959) called *vicarious introspection,* through the three previous steps, which permit one to take correct account of both the content and the affective import, whether overt or covert, of the message a person is sending (Basch 1983*a*). In that sense, I believed that I had now come to have an empathic understanding of my patient's communication. However, common usage in psychotherapy subsumes under *empathy* or *being empathic* not only understanding but also the therapeutic employment of that understanding. This involves two further steps: establishing what the patient is trying to say about himself or herself; and then deciding *whether* and, if so, *how* one will respond to the need being signaled by that message. Although, bowing to established custom, I will accept this expanded view of empathy, steps four and five are by no means just dependent on the therapist's ability to hear the full import of the patient's communication. Conclusions about the deeper meaning, the developmental implications, of what the therapist hears and experiences and how then to deal with the patient therapeutically, are governed by the therapist's theory. That is, they are dependent on the therapist's concept of what therapy is meant to accomplish, a theoretical position that he or she has learned and accepted and now superimposes on the patient's material.

ESTABLISHING THE SIGNIFICANCE OF A PATIENT'S MESSAGE

In the context of the model of childhood development I have described, I asked myself, "What is Mr. Albright saying—not only about his present mental state, but about the underlying concerns that gave rise to it?" Here I considered that, far from being bored and uninterested, as he initially claimed to be, my patient was really sad and disappointed. I compared his behavior to that of a child who responds to the solicitous inquiry, "What's the matter?" with "Oh, nothing," while at the same time hoping that, though he is ashamed to admit it, his anguish is evident to the parent who will take the trouble to show concern by exploring it further.

Mr. Albright came from a very large family. His father had to hold two jobs to make ends meet, and, although a decent, well-meaning person, was seldom emotionally available to his children because of his schedule. As a child, Mr. Albright turned to an older brother for masculine support and was bitterly hurt when this brother left the family's hometown when the patient was about eight years old. In therapy, the patient had formed an idealizing transference, finding in me the available father he never had. I thought that my tardiness, minimal as it was on the adult scale of things, brought together both the disappointment of losing his brother and probably the much earlier one of reaching out for a father who was not there. Now I understood why I had had a momentary flash to a memory of my own in which an older brother left his younger sib in the lurch. Because of the context in which the patient's disappointment occurred, I thought that it was related to attachment needs rather than to either psychosexual wishes or needs for autonomy.*

DECIDING ON THE MOST EFFECTIVE USE OF WHAT ONE HAS LEARNED

My decision now was based on the theory elaborated previously: namely, that human behavior is affectively motivated; that affect has a line of maturation; and that the therapeutic situation takes into account both the content of the affective memory and the patient's level of affective maturation.

Had basic tension control been an issue in Mr. Albright's situation as he talked to me during that interview, I think I would have been much quicker to formulate for him what I thought was going on in an effort to forestall the angry, painful, and usually unproductive reactions that such primitively organized patients often have when they feel affectively deprived.

Had the patient been one who could not articulate feelings, I might have talked about the feelings stimulated in me—how sad and guilty I felt myself to be when I saw how upset he was—so as to give him an example of how one turns an affective experience into feeling, and then I would have asked him to do the same if he could.

Had I come to the conclusion in my past work with Mr. Albright that he was suffering from some psychoneurotic disorder, then there would have been no need to focus on his affect per se, except to permit it to emerge. I might have said nothing and waited. If the

*Kohut (1959) usually defined empathy as *vicarious introspection* and considered it to be a method by which psychoanalysts gather data. He often also, however, used *empathy* or *being empathic with the patient* when he meant *being therapeutic* in the sense I describe here: that is, when the therapist's interpretation involves calling attention to his or her own failure as a selfobject, a failure that has caused the patient to respond with withdrawal, anger, dysphoria, or some other sign of hurt. Kohut's (1971, 1977) introduction of this innovative notion into the therapeutic armamentarium of psychoanalysis was both revolutionary and evolutionary, in that it corrected the traditional psychoanalytic assumption that the patient's reaction to the analyst's words, personality, or behavior always represented a transference manifestation pure and simple, to be interpreted in terms of the patient's past conflicts around discharging sexual and aggressive tensions. It is, however, precisely in the part the therapist plays in the patient's experience that the idealizing, mirroring, and alter ego needs of the patient can be understood most clearly. It is unfortunate that Kohut did not distinguish this contribution with a term better suited to describe it. (Harry Stack Sullivan [1940] called attention to the therapist's contribution to the patient's reaction by calling the former a "participant observer"; George Atwood and Robert Stolorow [1984] discuss the therapist's influence on the clinical exchange under the rubric *intersubjectivity*; and Howard Bacal [1983] subsumes it under *optimal responsiveness*.)

patient remained silent, I would have made the traditional psychoanalytic noises—such as "Yes?" "Hmmm?" or "Just say what you're thinking"—which are usually enough to mobilize associations in such a patient.

However, having determined during previous therapy sessions that Mr. Albright fit into the group of people who lacked appropriate affective attunement when this was crucial for development, I decided neither to remain silent nor to articulate the affect I thought was present. Instead, I proceeded to question him actively but in such a way that for the moment at least he could overcome the shame of his need for me and bring that need into consciousness. What made it possible for him to take this step was my understanding and openly acknowledging in a nondefensive manner my recognition that by keeping him waiting I had precipitated his dysphoric reaction. That I had reason to feel I was on the right track with my interpretation was indicated by the patient's "Why didn't I think of that?" and his spontaneously associating to other incidents that could be understood in a similar manner (Freud 1937).

Now that I have presented the scientific basis for psychotherapy and outlined a technique for its use based on the examination and management of the therapeutic transferance, let me turn to the art of psychotherapy—the in-depth application of the theory to specific cases. In chapters 7 to 10, I will present case material illustrating the four groups of patients who are most frequently seen and helped in the offices of psychotherapists: patients with early failure of affective bonding (Jim Zurf, Bob Granger, Tina Pearl); those who, blocked from healthy affective development, have become ashamed of their potential feelings and retreated into depression (Roger Flynn); patients whose affective needs are hidden within a defensive shell of achievement and seemingly successful social adaptation (Esther Romberg); and those patients in whom a definitive affective trauma and maturational arrest occurred during the oedipal stage of psychosexual development (Otto Neubach, Irma Waller, Norma Newton).

7

Failure of Affective Bonding and Withdrawal from Attachment

Overcoming Resistance to Treatment: Jim Zurf

Dr. and Mrs. Zurf came to consult me about their sixteen-year-old son, Jim, who—to judge from their description—was in serious developmental difficulty. His grades in high school were poor, he was a disciplinary problem for his teachers, and he seemed to have no friends. At home he continually goaded his parents, going out of his way by word and deed to show his contempt for their values, especially their ambitions for him, their only child. They thought that until he was about thirteen years old Jim seemed to be developing in a fairly average manner; at least he never created any significant difficulties for them. A boy of obviously high intelligence, he had up to that point always done well at school without having to work hard. I had the impression that the family was not close, and that the parents had felt that, by putting their son into a suburban environment where he could enjoy what they considered to be the best in terms of company, education, and recreational facilities, they had done what was needed and could be expected of them. They seemed willing to accept the advice of the school that Jim be psychiatrically evaluated and, if necessary, treated; not particularly curious, they behaved as if psychiatric therapy was one more service that they would provide for their son if it was recommended by the authorities.

INITIAL INTERVIEW: ELICITING THE PATIENT'S TRUE FEELINGS

THERAPIST: Well, Jim, so far I've only heard about you from your parents. Now I'd like to hear from you.

JIM: Like what?

THERAPIST: Oh, what you think about the problems that brought you. How you see me being useful to you. How you feel about being here. Stuff like that.

JIM: I'm here 'cause they sent me. I don't have any problems. *They* think I got problems.

THERAPIST: They decided you should come?

JIM: That's right.

THERAPIST: And you had nothing to say about it?

JIM: Right.

THERAPIST: Well, that's trouble.

JIM: Waddaya mean?

THERAPIST: When your folks first came to see me and told me how unhappy you seemed to be and the difficulties you were having getting along both at home and at school, I suggested they talk it over with you, offer you the opportunity of coming here, and let you decide if you would like to give it a try.

JIM: What's the difference? Nobody likes to come to a shrink.

THERAPIST: Oh, it's quite possible to like coming here, but at the moment I'm not talking about likes and dislikes, but about deciding to come or deciding not to come.

JIM: What's the difference?

THERAPIST: If there are problems in getting life on the right track, and the help that friends, parents, teachers, and others are able to give doesn't seem to be working out, then a decision to see a psychiatrist may make good sense. You don't have to be happy about it, but it has to be your decision. Psychotherapy is a cooperative business and that requires that each of us make up his mind to participate.

JIM: I'm not crazy.

THERAPIST: Exactly. There are two kinds of people who are seen by psychiatrists: those who have decided they need and want that sort of help, and those who cannot be trusted to make their own decisions and have to be brought against their will to see the doctor. It's the latter who are often suffering from what we call psychotic illnesses, what the man on the street calls "crazy." I am only set up to work with the first type of person, the patient who has decided to come to see if I can be of help.

JIM: That's bullshit! Kids don't decide anything. I guess we fit in with the crazies.

THERAPIST: Not true. Babies already make decisions, so do children, and of course teenagers like you. Naturally, the kinds of decisions that can be appropriately made vary with the level of development and the circumstances of the people involved. At your age, you certainly have something to say about the way your life is going and what you will or won't do about it.

It became obvious to me almost immediately that Jim, rather than cooperating with my attempts to get to know him better, was bent on frustrating my efforts by either aborting the process or turning it into a replica of the relationship he was reported to have with his parents. It is especially in situations like this that a general theory of how and why therapy works provides an orienting framework. The therapist can use the theory to focus the session and engage the underlying problem before he or she knows the specifics of a patient's dynamics and their origin.

What surprised me was that I was not put off or angered by Jim's oppositional attitude. His defiance reminded me of nothing so much as that of a little boy who tries to conceal his fear behind a show of bravado. I experienced a rush of sympathy for his plight and, figuratively, wanted to hold out my arms to him: to assure him that I would and could respond to his need; that I realized how much he wanted to feel close to someone who could understand his longing; and that I understood how fearful he was that any attempt in that direction would meet with frustration.

At the same time, I realized that, even if my affective understanding of Jim's condition was accurate, it was based on identification and should not be confused with empathy (pages 146–50; see also Basch 1983*a*). Jim's behavior and attitude reminded me of experiences in my own past, but, though I had learned not to dismiss them, in and of themselves such reactions are not useful guides for therapeutic intervention. In other words, what I might have wanted, or thought I needed, when as an adolescent I behaved like Jim, did not necessarily coincide either with what he needed or could use. Continuing with the decentering process, I decided provisionally to accept my reaction to Jim as an indication of what might be going on at some deeper level within him, while I took into account the immediate message he was sending to the effect that he was not ready to deal with me as a helpful person. He needed to maintain distance between us and must have good reason for doing so.

I was now in a position to formulate a working hypothesis that would guide me in my approach to Jim, at least in this initial session. I asked myself, "Why should anyone behave in a way that will probably antagonize the person who is at the receiving end of this sort of oppositional behavior?" And answered, "For the same reason that anyone does anything: to achieve competence and enhance or protect self-esteem." The question then became: "Why does Jim, in an effort to prove himself, have to establish a behavior pattern that, if effective, would result in his being disliked and rejected?" "Because he has no choice," seemed to me the only sensible answer.

For the moment, then, I took at face value what I had heard about Jim's failure to adapt to school, his lack of friends, and the difficulties he had with his parents. Combining this information with his need to withdraw from me by responding angrily to my attempts to bring us closer together, I came to the tentative conclusion that his capacity for trust in affective communication had been significantly damaged early in his development—a time when withdrawal was the only defense available to ward off pain. His angry behavior, which led to his now being shunned and isolated, served to shut out stimulation. In his own way, therefore, he was competent. The problem was that such a global, primitive defense would not be likely to lead to meaningful self-esteem, to continued development of his character, or to fulfilling his potential as a person. It would be useless, however, at least at this early stage of treatment, to confront him with the fact that he was courting disaster for, as far as *his* pattern of expectation was concerned, he was achieving his goal.

To gain therapeutic leverage, I created a situation in which he could not depend on me to tell him what he should do so that he could then refuse. Instead of accepting his implicit invitation to enter into a power struggle, one I was sure to lose, I engaged him by insisting that, far from trying to exert authority over him, I recognized his right and obligation to decide what he wanted for himself and why. I thereby prevented him from deluding himself that he had decided what—or, more correctly, what not—to do when actually he had made no choice. In this way I was able to short-circuit the efficacy of his maneuver: I did not give him the feedback, so to speak, that would let him match his unspoken goal, which, at least as I saw it, was something like, "Made you angry and upset, didn't I? Now who's helpless and weak, and feels bad about himself?"

However, at the same time that I was frustrating his accustomed way of functioning, I entered the developmental spiral by acknowledging his right and obligation to make decisions about his future. I did not insist that I knew best; and, indeed, I was prepared to let our first session be the last session if that was his choice. In the long run, that would have been preferable to having him continue with me under what he felt to be duress. I did not think that he would take that road, however, for I believed that he still had hope for a life different from the one he was leading. First of all, he had come for his appointment with me; second—and I thought this very significant—was the reaction he had been able to mobilize in me. His adversarial demeanor, far from antagonizing me, made me feel that

I wanted to reach out to him: I felt that there was a little boy who could grow inside that angry young man, but one had to reach that child in a roundabout way.

By not responding to Jim's provocativeness and thereby simply fulfilling his negative expectations, but, instead, treating him courteously and dealing with him as if he were not out to make me angry but was really looking for explanations (which I did feel was probably true for him at a deeper level), I tried to stimulate a need to order or organize the signals I was sending. This procedure met with some success.

JIM: It's my life, and I can do what I want with it. They act like I'm the problem, but they were at each other before I was born.

THERAPIST: How?

JIM: They get a couple of drinks in 'em and I hear her yelling: "I never should have let you talk me into getting married. I should've divorced you years ago." And him: "Think you would have been better off with that bum you were with when I found you? At least I make a living." They can't blame that one on me, I wasn't there then.

THERAPIST: Sounds bad. I hear real pain in your voice as you tell me what you've had to hear.

JIM: I don't give a fuck.

THERAPIST: When they yell at you, they can't be yelling at each other. Maybe as long as you give them trouble and they're bitching at you, they're too busy to fight with one another.

JIM: Aw shit!

THERAPIST: I agree with you, but what can be done about it?

JIM: How is my coming here supposed to change anything?

THERAPIST: That's hard to say, but we do find that when there is a significant change in one member of a family locked in combat, then the whole system has to find a new balance, usually for the better. It's possible of course that your parents need you as a lightning rod for whatever unhappiness there is in their lives, and that without meaning to do so they will effectively block you in finding a resolution for your difficulties. On the other hand, when I talked to them, they did seem to want to help you. They may be willing to let you grow and give us a chance to do together what they and you could not do unaided.

JIM: What do you want me to do?

THERAPIST: You've decided to give it a try?

JIM: I guess . . .

THERAPIST: Good. So have I.

I believed that I was on the right track with Jim, not just because he made a decision to continue working with me, but because he spontaneously began to talk about what sounded like a central problem for him—his parents' dissatisfaction with one another. This enabled me to introduce him to the affective dimension of his difficulties. As I have noted with many male patients who have had early difficulties with affective communication, the closer they come to the issues troubling them, the more they find themselves cursing and/or using vulgar language. Most often it is not lack of vocabulary that forces the patient to do this, but the lack of experience in dealing directly with strong affect. It seems to be the only way they can give voice to what calls for sophisticated nuances of emotion. I read it as a call for help with communication, and usually respond by trying as best as I can to give language to what I think a patient is trying to say. When the patients themselves become more able to deal with their past experiences and to use more suitable language, I take it as a sign of their affective maturation.

Let me comment here on the language the therapist uses in the therapeutic relationship. I am not infrequently asked whether my emphasis on affective maturation and the early stages of development infantilizes patients and fosters an unhealthy dependence. As is evident, I spoke to Jim Zurf as I would to any adult, or child for that matter. *What* I say—and *how much*—varies with the patient's need and the stage of the treatment; *how* I say something does not. While I often talk to patients about the child within them, so to speak, I never address them as if they were children or infants. In making long explanations in response to Jim's monosyllabic comments, I was talking to the person he could be, not to the manner in which his problems led him to present himself. Far from infantilizing patients, I believe that this approach promotes development: it permits a patient to regress when necessary in the course of treatment, while, on another level, the patient also knows that I do not mistake his pathology for his entirety (see also Kohut 1987, p. 39; Gedo 1979).

SELF-DEFEATING WITHDRAWAL

Once Jim had committed himself to working with me, I continued to see him once a week. As I expected, he continued to try to re-create with me the same situation that existed at home and at school: namely, one in which he established what adults wanted from him, so that he could then frustrate those aims. A session early in his treatment went like this:

JIM: I don't have anything——
THERAPIST: Nothing happening worth talking about?
JIM: I don't know what you want.
THERAPIST: What I want? I just want to have some fun.
JIM: Huh?
THERAPIST: Some people get their kicks out of solving crossword puzzles. I like to help people look at their lives as if they were puzzles, and figure out what it is they really want and why they're not getting it. Once that's done, they can plan their future.
JIM: I know what I want.
THERAPIST: Hmm?
JIM: I just want to be left alone.
THERAPIST: Left alone to do what?
JIM: How should I know?
THERAPIST: I think that since you don't know the answer to that question, being left alone may not really be what you want. I mean, if someone told me that he wanted to be left alone to watch a TV program, or build something, or just enjoy nature, that might well make good sense; but when you tell me you just want to be left alone but

don't know why, then I think there is more to it than
that.

JIM: Like what?

THERAPIST: Oh, like you really want to be left alone not because you
want to be left alone, but because you haven't been too
successful in getting anything out of not being alone.
That being with people doesn't work for you. That your
goal is not so much to get something as to avoid something—avoiding the frustration and pain of feeling
*un*understood, for instance.

JIM: Yeah, it's a pain in the ass.

THERAPIST: What?

JIM: Oh, people, y'know.

THERAPIST: Are you thinking of a particular situation right now?

JIM: Yeah, I guess. This dumb-ass broad teacher I got, she
says I'm supposed to have a big discussion about atomic
bombs and stuff, taking sides, y'know, and I'm supposed to be on the side that says they're O.K. What the
fuck's the difference? What we say doesn't make any
difference anyway. If they drop it, they drop it; we got
nothing to say about it. Maybe it'd be a good thing. Get
it over with.

THERAPIST: In other words, you might turn the debate into a question of whether or not humanity is worth saving, and
answer in the negative.

JIM: Yeah, but what's the point?

THERAPIST: The point of any behavior is its goal. If the goal of your
debate were to decide whether atomic bombs would or
would not be used in the immediate future, you would
be quite right in saying that no matter what conclusion
the class reached, it would, in all probability, have no
impact on how nations conduct themselves. However,
I don't think that was the teacher's purpose in making
this assignment. Probably what she is trying to foster is
your skill in developing a coherent argument and delivering it in convincing fashion. The pros and cons of
atomic warfare are simply a topic that she felt would
make for a good discussion.

JIM: [*Contemptuously*] Yeah, I know that.

THERAPIST: Of course you do, but when you first began to talk about this assignment, you presented it as if the teacher were a real dummy for expecting you to take seriously a discussion of world affairs over which you know you have no control. Looked at that way, it makes no sense to study for the debate, and I would be a fool if I tried to persuade you to do so. But what about learning to marshall a cogent argument and to express yourself more effectively? Can you exercise control in that area?

JIM: You mean I should do what she says—go to the library and stuff?

THERAPIST: I can't make those decisions for you. All I am trying to do is to help you see clearly what the issues are, what options for action are reasonably open to you, and to think them through. Once you understand the meaning of some particular activity, what it is really about and how it will or may affect you, then I would expect that a person your age is quite capable of deciding whether or not to go ahead and pursue that particular goal.

JIM: Well, I don't have any goals, like you say. That's what my Dad always bitches about: "No direction!" I just can't see it. He wants me to be like him: "Get a profession, and make something of yourself." No thanks. When I see what it's gotten him. . . . It doesn't make sense to kill yourself for that.

THERAPIST: What do you see that doesn't make it worthwhile?

JIM: All his fucking money doesn't make him any happier with my Mom. She's got three fur coats, but she's not happy either.

THERAPIST: Do you notice how you always come back to the relationship between your parents whenever you try to make the point that hopefulness about life and planning for the future makes no sense?

JIM: I don't know. All they do is yell at each other—unless they're with their friends, of course. Then everything is real polite and nice. Phony shit!

THERAPIST: So they can be pleasant and polite, but not when they're alone with each other?

JIM: Yeah, that's what I said. So?

THERAPIST: It seems to me that you know what you don't want, but haven't quite figured out what might be worthwhile, what you might want to work for.

JIM: Are you happy?

THERAPIST: I know why I'm doing what I'm doing most of the time. That prevents a lot of unhappiness at least.

JIM: Well, my parents ain't happy.

THERAPIST: Sure doesn't sound as if they were.

JIM: Yeah, well, that shows you're wrong.

THERAPIST: How so?

JIM: They know why they're yelling at each other all the time. They can't stand each other's fucking guts, that's why! But knowing it don't make them less unhappy.

This was the first time that Jim had shown any curiosity about me as a person and made a move toward using me as a model, as opposed to the parental paradigm for feeling and behavior. I silently noted a tendril in the direction of what might some day become an idealizing transference.

THERAPIST: I doubt very much whether your parents know why they're at each other's throats all the time. If they knew, they would have done something about it a long time ago. Whenever you see people doing the same thing over and over again, even though it doesn't get them anywhere, you can bet they don't know where their feelings really come from or what the purpose of their behavior might be. I'd bet you that your parents' unhappiness has a lot to do with that.

JIM: That's what you do? Figure stuff like that out?

THERAPIST: All the time.

JIM: They ought to be here then, not me.

THERAPIST: What are you feeling right now, Jim?

JIM: Huh?
THERAPIST: Are you aware of feelings or emotions as you talk to me
             about your parents' need for treatment?
JIM: I dunno.
THERAPIST: Your face sort of clouded over, and you had a real sad
             look.
JIM: I guess.
THERAPIST: I think you're in a lot of pain about your parents' situa-
             tion.
JIM: Naw, I don't give a shit now. Maybe when I was a little
             kid. . . . Now I'm used to it. . . . Half the time I don't
             even hear 'em. Who gives a rat's ass?
THERAPIST: Some things you never get used to. You may not be
             aware of it or of your feelings, but that look on your
             face tells me that it still hurts plenty, and understand-
             ably so.

Here, again, in an attempt to help Jim articulate his feelings, I took
the opportunity to shift from his description of behavior and events
to his affective response to the situation.

Jim missed his next appointment. When I telephoned him that
evening, he told me that he had been kept after school as punishment for creating a disturbance. His voice conveyed a note of both
defiance and triumph. He said he would be in for his appointment
the following week. I suggested instead that, since I had time available, he come in the next day after school. He raised no objection and
accepted my offer.

When I saw him and asked for details about what had happened
the day before, he bragged how he had managed to aggravate his
"asshole teacher" until the man became angry and gave him a de-
tention. Exploring further, we found that this teacher was one who
had seen Jim's potential and had taken a special interest in him.

I suggested to Jim that his going out of his way to get into trouble
was a self-protective response to the distress he began to experience
in his last session when we were beginning to explore his true
feelings regarding his family situation; that he was both converting
his distress into anger, with which he was more comfortable and

could cope more easily, and also creating a situation that would prevent him from seeing me and possibly having to face once again feelings that he had done his best to bury and avoid re-experiencing. I told Jim I thought something like that was happening to his parents, that a confusion about their feelings led to continual quarrels, which could lead to no resolution because they never addressed the underlying reasons for their despair. It looked to me as if he had learned to deal with unhappiness in similar fashion; his oppositional behavior would serve only to create secondary problems and no personal solutions because it never dealt with the real issues troubling him: namely, the effect of living in a chronically tense, unsettling atmosphere, one in which he perhaps believed that he could get a show of concern from his parents only if he created problems that threatened to undermine the one thing they seemed to care about—maintaining the façade of a socially correct, conforming, upwardly mobile family.

At this point, about four months into the treatment, although I still felt that Jim could be helped and that he was benefiting from our work, the extent of his pathology also became clearer. Paradoxically, but understandably, my ability and readiness to deal with him in a tender and understanding fashion represented a threat that he had to neutralize. I surmised that his behavior meant that if he could offend or discourage me, he would be spared the pain of his longing for the very love and affection he seemed to fear. Accordingly, I continued to focus whenever possible on what I suspected were his true feelings, and tried to show him that I could be comfortable with the expression of his affective needs.

Withdrawal was indeed Jim's main defense against anxiety, but an even more serious problem was that withdrawal was not effective. Apparently, no aspect of his life had been protected by this defense; in no area was he free to function competently and promote some modicum of self-esteem. He seemed to have no control over affective tension; all he could do was flee when he experienced such involvement.

By contrast, let me briefly discuss a case superficially similar to Jim's, but one in which withdrawal was able to exercise a protective function.

Adaptive Withdrawal: Bob Granger

I was once consulted by the parents of a young man who, while away at college, had refused to communicate with them, and had not been home for two years. He had returned this time during the summer vacation only because the parents had threatened that they would no longer pay his bills if he did not come home and agree to go to a psychiatrist for an evaluation. They painted a bleak picture of their son: like Jim Zurf, Bob had been nothing but trouble at school and at home; he was isolated from the family and had few or no friends. The college he wanted to attend, and the only one they thought would be willing to take him, was a small, relatively unknown, out of the way institution that gave a chance to students who had been academically unsuccessful but showed talent in the visual arts. His parents had reluctantly agreed to send him there for a year, and then for another, though he gave them no idea of how he was doing or what his ultimate career choice might be. After their family physician and a psychologist friend had warned them that their son Bob's apparent withdrawal might indicate a psychotic process, they insisted on a psychiatric consultation for him.

My heart, encased as usual in a three-piece suit, fell when Bob Granger presented himself in my waiting room. He was a scrawny, unprepossessing fellow. His long hair, tied back with a ribbon, did not look any too clean. The wisp of moustache on his upper lip looked ridiculous on his pimply face. The ragged T-shirt and the stained cut-off blue jeans that young men that year were wearing to show off their athletic physique only accentuated his lack of same. In sum, he looked bizarre, and this appearance, along with his intensely staring, slightly protuberant eyes, readied me to believe that his external appearance reflected an equally chaotic inner world. My fears were quickly allayed. Bob and I subscribed to different life styles, but I soon learned that he in his way, just as I in mine, had found his niche in life and was functioning in a way that satisfied the conditions of his particular environment while bringing him closer to his personal goals.

Like Jim, Bob was understandably wary at first, seeing me as an agent of his parents. I dealt with this attitude by being straightforward about my preliminary interview with them, but assuring him that I would have no further contact with his parents without first getting his permission. As had Jim, Bob declared that he was seeing me only at his parents' insistence. They had made his future support dependent on the outcome of such consultation; as far as he was concerned, he had no problems and needed no psychiatric help. I said something like, "In essence, what you're telling me is that you're satisfied with yourself and where you're going." "Yes." "Fine, I'd like to hear about that. What are you doing now? How do you feel about it? And where do you see yourself down the road five years from now? Ten years from now?"

Bob, significantly unlike Jim, now seemed convinced that I really wanted to hear about him from him, and was able, without anger or antagonism, to tell me quite a bit about himself. He said that he had been a successful achiever at college and got along well with a group of like-minded students. He had made friends, male and female, and was on good terms with his instructors, although he was essentially following a course of independent study and was responsible only for final examinations at the end of the term. He was apparently so gifted that he had been given permission to pursue his interests as he saw fit. The main reason he gave for not coming home for the summer vacation between his freshman and sophomore years was that he had been approached by a commercial concern that had use for his talents and hired him on a full-time basis for the summer and part-time during the school year. In this way, he earned money to pay all his expenses except tuition, a fact that his parents had not mentioned to me. Bob was resentful that he had to come home during this vacation and miss the opportunity to work at what both interested him and at the same time earned him a tidy amount of money.

To hark back to the phases of psychotherapy (pages 19–23), in this initial meeting with Bob, consternation had preceded orientation. Therapists all run into situations where a patient's appearance, viewpoints, life style, and/or background are so foreign that one feels less curious and interested in the person and more in the grip of "stranger anxiety" with a need to defend oneself against this intrusion. How can one hope to reach empathic understanding under these circumstances, get the necessary distance from one's reaction to the patient without withdrawing from him or her? As in Bob's case, one can reinstitute efforts toward orientation and eventually bring about collaboration if one is aware of the universality of the need for competence as measured by the patient's level of self esteem and his ability to make decisions and engage in behavior that furthers the developmental cycle. By using the patient's self-esteem as a measuring stick, one can largely avoid both introducing one's own values, moral standards, or other predilections, and the solipsistic position that what is psychologically healthy, normal, or optimal closely resembles what one sees in the mirror. So when I asked Bob such questions as "Where are you now, and where do you see yourself some years from today?" I was not only interested in gathering facts about his development and his future goals. I was also letting him convey to me his picture of himself as differentiated from how I might judge him based on my own background and experience. Bob satisfied me that he thought well of himself and had reason to do so. Given the people who were important to him and the work he was interested in, he had established a hierarchy of goals and programs geared to reach his objectives. Only the area of his relation with his parents was not clear to me. When asked about this, Bob, who had been forthright and informative, suddenly became shallow and noncommital, talking in generalities—"We just don't get along"—statements from which I could not lead him to specific examples. Also, he again became suspicious of me and wondered what I had up my sleeve.

Such closure in selected areas as Bob's is more common in psychotherapy than the global arrest Jim suffered. Bob was able to "hear" me. He was able to compare (1) the pattern of expectation created by whatever prejudgments he may have made about me, based on his connecting me with his parents' demands and whatever other associations the word *psychiatrist* may have aroused in him, with (2) the actual manner in which I presented myself; he was able to see that the two concepts *agent of my parents* and *Dr. Basch* did not coincide, and then to sort through the behavioral scripts he had available to make productive contact with me. But when his parents came into the discussion, he mobilized, in machinelike fashion,

avoidance behavior that signaled trouble. He could not think about
that subject. When this sort of cognitive block occurs, and sooner
or later it always does, the therapist has struck paydirt—*resistance* in
the technical jargon—and can begin to plan how to mine that lode.

I explained my puzzlement to Bob and suggested that maybe I
could become clearer in my own mind about his situation if our next
meeting could be a family session attended by him and his mother
and father. That way I could talk to his parents without his needing
to be worried about what I was saying or not saying to them. Bob
agreed to this plan.

With his parents, Bob became a different person. He whined,
complained, sulked, all in all presenting a much more immature
picture of himself than he had before. His parents who, when I
talked to them alone, appeared to be pretty reasonable and fair-
minded people, if emotionally distant, now seemed bent only on
venting their anger at Bob, finding fault with everything he did, and
criticizing his behavior past and present. As I let the three of them
go on for a while, gradually a clearer picture of the family relationship emerged. There was, indeed, a psychotic or nearly psychotic
person in the family, but it was Bob's mother, not Bob. It seemed
that she could maintain herself only by exercising absolute control
over her home and everyone in it. Though she complained mightily
that Bob was not helpful or cooperative and isolated himself from
the family, what emerged was that she could not tolerate his touching—literally touching—anything in the house. If he made up his
bed, she remade it, complaining that it had not been done properly.
If, at her urging, he started to bring dishes to or from the table, she
screamed that he was sure to drop them and snatched them out of
his hands. Bob's father had accommodated himself to the situation
by agreeing with whatever his wife said and adding his condemna-
tion to hers. As he ran his business from an office adjacent to his
home, he was essentially available to do his wife's bidding twenty-
four hours a day and was, psychologically speaking, undifferentiated from her in the son's mind. As this situation became clearer
and I began to probe a bit, an egregious example of the chronic
sacrifice of Bob's self-esteem to his mother's compulsions emerged.
Bob apparently was mechanically gifted: from an early age, he had
trained himself to build and repair all sorts of machines. In high

school, he and a classmate, working in the classmate's parents' garage, took a car that was just about ready for the junk heap and totally rebuilt and rehabilitated it. Yet, on one occasion, when something went wrong with the family automobile, the mother rejected Bob's offer to troubleshoot the car, insisting that he would be sure to compound the damage. The father agreed, took it from one mechanic to another at considerable expense but without results, and eventually traded it in for a new model, taking a hefty financial loss in the process. When this matter came up in the interview, Bob could not suppress a delighted grin, which his mother immediately seized upon as an example of his hostility to them. Neither parent had any grasp of how Bob's manifest pleasure in their discomfort had its origin in wounded feelings precipitated by their inability to recognize, admire, and give scope to his skills.

It became increasingly obvious that vis-a-vis the mother's pathological behavior, which precluded Bob's gaining any self-esteem through competent behavior, there remained only the alternatives of surrendering to the mother, as the father had done, or, as Bob had chosen to do, isolating himself psychologically while with them and escaping from home as soon as he possibly could. My impression of the situation was that, under the circumstances, the patient had done what was in his best interest. Probably only his unusual talent and high intelligence had enabled him to grow up in this atmosphere and survive psychologically to the extent that he could still make a life for himself.

I told the parents while we were all together that their fears about their son's mental derangement were unfounded; that they should by all means support his education and let him find his way in the world; and that, in the face of the obvious tension between all of them, it might be helpful to seek qualified family therapy. The last suggestion was rejected unanimously. I then concluded that, since they could not get along as a family but seemed to have adjusted individually, they continue in that mode and not force prolonged family togetherness. I offered to continue to see Bob on a weekly basis, and he did come in a few more times. However, assured of continued help with his tuition, he felt he really did not have much more to discuss. I pointed out his personality change in the presence of his parents—how that sector of his personality had been traumatized—and suggested he explore with me the effect that this had had on his development. Bob would have none of it, and understandably so. He had survived by withdrawing from his emotional needs as they related to his parents and, as any other person, could not be expected to give up that defensive posture unless that defense ceased to work effectively and gave rise to anxiety. Such was not the case at the moment. Bob had found an environment that enabled him to function competently and enhanced his self-esteem, while his psychotherapy had neither persisted long enough nor become intense enough to permit him to reactivate the affective needs originally directed toward his parents in a transference experience with me. Bob protected himself against any transference attachment by starting to miss every other therapy session on one pretext or another. He readily agreed when I suggested, after I had seen him three more times, that he might well feel he had accomplished what he came for: namely, he had independent confirmation that he was more than capable of functioning effectively as a college student; that his goals were realistic; and that his parents had no reason for not continuing to support his studies.

To return to the point I was making when I digressed to compare Jim Zurf's situation with Bob Granger's, that is, that the presence of a defense, in this case withdrawal, is not indicative of the level of pathology: in both cases the parents, serving as the initial informants, had painted a dim picture of their respective offspring. I found it easy enough, however, to separate Bob from the implied picture of him presented by his parents and from the equally negative impression he made on me when I first set eyes on him. Like Jim, Bob denied that there was anything wrong; but when I said, "O.K., tell me what's right—what you have been doing, and where you think you're going with your life," he quickly told me what I needed to know to understand how he was able to achieve meaningful competence, and how the resulting self-esteem led to further decisions and behavior that permitted increased growth academically, socially, and personally. Bob had removed himself from a family situation in which he felt stifled and misunderstood; he had also learned to become a different person in relation to people in his new environment. Bob could trust a new situation sufficiently to see whether the people with whom he was dealing would or would not behave toward him as his parents did. Jim could not do so; he was locked into a particular behavior pattern. I had the impression that Jim was much attached to and dependent on his parents. He had not managed to promote interests or acquire skills that might have let him, as had Bob, develop as an individual in his own right. That Jim's attachment to his parents took a negative form is beside the point, for though he always took a contrary position to what they wanted from or hoped for him, he was just as dependent on their direction as a child who is compulsively compliant with his parents' wishes. Like such a child, Jim's behavior was always a response to his parents' script rather than to his own. It looked as if he saw other authority figures, like teachers and myself, simply as parental surrogates and did not deal with them as individuals in their own right who just might offer him the possibility for a different and better relationship than he had with his parents.

As Bob's case shows, opposition to the powers-that-be is not problematic in principle; Jim's difficulty was that his rebellion did not lead to any worthwhile increase in his self-esteem. He was going nowhere; seemingly, all he could do was demonstrate over and over again that no one could make him succeed. Jim's concept of himself did not let him function as a center for initiative (Kohut 1971); his oppositional behavior was governed by what he thought others wanted or expected of him, not by any goal-directed program expressing his own aims. His was a closed system, one not open to generating new information and thereby altering patterns of expectation that were no longer adaptive.

Toward Transmuting Internalization: Jim Zurf

A CRUCIAL TURNING POINT IN THE TRANSFERENCE

After having seen Jim Zurf for about a year, I was satisfied that his willingness to attend and participate in our sessions—although he spurned my suggestion that we meet more frequently, and refused to come in more than once a week—meant that he was

getting something meaningful from our work. Outwardly his behavior did not change much, but he was increasingly able to hear
me out when I discussed with him what I saw as the connection
between his current isolation from potential friends and mentors
and the hurt and disappointment he experienced when he had tried,
in years past, to arouse his parents' interest in his life. It became
clear that the parents' report of Jim's essentially trouble-free childhood was a fond illusion. While he had not made trouble for them—
that is, interfered with their lives or plans, which seldom involved
him—there was no doubt that the boy was chronically withdrawn
and depressed, escaping into sleep whenever he could, and easily
distracted and inattentive when awake. (As a matter of fact, Jim
remembered, though his parents had not told me, that in grammar
school he was thought to have an attention deficit disorder and had
been medicated by their physician at the suggestion of the school
psychologist. However, this medication seemingly had no therapeutic effect on Jim.)

At this time, Jim, who was doing no better in his schoolwork than
when he first started with me and was failing most of his courses,
decided to drop out of high school. I first heard about this in a
telephone call from his father, who threatened to end Jim's treatment, for this turn of events clearly indicated to him that my work
with his son had been a failure. I temporized; and before anything
further occurred, Jim's mother fell ill, was hospitalized, and had to
undergo breast surgery for a malignancy. Although her surgeon was
optimistic for her long-term survival, she fell into a depression that
necessitated transfer to a psychiatric hospital.

Jim was now left alone much of the day and evening. His father
was either in his office or with his wife in the hospital. Jim was no
longer in school, and had not made friends. Long since discharged
were the various housekeepers who had cooked for the family and
supervised him during his early years, so there was no one now even
to care for his basic needs, and he ate most of his meals in a local
restaurant. One day the manager of the restaurant asked him if he
wanted a part-time job as busboy and dishwasher—an offer Jim
accepted, perhaps out of boredom, perhaps because there was no
one around to fight with him about his doing something productive.

From what he told me, he expected his father to be upset that he was settling on the bottom rung of the employment ladder; and indeed, the father did at first make some contemptuous remarks about the fate of high school dropouts. But he eventually let Jim know that his own first regular job had also been as a busboy. Indeed, it was the interest taken in him by one of the restaurant's patrons that eventually led Jim's father, who came from a poor and uneducated background, to go to college and then to dental school. With his wife in the hospital and memories of his youth awakened through Jim's work, Dr. Zurf made an effort to talk with his son, telling a few stories of his days as a restaurant worker and showing some interest in comparing his early experiences with those Jim was having now. It was at this time that my therapeutic efforts had some fairly dramatic results. The father's heretofore unheard-of attempts at forming some sort of relationship with his son remobilized Jim's early longing and disappointment in that area in a way he could no longer disown.

JIM: Yeah, now he wants to sit and talk with me all of a sudden. I'm watching television, and he sort of comes in with the paper and sits down like he wants to read, but I know he wants to talk with me. He makes comments, y' know, like, "Is that a good show?" or, "I think I saw that guy on last week. What's his name?" I just fluff him off.

THERAPIST: What do you say to your Dad?

JIM: Nothin'. Just "yes" and "no" or "I don't know."

THERAPIST: Sounds like you're giving him a dose of his own medicine. He wasn't there when you needed him, and now the tables are turned.

JIM: Yeah, where are all their fancy friends now? The first couple of weeks she was sick they'd call, or they'd invite him for dinner——

THERAPIST: Did they invite you, too?

JIM: Yeah, but I never went. They didn't want me anyway, just being polite.

Anyway, now the place is like a fucking graveyard.

Nobody calls. I get a kick out of it. When he hears the phone, he runs for it, but most times it's the restaurant asking if I can come in an hour earlier, or stuff like that.

THERAPIST: You know what that's like for your Dad—how lonely it is when nobody wants to know what or how you feel, or cares about what you've been doing.

JIM: You want to know something?

THERAPIST: Sure.

JIM: I'm not making this up. When I was in fifth grade, about eleven fucking years old, they took off for Europe for a month. The maid they had quit, so a couple of days before they leave, they get this fat piece of shit from an ad in the paper who's supposed to watch me and take care of the house, y' know. This fucking broad is nuts! The first night we're alone in the house, I wake up, she's screaming about someone being after her. I'm lying in bed, scared shitless, she keeps hollering. Finally I get out of my bed, quiet like. She's not in her room. I sneak downstairs. There she is in the kitchen, holding a fuck- ing carving knife, yelling at some guy who isn't there that she's not going to let him get away with it, and stuff like that. What am I supposed to do? Finally, I figure I'll try to see if I can get her out of it. If she comes at me with that knife, I know I can run faster than her, and there's a window I can jump out of and land on top of the garage. No good trying to get out the front or back door. By the time I'd get it open she'd have cut my goddam nuts off.

So I'm going to call her, but I was so fucking scared I forgot her fucking name. She's hollering, so finally I say, "Hey, Lady, there's nobody here but me." But I'm so scared it doesn't come out. But she hears something and starts looking over where I am on the stairs, and her eyes have that crazy, stary look like she doesn't know where the hell she is. Now I'm really scared and I yell, "It's just me! Jim, the kid!" That seems to bring her around a little, she sort of seems to remember who I am, but she doesn't put down that fucking knife. She says,

"You've got to help me. He's in here." I've got to help her? Oh, shit! But at least if she thinks I'm on her side she won't knife me. So I say, "I'll help you. We'll check out the rooms." So at one o'clock in the fucking morning I'm taking this fat bitch from one room to the next, turning on the lights, looking behind the curtains and out of the window, trying to convince her whatever she thinks is after her ain't there. I'm trying to find out who this guy is, but she ain't talking. Just follows me around, and she won't let go of that fucking knife.

After a while, though, she starts crying and she says to me, "Little boy"—she couldn't remember my name either—"do you know where your daddy keeps the whiskey? I could sure use a little drink." Well, I put two and two together. I knew about these alkies who go crazy when they try to dry 'em out, and I figured maybe this broad sobered up to get this job and now she's got the shakes. So I said, "Sure, you look a little sick, just sit right down and I'll bring you something." Well, I knew where the old man kept the stuff behind a phony section of the book case: You push a button and it swings out, and that's where he stashes the booze. They didn't know I knew where the button was, but I did. Thank Christ!

So I bring her a bottle and a glass, and she can hardly pour the goddam stuff she's shaking so bad. So I fill it up for her, and she drinks it down like in one swallow and asks for more. After a couple like that, she falls back in her chair and her eyes sort of roll up. I'm thinking, "Oh fuck, she's dead!" But she starts snoring so I know she's only passed out, and finally that fucking knife falls out of her hand. I grab it and run to the kitchen, and I take all the sharp knives and I hide 'em in the basement. Then I just leave her where she is and go upstairs, push the dresser against my fucking door in case she wakes up and starts looking for whoever, and get into bed—I got to get some sleep before it's time to go to school. That's when I find out I'm all wet. I was so scared I must

have pissed my shorts and didn't even know it. But I
was so fucking beat by then. I just threw 'em on the
floor and went to sleep anyway.

Jim went on to tell me how in the morning he found his supposed
sitter still asleep, made his breakfast as best he could, and went to
school. When he came home at midday for lunch, she was still
asleep, but he knew she must have gotten up sometime during his
absence, for she was now snoozing in front of the television set. The
bottle, which had been full when he removed it from his father's
cache, was now almost empty. Jim then realized that this woman
was not going to recover, that she was essentially incapable of
taking care of herself, much less of him and the house.

Although his parents would call him every Sunday to see if everything was all right, Jim quickly understood that they did not
want to hear anything that was not reassuring. The first time they
called, he hinted that there was a problem with the "sitter"—only
to have his mother cut him off by telling him to be cooperative and
not make trouble for the woman.

In the month that followed, Jim was in charge of himself and this
invalid. He did his best to provide meals for both of them, going to
the store to buy supplies and preparing them as best he could. With
his limited imagination and culinary skills, they lived on peanut
butter sandwiches, hot dogs, which he knew how to boil, potato
chips, milk, and candy bars. Each day he provided her with what
he felt was enough alcohol to maintain her tenuous mental equilib-
rium, limiting the amount both to keep her from going into a total
stupor and to make the dwindling store of liquor last until his
parents returned. When he saw that, at her rate of consumption, the
hard liquor would not last the month, he judiciously stretched her
ration of bourbon or scotch whiskey by supplementing it with
brandy, wine, and the various cordials he found stacked up in the
back of the liquor closet. His guest did not seem to mind, imbibing
indiscriminately whatever she was given, seldom rousing herself
from her station in front of the television set except to go to bed
whenever the notion struck her.

A few days before his parents were due to come home, Jim alerted
her to their imminent return, and she made an effort to sober up.

Together they tried to get the house in shape, but their attempt was not too successful. When his parents arrived, however, they said nothing to him about the shambles that greeted them, nor did he hear a word then or later about the almost total depletion of what had been a more than generously stocked liquor cabinet. Indeed, they never asked him anything about what had transpired during their absence, and he never volunteered any information. Within hours of his parents' return, he developed a high fever. The pediatrician who was consulted could find no specific physical illness to account for his symptoms. Of the week he spent in bed he had no recollection. The presents and souvenirs his parents had brought back for him from their trip were not particularly interesting to him and were soon either lost or broken.

Until he told me this story, Jim had never spoken about himself for more than a sentence or two, and those I usually had to drag out of him word by word. I took his confiding in me now, and at such length, as a sign that he had learned to trust me over the months I had worked with him; but more important, I assumed that his barriers to expression came down at this particular time because his father's lonely, lost behavior had reawakened and mobilized similar feelings in him. The incident he recounted represented dramatically the chronic sense of isolation and danger in which a child of uncomprehending, unresponsive parents may live out his or her formative years.

(I usually end my sessions on time, but this was an exception. Jim had begun to tell me the story of his abandonment some ten or fifteen minutes before his session would normally have ended. I listened attentively and without comment and made no attempt to hurry or interrupt the flow of his thought. It probably took him twenty or more minutes to complete his tale in all its details. Fortunately, I was scheduled to attend an administrative meeting after his appointment, and simply made up my mind not to go to it. I would not for the world have interrupted Jim at this important juncture; and I knew that after he finished I would need time to respond to him, to make sure he had suffered no adverse effects from this unaccustomed openness, and to do what I could to keep this path to the affective depths open to further progress. Had I had another patient scheduled following Jim's appointment, I simply would have had to keep that person waiting, started late, and then dealt with the psychological implications my tardiness had for that patient. I could not have let Jim go before we had reached reasonable closure any more than a surgeon could leave a patient in the middle of an operation to tend to another case.)

THERAPIST: In one way, that is of course a very sad story, Jim. On the other hand, you were sure a resourceful fellow . . .

JIM: Yeah, I guess.

THERAPIST: Are you aware of your feelings as you recall this time in your life?

JIM: Yeah, I'm mad. Wouldn't you be?

THERAPIST: Mad that you weren't better cared for by either your parents or the woman they hired? But could you also feel again some of the fear and the loneliness that you must have experienced then? You did remember how scared you were when you found out the sitter was worse than incompetent.

JIM: I guess. But what's the good of bringing it all up anyway?

THERAPIST: It does a lot of good. I think you are getting reacquainted with a lot of emotions that were very painful and, for that reason, had to be pushed out of your consciousness. But when you have to make yourself sort of dead inside, that takes a lot out of you and unnecessarily limits your life.

JIM: Well, it's his turn now.

THERAPIST: In a way, though, maybe it makes your father more human. Perhaps your experiencing him as having some of the same feelings you had at least lets you know that there's nothing intrinsically wrong or shameful about being frightened and distressed when you feel all alone.

In the months that followed, we often came back to this episode; it became what Stern (1985) has called the *organizing therapeutic metaphor,* a significant incident the patient relives in therapy that represents, or in some meaningful way sums up, his life story. It certainly was a watershed in the treatment: it introduced the phase of *integra-*

tion in that Jim and I were able to see his past and present joined by a pattern of avoidance that he had at one time adopted as absolutely necessary for psychological survival (pages 120–23). I concluded that it also represented the first sign of a *mirror transference* (page 141): Jim was reliving this incident in impassioned tones so as to have me validate the reality and the significance of his experience. I believed that a conviction that I would not fail him permitted him to transfer to me the hope that he might be understood after all.

Henceforth, Jim's developmental process was not always so dramatic but, rather, manifested itself in incremental changes in the sessions. Although he remained cynical and negativistic for a long time, his abusive language lessened, and his English became more grammatical. His general improvement was reflected in his being promoted to apprentice waiter at the restaurant.

In subsequent sessions, he did not volunteer information on freely as he had during that crucial meeting; but as I emphasized the affective aspect of the various things he did talk about, he showed increased capacity to experience and think about his feelings in a much more flexible fashion. No longer limited to an all-purpose angry response, he became able to assign affect appropriately to the particular situations in which he found himself.

I took all this to mean that he had been able to establish better control over affective tension. His readiness now to share his experiences with me and seek my view of what was happening indicated that his self system had consolidated and matured to the point that he could look to me for help with and validation of his feelings.

GROWTH IN THE TRANSFERENCE: COPING WITH AFFECT

One day Jim came into my office and sat down, dressed in his overcoat with a scarf still around his neck. Though it was a cold day, the office was certainly warm enough. I wondered what was going on.

THERAPIST: Aren't you going to take your coat off, Jim?
JIM: Naw, it's O.K.
THERAPIST: You'll roast.
JIM: [*Flaring briefly*] That's my business!

THERAPIST: I'm not going to stop you, that's for sure. But what you're thinking is our business. Say, do I see tuxedo pants? You wouldn't run off and get married without telling me, would you?

JIM: [*Blushing and laughing sheepishly*] We're working a party tonight. Place is closed except for this wedding that's rented the whole joint for the evening.

When Jim first came into treatment, I would not have dared to comment on his clothes, much less make suggestions about how he might make himself comfortable. Such behavior on my part would have provoked him to a rage attack and severely compromised the therapy, perhaps even brought it to an end. For many months, our relationship was based on what Kohut (1971) has called *empathic immersion,* an often long preparatory phase necessary when a patient's self-esteem is fragile. It is the therapist's empathic immersion that gradually dissolves the patient's defense against the transference. During this time, a therapist tries to show understanding of a patient without directly examining the patient's behavior or interpreting what the therapist thinks might be the deeper meaning of what the patient is saying. That I was now able to take this different tack with Jim showed how far he had come. His old propensity for angry withdrawal was there, but only briefly: he could trust me not to want to hurt him and so did not have to mount a massive defense as soon as he was made even slightly uncomfortable.

My next comment, and my joking with him, were directed to preparing him for a further phase of his maturation—the symbolic manipulation of affect. That he blushed in response to my kidding him, but then clarified why he was wearing a tuxedo, was encouraging: a sense of humor about oneself indicates the ability to move far enough from one's self-preoccupation to begin at least to look at oneself through others' eyes.

THERAPIST: So all the waiters have to wear tuxedos?

JIM: Yeah. I got to go there right from here and help set up. No time to change in between. It's not really a tuxedo, y' know, not fancy. We rent them at a uniform place they send us to—that is, if y' don't have one.

THERAPIST: I suppose the old timers work so many parties they have to own one.

JIM: Yeah, shelling out twelve bucks each time for the outfit, it pays to get your own.

THERAPIST: I suppose the tips make it worthwhile.

JIM: Oh yeah, with a party like this, they guarantee the tip right in the contract. It's good money.

THERAPIST: Do you think you'll invest in one?

By engaging Jim in a serious conversation about the significance of wearing such a uniform, I made sure that he realized I was not trying to belittle him with my attempt at humor. Indirectly I was showing him that I realized what this signified in terms of the competence he had achieved and the pride he could take in it. This mirroring, in Kohut's terminology (1971), supports the patient's sense of genuine self esteem until the patient is able to give himself credit when credit is due; or, as Kohut called it, a transmuting internalization of the therapist's selfobject function lets the patient do for himself what he previously needed the therapist to do for or with him.

JIM: I'll have to see. Some of the guys work on the side for caterers on their days off. I'm not good enough for that yet.

THERAPIST: Think you will be?

JIM: Yeah, maybe. That guy Max, y' know, he's been teaching me a lot. There's a lot of little things that if you know 'em makes it a lot easier.

Here Jim demonstrated a capacity for idealization: he could look up to and learn from this older, wiser man and feel enriched, rather than endangered, by the exchange—another important sign of Jim's progress.

THERAPIST: Oh, yes. Like in any other business. But I guess this is your first time working in such a formal setting?

JIM: Yeah.

THERAPIST: Sort of exciting, isn't it?

JIM: Oh, I don't know.

THERAPIST: Well, sure. I would imagine it's sort of like a graduation ceremony. By getting to work this party, wearing the uniform and all that, you're being acknowledged as a real waiter, entitled to make good money, and expected to do a professional job.

JIM: I suppose.

THERAPIST: I remember, when I was about your age, I had a job working in a hospital cleaning and sweeping up. After a while I got to help out the orderlies wheeling patients around, delivering X rays, things like that. That was a lot more interesting than pushing a broom, and when they saw that I really applied myself and worked hard, I got promoted. I'll never forget how excited I was when I got to go to the surgeons' lounge and put on a white scrub suit and a lab coat, the standard uniform for my new position. I was very proud and thought I looked great, but at the same time I felt ashamed, wondering if people would laugh at me and not take me seriously. Nobody laughed. Nobody said anything either, which I think disappointed me. They just accepted the fact that I was now an orderly, but it took me a while to accept myself. It's that excitement that's hard to deal with for some of us, wanting to be admired, yet afraid we won't be. Well, anyway, you look great. Did you have to tie your own bow tie?

As Jim matured, he let himself experience affects he would have fled from before. The fact that circumstances dictated he had to wear his tuxedo to the session was serendipitous. These occasions offer opportunities for therapeutic interventions that, if not used to advantage, can severely injure a patient's budding self-esteem. In my comments I tried to match what I believed were Jim's feelings at this affectively charged time, much as a mother shows attunement by matching the pitch and rhythm of her voice to her baby's activity (Stern 1985): I told Jim how I had felt when many years ago I was in a position similar to his present one. The memory of that time in my life had been reawakened when I saw Jim so proud and yet too shy to let me know how good and important he felt—his tuxedo the visible evidence that he was considered competent enough to be promoted to this higher status. Having had my say, I did not want to embarrass him by making him feel he had to reply to what I had told him; it was enough that he heard that I could understand and share his feelings. Therefore, I switched back to the more neutral aspect of the discussion and invited him to tell me more about the details of his outfit and the work ahead of him.

When the therapist has the impulse to share a personal experience with a patient, the question arises whether it is truly in the interest of the patient, or arises out of the therapist's need to be understood (that is, whether the therapist is using the patient to recruit a self-object experience). When in the latter position, I have certainly felt chagrin at that break in technique, though it never seemed to do any harm to the patient. I have learned over the years to contain myself when I feel a great urgency to impart to a patient something about myself or my life's experiences. That strong urge indicates to me that I have not sufficiently decentered my affective response to the patient, and that I would be well advised to sort out my needs from his or hers before I speak. Here, in Jim's case, I found myself quite able to weigh the pros and cons of confiding my experience to him, and decided to do so: firstly, as I already said, because it seemed to me the most phase-appropriate way to show I was attuned to his affective message; but, secondly, because I also wanted to convey to him that the fantasy life I suspected was now becoming possible for him was, in and of itself, not shameful. Far from separating him from me, I felt kinship with such experiences. Too often adolescents, especially those who do not read much fiction, never learn that they are not so different from their peers or their elders, for that matter—in drawing on fantasy when needed to support, soothe, or mobilize themselves (see also Basch 1980, pp. 143–45).

JIM: Naw, they give you a clip-on.
THERAPIST: Think I could see it?
JIM: It's hot in here.
THERAPIST: Yes, it is warm in here—but also the conflict between wanting to be seen and fearing that that wish will lead only to disappointment creates an inner tension that

increases your heart rate, makes the blood flow faster, and gets you to feel hot, sweaty, and overstimulated. In other words, we tend to feel ashamed when we're not quite certain how we will be accepted in a new and unfamiliar role.

[*Jim said nothing, but took his coat and scarf off and dropped them on the floor.*]

Good. Now I feel more comfortable, too. Stand up a minute again. [*Jim did so.*] Not bad at all. They did a good job of fitting you. I think you look handsome and very professional. What are they going to serve at this party?

Here I was helping Jim to deal with shame: not pathological shame—the shame about shame and feelings generally that led to the massive withdrawal and isolation present when he first came to see me—but the much more normal, expected shame that often accompanies healthy exhibitionism, the feeling that one has earned admiration but, at the same time, fears it will be withheld. I both explained to Jim what I thought was happening to him and also put pressure on him to act and face his fear in my presence. I *desensitized* him to his shame, in other words, in the hope that he would find it a little easier to deal with when it recurred in other, similar situations where his new-found competence made him justly pleased and proud of himself.

Acquaintance with and increased acceptance of his feelings freed Jim to do more with his life than simply turn it into a repetition of earlier disappointments. I began to hear more about the manager, fellow employees, and customers of the restaurant. Instead of just responding to what I said, Jim initiated topics of conversation. At first, he talked at me as if he expected me to have no idea about what he was saying; eventually he sought my opinions about his interactions with various people at the restaurant.

It was apparent to me that a block to Jim's psychological development had now been overcome, and that he was letting himself learn from experience instead of simply depending on preconceived convictions to govern his behavior. There had never been any question of his lacking the intelligence to do this; my initial hypothesis, which I then tested in the therapeutic situation, was that he had been blocked from achievement by the need to avoid affective stimulation. Based on the way Jim conducted himself with me initially, I thought that his expectation that the mobilization of hope, excitement, enthusiasm, or commitment would lead only to bitter disappointment precluded his participating in the opportunities for social and intellectual development that presented themselves to him. When his mother's illness and his father's subsequent reaction offered the possibility of working on this aspect of his development, I seized it. I believe I was correct in doing so, for once he was able to relive and begin to confront the affective experiences that had shaped his life, he was freer to resume his maturation.

CLOSURE AND TERMINATION

Jim began to think that he might want to make a career out of restaurant and hotel management. When he investigated the schools that offered programs leading to certification in that field, he found that a high school diploma was a prerequisite for admission. He tried first to complete his coursework through correspondence courses, but did not have the discipline to study and then complete the assignments that had to be mailed back to the school's headquarters. He was too proud to apply for reinstatement to the suburban high school that he had left; he did not want to become a classmate of his former peers' younger brothers and sisters. Eventually he did locate a school in the inner city that offered a program for people like himself who, having previously dropped out of high school, found that the disadvantages of not having graduated gave them reason to try again.

When he first sampled some classes at this school, he was full of angry braggadocio: he was going back to school and would be with a bunch of other tough guys who wouldn't take any crap either, and any teacher who gave him trouble . . . I saw this as a regression to the belligerence he had displayed in his beginning interview with me, his way of trying to cope with demands that seemed too great to face when he felt so alone. I shared this idea with him and explained that what was happening to him was neither unusual nor unexpected. Anyone, when threatened by strong feelings, may temporarily lose his or her logical way of solving problems and instead cover his or her fear with anger and the like. In other words, one behaves more like a little child who has not yet reached the point of helping himself or herself by thinking through the cause of the fear. So, I told Jim, the first order of business was to establish the nature of the affect with which he was trying to deal. The anger, I suggested, was secondary to deeper feelings, namely, doubt and shame: doubt as to whether he could now succeed even though he had not completed his home study course; shame in that he found himself having to acknowledge that he had to return to the conventional path he had previously spurned.

That at this juncture Jim was less able to cope with his affect, and as a result lost some of his coping skills, was not unexpected. As Kohut (1987) has pointed out, the self is especially vulnerable at a time maturational advances have been made but are not yet consolidated. At such times, the therapist must support the patient by helping him or her to understand that a temporary loss of function is expected and, far from vitiating the patient's progress, only confirms it.

JIM: If he [*his father*] says, "I told you so," I'll lay him out.

THERAPIST: I think your feelings would be very hurt. When you're vulnerable, you need understanding. Your parents' record is not so great in that regard, as we know. You always have to be prepared to be put down. This makes it difficult to retrace your steps and try again when you think you've made a mistake. But I don't think you have to worry about hitting your father, laying him out. You have never overstepped that boundary before, and I don't think you'll do it now. But if your father fails you emotionally again, it would hurt a lot, and what we have to do is to prepare you for that disappointment so that, if it does come, it does not have to be an occasion for hurting your cause, or undermining your ambition, just to get even with him.

JIM: I guess I can handle it.

THERAPIST: I think so, too. But the question is how hurt you'll get in the process. By thinking about what you can expect, how you might feel about it, what you will do, and how you'll feel about what you've done, you will prepare yourself to handle things and won't be at the mercy of the moment.

JIM: I do that at work. It's like a game. By now I can size up a table and how I'll approach 'em just by the way they look and act. Some of the guys can tell you what people are going to order before you give 'em the menu, and how much of a tip you're gonna get.

THERAPIST: Do you ever try to turn them around—make a sourpuss smile and end up giving you a big tip in spite of himself?

JIM: [*Laughing*] Like you do with me. When I've got nothing to say, you end up getting it out of me anyway.

THERAPIST: Exactly—and everybody feels better.

JIM: It's easier when it's not your family.

THERAPIST: That's true. You can step back, be more objective about people who haven't been in your life from the earliest days. They don't mean as much. That is, they can't so easily awaken the depth of the basic disappointment of being misunderstood when we were helpless babies or little kids.

That Jim's regression was temporary is underscored by the fact that we were able to deal with his difficulties on a verbal, interpretative level: he did not have to show me through action away from the treatment situation that he was troubled and needed help. Furthermore, I was able to call on his now-developed ability to deal with problems through imagination and fantasy. He was able to use analogy to clarify for himself what was happening, and in the process show some humor at my expense. His recognition of the similarity of his and my strategies for dealing with our respective clientele indicated that at this point he was drawing support from an alter ego transference to me.

Not surprisingly, Jim did quite well when he returned to school. Being extremely bright, he found his classes presented no great challenge to him once his affect was under better control. He was more and more able to use our sessions as a buffer to prevent his overreacting or reacting inappropriately to difficult interpersonal situations. Several times he almost dropped out of school again in response to feeling treated unfairly by teachers or administrators. But it became easier for him both to recognize the feeling behind his rage—the hurt he felt at not being understood, and what this reawakened in him—and then to separate the past from the present before deciding on a course of action.

He now began to socialize more and made male and female friends. For the first time in his life—he was now in his nineteenth year—he felt confident enough to ask girls for dates. He found himself sufficiently popular to tolerate the occasional times that his invitations were refused or dates with him were broken.

In due time, he not only obtained his diploma but completed his senior year with distinction. In honor of the occasion, I presented him with a history of the most famous hotels in the world and inscribed it with a congratulatory message that recognized that his degree represented not just a scholastic achievement but a personal triumph, which I had felt privileged to witness.

Shortly after graduation, Jim entered a restaurant management school, but soon realized that the training he was looking for could best be obtained in Europe. A small trust fund established earlier for his education by his father had grown sufficiently to let him study abroad. Shortly after completing basic training in his chosen work and having taken an intensive course in the language, he left—with glowing recommendations from his teachers and his former employer—to apprentice himself to a world-famous chef in France.

I had invited him to correspond with me, or call me on the phone if he felt the need, and I received a positive letter shortly after he settled overseas. I answered it, but heard no more from him until Christmas, when he sent me a short note to which I replied. For the next few years, we wrote each other briefly at Christmastime.

I saw Jim only once more, about five years after his therapy ended. He had returned for his mother's funeral. Supposedly she had died after a sudden and unexpected cardiac arrest, but he had reason to suspect that she had committed suicide. He did not feel particularly affected by her death, and expressed no sense of loss, only a vague pity for her unhappy life. He felt as if he had shed his childhood and all that went with it when he moved to Europe; his involvement now was elsewhere.

On this return visit he also showed me some pictures of himself and a woman with whom he had lived for about a year. She was a widow and had two small children to whom he became very attached. He had wanted to marry her, but she had refused him, saying that the difference in their ages—she being fifteen years older than he—would lead only to insoluble problems. He had mourned her loss, but felt the absence of the children even more keenly. He was aware that in his relationship with them he was giving what he had never had, and that the opportunity to do so went a long way toward healing his wounds. It was clear to me that his affective maturation had continued after his therapy with me had ended, and that he was now capable of experiencing and articulating complex emotions.

He told me that his career was progressing well, that he was satisfied with his life, and that he did not think he would ever return to the United States to live. He planned to continue working and expanding his expertise in various famous kitchens in Europe and eventually hoped to be able to open his own restaurant and inn on the Continent.

In four and one half years of once-weekly psychotherapy, Jim Zurf progressed from a confused sixteen-year-old who could only defend himself angrily against his longing for human contact and affection, to a young man who could not only tolerate but successfully solicit meaningful affective responses. He became capable of articulating his feelings and manipulating them symbolically. In addition, he was able to use both his imagination to plan for the future, and fantasy to soothe himself when overstimulated or understimulated. The content of both the defense against, and the expression of, his needs in the transference related primarily to issues of attachment. Once these could be dealt with openly, development in the areas of autonomy, creativity, and psychosexuality seemed to proceed satisfactorily without requiring specific intervention on my part. The primary transference, once it had formed, was a mirror transference, but elements of the idealizing and the alter ego transference also came into play. In Jim's treatment the transference was not resolved through interpretation. It was instead used to permit him to heal the gaps in his development that had been brought about by the traumatic deprivations of his childhood. Through *transmuting internalization* of the therapist's selfobject func-

tions the transference was replaced by what Kohut (1977) called
compensatory structure, coping skills that are no longer defensive, but
can be relied upon to maintain the cohesiveness of the self system.
I would certainly not have been able to predict at the beginning of
our work that Jim had either the resilience or the capacity to grow
so dramatically with the aid of psychotherapy. I have seen many
patients who seemed initially to be much less disturbed than Jim
was who did not do nearly as well. All in all I found his treatment
to be a most instructive and gratifying therapeutic experience.

8

A Depressive Retreat from Feelings

The Man God Did Not Want: Roger Flynn

Roger Flynn, age forty-four, was sent to me for evaluation because he was in danger of being dismissed from his job. His employers felt that his increasing absenteeism and his inability to function cooperatively when on the assembly line were grounds for dismissal, while his union took the position that his difficulties were a medical/psychological matter for which he should be given sick leave without prejudice. I was told by the referring physician from the union's health plan that Mr. Flynn had had a complete physical workup, including neurological tests and that, with the exception of a mildly elevated blood pressure, he seemed to be in good health.

When he called me to schedule an appointment, Mr. Flynn sounded angry. He made no bones about the fact that he was coming to see me only because he had been told he must. When I suggested we find a mutually convenient time to meet, his voice was gruff and bitter as he said, "Doesn't matter, they laid me off of work. I got nothing else to do anyway."

INITIAL INTERVIEW: FROM CONSTERNATION TO ORIENTATION

On the appointed day, when I went to fetch him from the waiting room, it immediately struck me that Mr. Flynn looked too big for the furniture. He slouched in the chair, his legs extending well into the room so that it would have been easy to trip over them. He was dressed in denim overalls and a plaid sportshirt, open at the neck. A visor cap, pulled forward, half hid his face. He had just begun to light a cigarette. He took no notice of me, finished with the match, located the ashtray, and then finally looked—or rather, scowled—at me. He barely acknowledged my greeting, reluctantly shook my proffered hand, took off his cap, and followed me into the office. (Mr. Flynn's appearance and behavior confirmed the initial misgivings I had already formed during our phone conversation; and I was aware, as I ushered him in and got him settled, of my muscles tensing, as if I were preparing to ward off an attack. Only later did I realize that I had registered with approval the fact that he took off his cap as he came into the consulting room.)

THERAPIST: So, Mr. Flynn, you know of course that your union has asked me to make a report on your psychological condition insofar as it applies to your work situation.

MR. FLYNN: That's what they told me.

THERAPIST: Why don't you tell me your view of what's been happening at work and why you were sent to see me.

MR. FLYNN: They were supposed to send you a report about all that.

THERAPIST: Yes, I have that here, but I haven't studied it yet. I would much rather hear what you have to tell me about yourself first.

I noted that whereas his expression had so far been uniformly sullen, at this point his face lighted up, albeit only momentarily. Yet, brief as it was, this made me feel hopeful. It reminded me of a young woman I had seen some years before who began our first session with a diatribe against physicians generally and psychiatrists in particular. When she ended by accusing me of wanting only her money, I told her that, since she had brought it up, we might as well deal with the financial aspect of our transaction. I told her my fee, asked her if she was prepared to pay it, and informed her that, just as she had suspected, I expected to be paid promptly. Her face brightened for a moment, just as Mr. Flynn's had, and a productive two years of psychotherapy followed. It was only after several months of treatment that we were able to deal with the symbolic significance of her opening attack: namely, the fear that I, like her parents, would be a hypocrite, denying my needs and expectations, claiming to be interested only in her welfare, and then demanding equally self-sacrificing devotion from her. All this came back to me in the split second that Mr. Flynn's face lit up.

I now held two contrary patterns of expectation—one pessimistic, the other optimistic—and was ready to match these against whatever signals Mr. Flynn might send as we proceeded. I found myself becoming less tense and more interested in what might turn up next in our interview.

THERAPIST: [*Continuing*] Your doctor told me on the phone that there has been some problem at work, that your company wants to fire you, that your union thinks it's a medical matter, and that you are apparently in good physical health. I wish you would take it from there.

MR. FLYNN: Will you tell them what I say?

THERAPIST: Not necessarily. After we talk, whenever I feel I'm ready to make a report, I will discuss it with you and we can decide together whether you want my report to be sent. As I told your health service, that's the only way that I will participate in this evaluation.

MR. FLYNN: I can't tell you what to say, but I can tell you not to send it?

THERAPIST: Exactly. Also, I'm perfectly willing to have your input and modify my report in such a way that, if we send it, it will reflect fairly what we have talked about and the conclusions we reached.

I was impressed by the manner in which Mr. Flynn was able to look after his own interests. He was more intelligent and sophis-

ticated than, judging from his attitude and appearance, I had expected him to be. The original pattern of expectation engendered by
his appearance and demeanor was countermanded by experience.
Thus, on scanty evidence, I first cast the patient into a mold based
on my own past experience which, as the session proceeded, was
less and less satisfactory. I then began to build a model of the patient
that, though at this point in the interview still vague, probably had
some resemblance to what he was really like. Thus, the evaluative
process proceeded in a manner quite the reverse from what I as a
student had been taught to expect: that is, that the psychiatrist
suspends judgment and comes to conclusions about a patient only
as the facts accumulate. In my experience, judgments are initially
easy to make—the patient is this or that kind of person—but as the
patient begins to reveal himself or herself, things get less clear, and
I have no thought of reaching conclusions but settle back to see how
my mental model of the patient will shape itself. Of Roger Flynn—
incidentally, but not unimportantly—I registered the facts that he
seemed to manifest no obvious thought disorders, his affect was in
keeping with how he was behaving and with what he was saying,
and he accommodated himself effectively to the interview situation.
Though I could not yet be certain, in all likelihood he had no major
psychosis.

MR. FLYNN: Where should I start?
THERAPIST: Try to tell me in your own way what I need to know
to understand you and the circumstances in which you
find yourself. How do you see the events that brought
you here, for example?
MR. FLYNN: I'm not much for talking, just working. Now they want
to get rid of me.
THERAPIST: And you want to stay on the job?
MR. FLYNN: I got nothing against my job: Sure I want to stay. Anyhow, I got no choice, I've got to work for a living.
THERAPIST: What exactly is it that you do?
MR. FLYNN: Machines. Troubleshooting, quality control. If the
transmitters aren't assembled right, I have to figure out
why not. Sometimes the new guys don't know what
they're doing, and I have to show 'em. Other times you

get defective parts and you have to figure out what
went wrong up the line. Stuff like that.

THERAPIST: And you like the job?

MR. FLYNN: I worked hard enough to get it, I must like it.

THERAPIST: How do you mean?

MR. FLYNN: It took me twenty years to work my way up. I did every
job there was in the shop. There's nothing I can't do on
that floor. I didn't even finish high school. There's nobody else who ever got where I am who didn't finish
high school. Some even had some college engineering
courses.

THERAPIST: No wonder you're proud of your achievement.

MR. FLYNN: I guess it's the only thing I ever did that I've got to be
proud of.

It sounded as if Mr. Flynn's belligerent attitude was not characteristic of his usual manner of adaptation, but was rather a reaction
to finding himself in danger of losing his job. He seemed to be
saying that the work situation, where he demonstrated a high level
of competence, was his source of self-esteem. If this was so, then
his anger might in its own way be a healthy sign, representing an
active struggle against despair and a depressive solution.

THERAPIST: And yet there's trouble of some kind? Is that something
new?

MR. FLYNN: Just the last six months or so, maybe a little longer. I
never had trouble before, you can check that out. I
wouldn't be where I was if I was a troublemaker.

THERAPIST: What kind of trouble?

MR. FLYNN: I just don't get along with the shift boss, that's all.

THERAPIST: How come?

MR. FLYNN: Because he's a chickenshit asshole! That's why! Can
you understand that? [*The patient, who had been matter-of-
fact up to this point, now became so enraged that I was quite taken
aback by the intensity of his passion.*]

THERAPIST: Not exactly. I've been plenty mad at times myself, so
I know how it feels to be so angry, but it doesn't tell
me the reason you would feel so strongly about your

situation. What sets me off might not bother you at all, and vice versa.

MR. FLYNN: [*Still very angry*] After twenty years I don't need to be told what to do and when to do it by some jag-off who hasn't been with the company any longer than I have.

THERAPIST: What's the boss bugging you about?

MR. FLYNN: He's no boss of mine! The shift boss is all he is! I could have been that, too, if I wanted it. A glorified foreman, that's all. Just because he wears a white coat doesn't mean he has to side with the front office!

THERAPIST: And what is he picking on you for?

MR. FLYNN: He never comes up with anything special. It's his attitude, high and mighty. The way he gets the count from me and writes on that clipboard of his. You can tell he thinks his shit doesn't smell. When something goes wrong, he acts like it's your fault. Writing up the report for the big shots to look at, blaming me for what a bunch of idiots that shouldn't have been hired in the first place messed up. If production is slowed up, it's not my fault! I got to straighten it out and then show them what they did wrong. I'm a fucking schoolteacher not a machinist. Instead of him running around in his fancy coat with the clipboard, he should help out, roll his sleeves up once in a while. Shit, I knew him when his hands were plenty dirty.

THERAPIST: He's been making trouble for you? Has your work been written up in such a way that the higher-ups have come down on you?

MR. FLYNN: No, nothing like that. He's too smart to come right out and try to pin something on me that won't stick. But it's the attitude—the way he looks at you. The others can see what he thinks, the son-of-a-bitch! How am I supposed to get anything done when my own guys are laughing at me?

THERAPIST: The men on the line have been laughing at you?

MR. FLYNN: They'd better not try. I might not be a kid any more, but anyone who wants to mess with me, they can come outside any time!

Mr. Flynn's outburst made me slightly anxious, signaling that something was going on that I should give special heed to. My anxiety was related to a mild disorientation brought about not just by the intensity of the patient's anger, but by the fact that it seemed to be rootless. In our customary scheme of things, the precipitant of such a violent reaction should be clear-cut and readily identifiable. If Mr. Flynn had said that he was furious because this man had been promoted instead of himself, or had cheated him out of something else that was rightfully his, or some such thing, I would at least have understood how the patient explained and rationalized his rage. However, in this case, regardless of my willingness provisionally to accept the patient's outburst on his terms, Mr. Flynn's anger simply made no sense as yet.

I briefly toyed with the diagnosis of paranoia. Perhaps I had been too quick to rule out psychosis. But, although a case could be made for a delusion of persecution, this was not in keeping with the overall picture Mr. Flynn presented. Compared with the paranoid patients I had seen, Mr. Flynn was far too passionate. He became increasingly angry and less organized as he spoke about the situation, trying to envelop me with his rage, instead of, as paranoids are wont to do, withdrawing into the cold certainty of a well-organized system that, as far as they are concerned, is self-explanatory.

I was left with the impression that Mr. Flynn was trying to rationalize something that had gripped him without his knowing why or how this had happened.

THERAPIST: Well, Mr. Flynn, you're very angry about something, but I think you're as much in the dark about why you feel this way as I am. Maybe you and I ought to take a look at this report the doctor at the health service forwarded to see if that will clear anything up.

MR. FLYNN: Suit yourself.

THERAPIST: [*Reading the report and summarizing its contents*] According to this report you're quite a guy! This thing reads like a speech at a testimonial dinner. Nothing but praise for you as a person, as a worker, and as a leader of your group. Apparently no one else can make heads or tails out of what happened to you either. Even this fellow you're so mad at, Paul is his name, I guess——

MR. FLYNN: Cocksucker!

THERAPIST: Paul can't say enough good things about you. You pretty much started at the same time, from what he says, and though you're not socially friendly, you've always gotten along very well as you both moved up the ladder.

MR. FLYNN: It's different now. That stuff they're saying is from *then*. It's all bullshit as far as I'm concerned.

THERAPIST: Paul can't figure out what happened between the two of you. As far as he knows, you just have become increasingly mean and uncooperative, production has markedly slowed down, and it's all he can do to keep your job for you.

MR. FLYNN: I said that's all bullshit!

THERAPIST: I'm just reading the report that was sent to me about you. I'm not saying that I accept it as an accurate reflection of what's going on. Shall we go through it first and then discuss whether you agree or disagree?

MR. FLYNN: Go ahead.

THERAPIST: The way it's presented here is that Paul, far from having it in for you, is doing everything he can to defend you to the higher-ups——

MR. FLYNN: He's just covering. . . . O.K., O.K., I'll shut up.

Mr. Flynn's ability to contain his rage demonstrated that he functioned on a higher level of affective maturity than did Jim Zurf when I first started to work with him. In the face of anxiety, Jim could only attack or withdraw; he could not wait to see what might happen, as Mr. Flynn was able to do.

THERAPIST: Paul seems to be the one who alerted the union and insisted that there must be something medically wrong with you to account for such a dramatic change in your personality. It also looks as if you've had a very thorough and comprehensive physical workup without discovering any problems.

MR. FLYNN: Why did they have those tests with the wires on my head, and that other gizmo?

THERAPIST: You had a neurological examination, a brain wave test, and a brain scan. Sometimes sudden dramatic changes in the personality are due to physical problems in the brain—infections, strokes, cancers, or other kinds of tumor. In your case, everything was negative—that is, there was no sign of any brain damage of any kind.

So, even though the report doesn't tell us what's wrong, at least some possibilities seem to have been ruled out.

MR. FLYNN: I suppose you'll write me up as a loony now, just a guy who went soft in the head.

THERAPIST: You don't fit that picture.

MR. FLYNN: So I shouldn't be here.

THERAPIST: On the contrary. Lots of people come here who are very upset with themselves, or with life, and don't know exactly why. Our job is to find out what's making you so unhappy.

MR. FLYNN: What's the good of that, finding out? If you're unhappy, you're unhappy.

THERAPIST: If you know why you're destroying yourself, there's at least a chance to improve things. If you don't know, you don't know where to start helping yourself either.

MR. FLYNN: I'm not destroying myself. It's him. And it's just my tough luck, that's all.

THERAPIST: As far as I can tell from the report, the only enemy you have is yourself, even though we haven't figured out why you're behaving in such a self-destructive manner.

MR. FLYNN: You're going to believe them and not me, is that it?

THERAPIST: No, not at all. The problem is that you have no explanation either. I'm used to hearing people complain about other people, blaming them for their problems, but they always have a case built up that, as far as they are

concerned, supports their position. So-and-so did such-
and-such, and that one did this and this one did that.

At this point, as several times before, I not only answered the
patient factually, but explained how I arrived at my conclusion.
That is, I showed him the pattern of expectation or theory that I was
using at that particular time to try to understand him. In this way,
I not only took the mystery out of what I was doing, but also
prepared the patient to use the same strategy eventually in examining himself.

MR. FLYNN: I told you that Paul is fucking me over!
THERAPIST: You're substituting curses for facts. Maybe it is Paul
              you're upset with, but so far you haven't been able to
              build up a very convincing case.
MR. FLYNN: That's your opinion.
THERAPIST: That's my opinion—so far at least.
MR. FLYNN: Now what are you going to put in your report?
THERAPIST: We're nowhere near being able to write one. We've
              made a good beginning, though. We know you are a
              well-respected, accomplished, and successful person
              who is neither physically ill nor insane, who seems to
              be doing his best to undo everything he has worked for.
              Why, we don't know, but in some way it is associated
              with this man at work, Paul, who until about six
              months ago didn't seem to bother you.
MR. FLYNN: I never put it together that way.
THERAPIST: It's not so different from what you do, though, is it? I'm
              a troubleshooter, too. If a person is not operating the
              way one would expect, first you look at the various
              parts and see why things aren't meshing.
MR. FLYNN: [*Visibly more relaxed and even smiling a little as the analogy
              registered*] Well, maybe there is a screw loose some-
              where. Maybe that's why I get so mad lately. I get so
              pissed-off all the time. I'm jumpy and irritable. I don't
              sleep good. I thought maybe it was the coffee, but
              when I didn't drink it for a week, it got worse, not
              better. I wish you could lubricate my head and make

things go smoother, but you can't. Maybe I'm just getting old.

THERAPIST: Oh, I wouldn't be so sure that you can't be fixed. We've got a basically good machine here, and it's not that old. Forty-four is young for the human machine, especially for one that has been working well and hasn't gotten rusty with disuse. But so far we've only looked at one part of your life. There's more to you than your job. Are you married?

MR. FLYNN: Twenty-five years this month.

THERAPIST: Children?

MR. FLYNN: One. One boy. [*He mumbled something.*]

THERAPIST: What did you say? I couldn't quite hear you. [*The friendlier, relaxed look of the last few minutes disappeared, to be replaced by the bitter angry face Mr. Flynn had displayed initially.*]

MR. FLYNN: I said I have half of a son. One half of a boy is what I ended up with! [*At this point the patient got up from his chair, his face so contorted with rage that for a moment I thought he was going to attack me; but I quickly realized that he was now oblivious to my presence. The outburst that followed was accompanied by Mr. Flynn's frenzied pacing, tearing at himself, and speech so explosive that spittle literally flew across the room.*]

Idiot! Wise ass! Asshole! [*These ejaculations continued for some time. His cursing was, as before, repetitive, filthy, and unoriginal, but in a tone of voice conveying such pathos and desperation that it did not seem offensive. I made no move to interrupt him, and gradually he began to talk in sentences again, but still more to himself than to me.*]

Oh no, you couldn't listen, could you? Mr. Big Shot always knew better than his old man, didn't you? You had to enlist! Be a marine, be a hero, make all the broads in your fancy uniform! Well, you're a hero now, you poor fuck, and the only thing you'll make is a load in your pants, that your father, the stupid old son of a bitch who didn't know anything, has to clean up! The big dummy who doesn't know better than to go to work eight, ten hours a day, and cuts the grass on weekends, and never goes anywhere, what does he know? You're going to see the world, live it up, be smarter than me—stuck in a rut and too dumb to know it! A hell of a lot you saw before you got yours! A stinking jungle, that's where you went. "Don't worry, Dad, I've got it made. They really need guys like me for the band that plays for all the bigshots." Sure, sure, my boy, you got it in writing? And even if you did, I still wouldn't give a shit if the President himself signed it. I would've wiped my ass with it. All liars. Anything to get you into uniform. Found that out, didn't you? But then it was a little too late, wasn't it? Did you think a little bit about what I told you when you were lying in that jungle? Did you remember how the dumb asshole came to your room and begged you? Yes, on my knees, your own father, on his knees, begged you, "Finish college, nobody is coming after you; they're killing people, it isn't our war, let the gooks fight it out." "Oh, don't worry, Pop, you worry about everything." You'll see the world all right! If I push your wheelchair, you'll see it. Maybe we'll roll it to Washington and hear the band play at the White House, the one you were going to be in for sure! [*Mr. Flynn now fell back into his chair, covered his face with his hands, and cried for some minutes.*] I'm sorry, this is the first time I've cried like this. [*Sobbed again uncontrollably; after a while he made a visible effort to pull himself together.*] This isn't getting us anywhere. It's not your concern.

THERAPIST: Please, there's no need to apologize.

MR. FLYNN: I've never been one to cry on other people's shoulders. We all have our problems, and nobody really cares about yours, so why bother?

THERAPIST: From the way you describe it, it sounds as if your son's spinal cord was damaged, and he's paralyzed.

MR. FLYNN: [*Nodding assent*] Below the waist. Paraplegic. [*His eyes again filled with tears.*]

THERAPIST: Any hope of some recovery of function?

MR. FLYNN: No, no hope. The doctors said they did everything. I took him to specialists. I didn't trust the government ones, but they said the same thing. [*He started to cry again.*]

THERAPIST: You know, Mr. Flynn, I think that it's quite possible that the anger and the upset at work are more related to what happened to your boy than anything that's happened at the shop.

MR. FLYNN: I don't know any more.

THERAPIST: When did your son get hurt?

MR. FLYNN: Two years ago September.

THERAPIST: I know it's not easy, but try to tell me more about what happened.

MR. FLYNN: First thing we knew was when we got word from the hospital that he got sent back from 'Nam. We heard from the social worker. Lenny, he didn't write and wouldn't take our calls. The social worker told us that's the way it always is, they have to get used to themselves the way they are. So I wanted to fly right out to the Coast, but she said wait. And so I talked to her every week or so, and a couple of months later she said O.K., come out. I went out; the wife has arthritis pretty bad, and when she heard Lenny was hurt the way he was, she had what the doctors call a flareup—she was in bed most of the time, and he told her she couldn't travel.

I guess I really hadn't believed how bad it was, but it really shook me up to see him that way. He'd lost a lot of weight, and he wouldn't hardly talk to me. It was like he was all different, like his whole personality was changed, you know. Oh, what's the use? I don't want to talk about this any more.

THERAPIST: When you describe these early months during which you had to come to grips with Lenny's condition, you don't sound as angry as you seem to be now about what's happened to him.

MR. FLYNN: I guess I thought it'd get better, that maybe somehow he'd be able to walk again. I don't know why. They explained to me even then already that there was nothing more they could do.

THERAPIST: And then they discharged him from the hospital?

MR. FLYNN: No, he was in the hospital for over a year, but we got them to send him to one that was closer to here. There was a lot of trouble with infections in his bladder and kidneys, and his skin broke down a couple of times— from all the sitting, I guess. But they finally got that much straightened out at least.

THERAPIST: The last two years have surely been very difficult ones for you, yet for some reason your problems at work only started six months ago?

I listened on several levels to what the patient was telling me. First of all, I heard the factual information that gave me an increasingly detailed picture of Mr. Flynn's life and the experiences that formed the background against which, I anticipated, I would better understand his present situation. Secondly, I listened for the emotional tone that accompanied Mr. Flynn's recital of these various events. I noted that he was able to discuss calmly and appropriately the manner in which he first learned of his son's illness. Nor did he get angry when he mentioned his wife's apparently serious arthritic illness which left him, at least initially, with the burden of coping with Lenny's injuries. Finally, I listened, and actively probed—so far in vain—for those motivational connections between Mr. Flynn's present problems at work and events in the past that would make his difficulties comprehensible.

THERAPIST: [*Continuing*] Is that perhaps when Lenny came home?

MR. FLYNN: No, that was about ten months ago?

THERAPIST: How did you feel about that?

MR. FLYNN: How the hell d'ya think I felt?

THERAPIST: Very bad, I would imagine. I would think that seeing your son crippled in surroundings that you probably associate with the usual running, jumping exuberance of his boyhood, must have been a very heavy burden to bear.

MR. FLYNN: You got it. You sound like maybe you might have had something like that happen to you, too. I don't know why I get so mad sometimes just thinking about it.

I noted how his anger melted away when I was able to respond empathically—that is, address the covert message of despair he was sending me—instead of being put off by the challenging, belligerent tone of "How the hell d'ya think I felt."

THERAPIST: You know, I noticed that when you were talking about your boy in the hospital, you sounded more puzzled and unbelieving than angry. Was it bringing him home that altered your ability to deal calmly with the situation? Perhaps having to face the fact that it really was true that he was paralyzed?

MR. FLYNN: No, it's more the not being able to do anything about it, I guess. Problems that I've had I've usually straightened out. Maybe worked harder or done something different than what I was doing. But with this I just felt so . . .

THERAPIST: Helpless?

MR. FLYNN: Yeah, helpless, that's right.

Here was further evidence that Mr. Flynn reacted with anxiety not so much to being faced by problems per se, but to his inability to exert some influence on them. The therapeutic task then would lie in helping him to somehow regain control and a sense of competence. I wondered whether his son's paralysis, this constant, concrete reminder of what it means to be helpless, was both something from which he could not distance himself and more than he could tolerate.

THERAPIST: You mentioned that your wife has what sounds like a very bad case of arthritis. She's handicapped, too, I would imagine. Yet you don't sound so angry or bitter about her condition.

MR. FLYNN: Well, sure, but that's different. It didn't come on all of a sudden, and you sort of get used to it. And then she has her good days.

THERAPIST: How long has she had it?

MR. FLYNN: Oh, since she was a kid. It used to come and go, now it's pretty much there all the time. Her hands are getting

real bad lately—stiff and swollen-like—and the medicine doesn't help as much as it used to. But you know
it's not something she could have helped. She didn't
volunteer for it, for Christ's sake! Jesus, to go ask for it,
how dumb can you get? [*He fell silent.*]

THERAPIST: Yes? [*But Mr. Flynn remained silent.*] Can you tell me
what's on your mind?

MR. FLYNN: Nothing.

THERAPIST: It doesn't have to be anything special, you know, or
connected to anything we've been talking about. Just
go ahead and say whatever it is.

MR. FLYNN: Nothing. I just don't want to start getting mad again.
When I think of this stupid kid of mine letting himself
get shot to pieces, I just lose control, that's all.

THERAPIST: We were talking about your wife's arthritis and your
reaction to it. You pointed out that she hadn't asked to
be hurt, and then started to get angry at your son again,
and then you stopped. That may indicate that a thought
came up that you didn't want to pursue——

MR. FLYNN: The doctor told her after Lenny she shouldn't have no
more kids.

THERAPIST: That's what you were thinking about when you
stopped yourself from speaking?

MR. FLYNN: I was thinking that it's not fair. I got one kid and he gets
it in the ass. Others, they have a lot and nothing ever
happens to them. But where's that going to get me,
talking about that? It'll just make me mad all over again
for nothing.

THERAPIST: Who has more kids and nothing ever happens to them?

MR. FLYNN: He got three, and none of them went! The oldest is
going to be a priest, and they don't draft them out of
the seminary. Another one in college, and one he put
on the line and they got a deferment for him when his
number came up. I could have got that for mine, too.
I offered it to him if he didn't want to go to school no
more, but he wasn't having any. It's not fair, goddam
it, not fair!

THERAPIST: "He" being?

MR. FLYNN: Who?

THERAPIST: Who has three sons that stayed out of the war?

MR. FLYNN: Who else, Mr. High-and-Mighty that pushes me around while his kids are safe at home!

A piece of the puzzle seemed to drop into place. Perhaps the anger the patient was experiencing at work was a displacement from his reaction to his son's spinal cord injury and subsequent paralysis. I had to assume for the moment that it was more than coincidental that the target for Mr. Flynn's rage was a man with three healthy sons; but, as is usually the case, every clarification brings questions in its wake. For example, why wasn't Mr. Flynn at least aware of the real source of his anger at Paul? Also, I wondered why no one at work seemed to have recognized that the patient's strange, unaccustomed behavior was related to the stress at home.

THERAPIST: Paul?

MR. FLYNN: That's what I said. It's easy enough to get on my back for coming late, or not being sharp like I oughta be, he doesn't have to be up half the night with his kids.

Having previously tried to investigate the patient's anger at his co-worker and finding it not open to rational argument, I now decided to keep in abeyance my conclusions about the relationship between his symptoms and his envy of Paul's healthy children. Instead, I chose to take some of the tension out of the therapeutic interaction while at the same time exploring a potentially valuable area that had just been opened up by the patient.

THERAPIST: You have to be up at night a lot with Lenny?

MR. FLYNN: Off and on he has pain and funny feelings that bother him. Then we have to figure out how to make him more comfortable. Some nights I lie awake and hear him crying in his room, not because anything hurts, it's just what happened to him, that's all.

THERAPIST: Then he's still very depressed about himself?

MR. FLYNN: Yeah, all he can do is sit around all day. He doesn't even watch TV or listen to his stereo.

THERAPIST: Do you ever talk with him about his situation and the future?

MR. FLYNN: Nah, we're not much for that. I never was much of a talker. Once in a while I try to with him, but we end up yelling at each other. What can he say? When you've fucked up your life, you've fucked up your life. That's that!

THERAPIST: What about rehabilitation, has anything been tried in that line?

MR. FLYNN: They'll come and pick him up a couple of times a week. There's physical therapy, and they show him how to do things for himself. Most of the time lately he says he doesn't want to go, he just wants to sit. I guess he knows it's all over. Who can blame him? What's the point of pretending?

THERAPIST: Sounds like he could use some psychotherapy as well as physiotherapy.

MR. FLYNN: He's got the social worker, and she told me that he ought to see the shrink they got there, but she can't get him to go. I'm trying the best I can to help the kid, but he won't be helped. I got a lead on a guy who makes special equipment that's a lot better than what they can get from the government. There's an electronic wheelchair that's supposed to be real good. It costs a lot, but it'll let him do all kinds of stuff and really get around. What's the point of getting it for him if he's just going to sit anyway? Anyhow, it doesn't look like I'll have a job, and you can't afford things like that when you're pumping gas somewhere.

THERAPIST: You'll have your job if we can help you to overcome the psychological problem that's weighing you down.

MR. FLYNN: How's that?

THERAPIST: In my opinion, your son isn't the only one who's depressed. It sounds to me as if whatever is going on at work is directly related to your psychological reaction to Lenny's misfortune.

MR. FLYNN: What do you mean I'm depressed? I'm not sitting

around like a bump on a log. I'm working my ass off around the clock.

THERAPIST: "Depressed" doesn't mean you have to be sitting there staring into space and crying. I think your depression is hidden behind your anger. When you're frustrated and lose hope, you start to swear.

MR. FLYNN: I know, that's what my wife says, too. Most of the time, I don't hear what I say, but I got to do something. I can't afford to sit around and cry about my problems. I got to take care of them.

THERAPIST: What I said wasn't meant as criticism. I'm just trying to think out loud, trying out what I think sounds like an explanation for what's happened to you. Of course there's an awful lot we don't know that we need to find out. Our work has really just started. One thing that puzzles me, for instance, is why the people at work haven't put two and two together. After all, it isn't difficult to figure out that a person's functioning at work might very well be affected adversely when he has to carry the unaccustomed, exhausting burden of taking care of an adult paraplegic day in and day out, to say nothing of the psychological burden of that invalid being his only child.

MR. FLYNN: It's none of their goddam business. I keep my troubles to myself, I told you! That fucking Paul! I'm not going to give him the satisfaction—him with his three kids and his white coat and his clipboard!

THERAPIST: You mean nobody knows?

MR. FLYNN: Shit, no! Nobody cares anyway. I do my work and I keep to myself. My business is my business.

THERAPIST: So you've been carrying this around inside of you all by yourself?

MR. FLYNN: I stand on my own two feet. I never had nobody do anything for me, and I'm not going to start now. What do you want me to do, start whining and carrying on?

THERAPIST: But you had to take days off—to go to the Coast, for example—when you visited Lenny in the hospital the first time. I imagine there have been other times since then that you've had to be out on his account. Didn't you have to explain why you were taking off?

MR. FLYNN: I don't have to explain nothing. I got plenty of vacation time coming. I get three weeks a year, four weeks next year if I'm still around, and I don't take more than a week usually. So now I take it when I need it, sometimes a day or two at a time. That's why they don't have any beef coming when I show up late once in a while. Let 'em take the hours off that. And sick leave, I never took a day of sick leave in all these years. Everybody else takes time off to go shopping and calls in sick. I come late or something, and they get on my back.

THERAPIST: So they *don't* know why you're late or absent—that something went wrong with Lenny, or that you had to stay home to get him settled or get him to the hospital, and so forth.

MR. FLYNN: Why should they? It's none of their business.

THERAPIST: So no one at work knows?

MR. FLYNN: No one.

Here I got a glimpse of the patient's deeper character structure. How lonely it must have been to have worked twenty years in a place and still have no one in whom to confide or turn to for understanding. How did Mr. Flynn become so alienated and isolated? I felt an inward shiver as I tried to imagine the lonely and cold world in which he seemed to be living.

Apparently, Mr. Flynn was unable to reach out to others for the selfobject experiences he would need for support in the face of severe stress. When his resources were not sufficient to achieve competence, he was lost. To understand why this was so, how it came about, and what if anything could be done about it struck me as the central issue for therapy. Now I felt I had overcome confusion and consternation and reached the reorientation phase, the point where the therapist can go beyond the patient's complaint and the precipitating circumstances to reach, at least provisionally, sufficient insight into the patient's dynamics to make an educated guess about why and how the particular circumstances of his life at this time have led him into his present difficulties. At this point, I felt it was time to bring the diagnostic interview to a close by outlining my conclusions and a treatment plan in a way that would make sense to the patient.

THERAPIST: Well, Mr. Flynn, our talk has cleared your situation up for me quite a bit. As far as I'm concerned, your difficulty at work is indeed a medical problem, one that stems from some psychological difficulties that have temporarily overwhelmed you.

MR. FLYNN: I should go on sick leave, you mean?

THERAPIST: Definitely.

MR. FLYNN: What about my job?

THERAPIST: I'd like to see you go back to it as soon as you're able to do so.

MR. FLYNN: What do you mean "able"?

THERAPIST: When we can tell your employers that they may expect you to function on the job as effectively and as competently as you have in years previously.

MR. FLYNN: I was going to see if I could take a demotion, step down and work the line on the late shift, just to get away from that fucking Paul. But the money isn't good enough, and I got to be at home at night to put the kid to bed, clean him up, things like that. . . .

THERAPIST: I don't think taking such a demotion would really solve anything, as a matter of fact, had you taken it, I think it would have made things worse. In any case, what you want back is your regular job.

MR. FLYNN: I don't see where going on sick leave and sitting around home for a while is going to make any difference. Not that I'd be sitting around anyway.

THERAPIST: What would you be doing?

MR. FLYNN: I got to change the bathroom around, and it's going to take a week at least, maybe more. His chair won't go between the sink and the tub, so he can't get to the can. It's a real mess. If I can change the sink around and build some supports around the stool, he can help himself. Their arms and their chests get real strong to make up for the legs, and they can get around pretty good, the social worker said. But I got to get the place fixed up for him first.

THERAPIST: Boy, you're a pretty versatile guy. You mean to say you do plumbing, too?

MR. FLYNN: When I figured out what I had to do, I went nights to the high school. Took a plumbing course. It's not so hard once they show you. I suppose it'll do me good to get that done, and maybe rest up some, but that still doesn't change anything.

THERAPIST: Quite right. The main purpose of the sick leave that I would request for you would be for us to start working on your psychological problems.

MR. FLYNN: There's nothing wrong with my head. I thought you said I wasn't crazy.

THERAPIST: Your head is fine and you are not crazy, but you are very troubled and need someone to sort things out with. That would be the first order of business in your psychotherapy, in your talking with me.

MR. FLYNN: You mean like we did today?

THERAPIST: Pretty much that way. Do you feel any better for it?

MR. FLYNN: I guess so. At least I don't feel worse like I thought I would when they told me I had to come here.

THERAPIST: I will say you didn't look too happy in my waiting room.

MR. FLYNN: Tell you the truth, I was scared shitless.

THERAPIST: How come?

MR. FLYNN: I didn't know what I was supposed to do, and if I didn't do it right, they'd never let me go back.

THERAPIST: And then what?

MR. FLYNN: What do you think? It's all I've ever done, it's all I know how to do. Somehow I got to go back. It's just every time he comes around, something happens inside of me.

THERAPIST: That's why I think it would be good to take a leave of absence. It will give us a chance to think about this whole business without your being rubbed raw by it every day.

MR. FLYNN: How do I know it will help me?

THERAPIST: What choice do you have right now, Mr. Flynn? Let's face it. This way you might have a chance. Otherwise, the way it looks, you're out anyway.

MR. FLYNN: I thought maybe you could give me some pills to quiet me down, maybe.

THERAPIST: Wouldn't do any good. If we do decide to use medication, it would only be in addition to our talking about things.

MR. FLYNN: What if I can't do it right?

THERAPIST: I bet you never thought you'd learn to do plumbing either, but when you had to do it, you did. As far as I'm concerned, you're already doing fine here. Keep it up, and I don't think there'll be any big problems. But first we have to figure out what to say in the report to your health service to get you that leave of absence. What I would like to tell them is that, the way I understand your situation so far, your problems at work are only secondary, and that a reaction to Lenny's injury is the basic cause of your depression.

MR. FLYNN: You don't believe what I told you about that guy, is that it?

THERAPIST: I believe that you believe that Paul is the cause of your problems. I'm sure that your feelings about Paul are very important and are a significant aspect of what we will have to look into. But first we have to get your company to give you the time and authorization for your psychotherapy, assuming you'll participate and really work with me.

MR. FLYNN: Like you say, I don't have much choice, and once I make up my mind to go along, I don't do it in a half-assed way. Do I come here to your office for it? I don't have to go in the hospital or anything, do I?

THERAPIST: What makes you think of the hospital?

MR. FLYNN: One of the guys a couple of years ago got real depressed and he had to go there for treatment. I can't afford to go to any hospital. Like I told you, I have a lot of work to do at home. Besides, who would take care of him? My wife can't help that much even when she's better, like now. She couldn't lift him anyway, and if she strains herself, then I'll have two in a wheelchair.

THERAPIST: The only reason I would think of hospitalization in your case is if you got so depressed that you started to think that killing yourself would be an answer to your problems.

MR. FLYNN: If I was going to kill myself, I would have done that before. I got to admit, I thought about it at first, it hurt so much—especially at night—but I couldn't do that. I wouldn't do that to them. Besides, I'm Catholic.

THERAPIST: So suicide is not an option for you now?

MR. FLYNN: No way!

THERAPIST: I didn't think it was, but I wanted to make sure. Now about my report. I have to tell them something to explain your problem and how it came about. How do you feel about my telling them about Lenny?

MR. FLYNN: No, I don't want nobody to know about that. Just tell them about Paul and how he upsets me.

THERAPIST: Perhaps it will be enough if I certify that you are depressed and need to be on medical leave to receive treatment.

MR. FLYNN: That would be O.K., I guess.

Following this session, I sent a report to Mr. Flynn's referring physician at the union health service, stating that he was suffering from a depressive reaction subsequent to certain personal problems not related to his work per se, but that the outlook for his recovery was quite good; and recommending that he be placed on medical leave so as to receive psychotherapy on an intensive, outpatient basis. As a result, Mr. Flynn was given a two-month sick leave, and he agreed to come for treatment.

These were my thoughts about the dynamics of the patient at this point. Based on his history and his behavior during the initial interview, it seemed to me that the early stages of self-esteem development and the capacity for organizing basic affective stimulation had probably proceeded satisfactorily. His prior ability to manage his life successfully in goal-directed fashion, to care for others, and to maintain impulse control, all suggested that his present difficulties were not coming out of either a borderline or a psychotic personality. On the other hand, he could not seem to deal on an interpersonal level with his distress at work. His inability to speak to anyone else about, or think through for himself, what might be troubling him, and his acting out his difficulties in such concrete fashion, told me that Mr. Flynn had not, in some significant respect, been able to translate the affect generated by his problems into feelings—feelings about which he could then think and talk. Thus, his predisposing difficulties appeared to be on the level of the subjective self (see pages 132–33), a hypothesis supported by his positive reaction to me when he felt momentarily understood, and by the shame that I thought I saw behind his inability—with the exception of his almost incoherent rage attacks—to let others know how he was suffering.

Paradoxically, although the paranoid quality and the self-destructive effects of Mr. Flynn's rage seemed much "sicker" than the low-level functioning and quiet helplessness and hopelessness displayed by many people suffering from chronic, disguised depressions, Mr. Flynn was better off because he was still fighting. Now the intensity and irrational nature of his rage seemed not so much paranoid as indicative of intense frustration—a frustration of the sort children feel in the face of a severe, painful illness, when they lash out at the very people who are ready to help them.

In terms of the sequence of the developmental spiral, his behavior at work was clearly counterproductive and incompetent, producing predictable results that further jeopardized his sense of self-esteem. The decisions he then made were not adaptive, further compounding the problem. On the plus side of the balance sheet was that for over twenty years he seemed to have adapted very well at work; at home he took pride in his job and in his accomplishments; and he was able to deal in what sounded like a caring way for a partially incapacitated wife.

Why, then, was all that he had built up in the way of self-esteem, based on genuine competence, not able to protect him against the psychological regression that he was now experiencing? I would have to see.

SECOND SESSION: FROM ORIENTATION TO COLLABORATION

MR. FLYNN: O.K., I'm here, what do you want me to do?
THERAPIST: Let's figure out what your goals are in coming here.
MR. FLYNN: That's easy. I've got to get my job back. You've got to tell them to let me go back. I need the money.
THERAPIST: Fair enough. We've got two months to really work on that.

In accepting the goal the patient set himself and proposing a time-limited therapy, I tacitly conveyed to him my conviction that in that period we could go a long way toward solving his problems.

MR. FLYNN: But what am I supposed to do?
THERAPIST: Once you and I together can find out what is making it so difficult for you to function on the job, figuring out what to do about that is usually not too hard.

Here I tried to help the patient focus on the immediate problem rather than leaving the therapeutic situation open-ended with such statements as "Why don't you just talk about whatever occurs to you?"

MR. FLYNN: [*Starting to get angry*] You don't believe me about Paul——
THERAPIST: That's not the issue in my mind at the moment. What strikes me is that you are acting out of character in the face of the provocation you're experiencing. I'm sure there have been many situations in your life that made you, or could have made you, angry that you handled less self-destructively. Or has your life always been a calm sea, undisturbed by any waves?

I could see now that any attempt to deal with Mr. Flynn's present problem directly would get us nowhere; he would only enmesh me further in his anger. Therefore, I posed a question that would divert him from the present without losing the affective focus; perhaps

letting me get some better understanding of how he had functioned
in the past when beset by other problematic situations.

MR. FLYNN: Are you kidding? Sometimes I think I've never had
anything but trouble.

THERAPIST: Even as a kid?

MR. FLYNN: Listen, I grew up in an orphanage. You think that was
a picnic? Think again.

THERAPIST: In an orphanage?

MR. FLYNN: Yeah, my mother died when I was born and my father's
people all came from Texas, so he put me in the Catholic Home here.

THERAPIST: Did you see your father much growing up?

MR. FLYNN: Nah, I didn't. I don't remember him much. He stopped
coming 'round by the time I started school. He might
have went back to Texas, he didn't leave no address.

THERAPIST: Did you miss him?

MR. FLYNN: I didn't see him but a couple of times in my life that I
remember.

THERAPIST: What did he look like?

MR. FLYNN: I don't remember. If he came in here right now, I
wouldn't know him.

THERAPIST: What do you remember about your childhood?

MR. FLYNN: The nuns, I guess. I think that's the first sound I remember, the noise their habits make when they walk. Like
a wind all the time inside the place.

THERAPIST: The rustling of their habits.

MR. FLYNN: And they always smelled so clean, like laundry soap.
Some of them were nice, but some of the old ones could
be real mean, too. Everybody was scared of Mother
Superior, even the other nuns. She was something else.

THERAPIST: Were you particularly close to any of the sisters?

MR. FLYNN: There was one I visited till she died. I think I thought
she was sort of like a mother. They didn't like that in
the home. They didn't want any nun to get specially
attached to a boy. But Sister Mary L. liked me; she
stood up for me a couple of times when there was
trouble with fighting and things.

So, though the patient had suffered a double parent loss, he seemed to have the ability to use what was available to promote at least some of the affective responses and the selfobject experiences he needed. I expected that he would respond to me similarly, and that a usable positive transference would soon surface.

MR. FLYNN: [*Continuing*] On Sunday, after Mass, the nuns'd tell Father Murphy who'd been put on report the week before, then you'd get it with the switch. He knew how to make it sting. They weren't just waiting for Sunday either. You'd get it on the knuckles with the ruler if they thought you were out of line. Sundays was extra.

THERAPIST: Did you think that they mistreated you?

MR. FLYNN: They had their hands full. Sometimes we'd have close to a hundred kids in the home, and they knew if they lost control, the place'd be up for grabs.

THERAPIST: So there was strict discipline.

MR. FLYNN: We had a million rules, and not knowing 'em or forgetting 'em was no excuse. And it wasn't just the nuns. They had the older guys keep the younger kids in line, so you had to watch out for everybody. [*Pausing*] My God, I haven't even thought about all that in years. How's this going to help me get my job back anyhow?

THERAPIST: The more we know about you, the more we know what makes you tick, how you learned to get along. Then maybe we can figure out what went wrong that you couldn't handle your anger. Were you an angry boy? Were you in trouble a lot in the home?

MR. FLYNN: Oh, I could dish it out when I had to, but I found out early that it didn't do no good to fight the system. Most of the time I stayed out of trouble. I did what they wanted.

THERAPIST: And did they reward you when you were a cooperative, good boy?

MR. FLYNN: With candy? Nah! If you were off of report for a month, you'd get a holy card, you know, pictures of the Holy Family with prayers on 'em.

THERAPIST: I meant more emotional rewards—smiles, praise for being a good boy, for helping out. . . .

MR. FLYNN: They weren't much for that. I think they were afraid that if they were too nice, the kids'd think they were soft and take advantage.

THERAPIST: You said most of the time you were one of the good boys. Do you remember ever getting angry?

MR. FLYNN: Yeah, sure. Somebody was always giving it to you and waiting for you to make a fuss, then you'd be in trouble. So I learned, like they say, don't get mad, get even. One time I really did get mad, though, when somebody swiped my chain. You know, one of those metal ones they use for lightbulbs in closets and things. I always had it around my neck. It had a St. Anthony medal from my mother and a picture of her in a locket from when she was a young girl. I hung it on a hook by the bash while I was washing up, and when I looked up it was gone. I really got mad then, but the nun in charge didn't believe me. When I told Sister Mary L., she just said to pray to St. Anthony and maybe whoever took it would give it back. But it never happened.

THERAPIST: I would think losing the picture of your mother must have been very hard. No wonder you were upset. How old were you?

MR. FLYNN: I don't remember. It wouldn't have been so bad, but it was the only one I had—picture of her, I mean.

THERAPIST: You were angry, but no one understood that meant that you were terribly hurt. An important part of you was gone.

MR. FLYNN: Well, I didn't stay mad long. Didn't do any good anyway. They just didn't want trouble.

Roger Flynn made a good adaptation to his orphaned state. Given his circumstances, he got the most out of what was available by learning the rules and meeting the needs of the nuns, his surrogate parents. But I could also see that the price he had to pay was suppression of his affective reactions. He developed a compliant but false self, as D. W. Winnicott (1965) has called it—a self that survives by focusing on the needs of those on whom one is emotionally dependent (see also Davis and Wallbridge 1981).

His anger at his basic loss, however, could not be contained and resurfaced when his locket was stolen, a symbolic recapitulation of the trauma of his mother's death. He sought understanding from the adults around him, but one nun did not believe him; and Sister Mary L., although she obviously meant well, also failed him empathically. He missed some recognition of and response to the hurt and anger he felt at having been deprived of his only link to his mother.

Mr. Flynn's case provides a good example of how arrested development in the area of affect attunement should be dealt with therapeutically. Rather than waiting for the patient to come up with associations, I supplied the words expressing what my affective resonance with his account led me to believe he might have felt but could not articulate at the time. His responses then let me gauge whether I was anywhere near the mark. Once we had a picture of how he probably had felt under particular circumstances, it was possible to mirror or validate that state, albeit belatedly, to show him that the child within was understandable and understood.

As I explained in chapter 5, primal repression, so-called, operates by arresting development and is potentially more readily corrected than are the effects of either secondary repression or disavowal, where the therapist usually needs to overcome a patient's strong resistance to mobilizing once more ideas, wishes, and fantasies that the self system has previously rejected as traumatically disorganizing.

THERAPIST: When your prayers went unanswered, did that affect your faith?

MR. FLYNN: If it did, it didn't last. I was very religious. I was an altar boy, and I thought I was going to go to the seminary and become a priest. A lot of the kids thought I was just doing it to brown-nose the nuns, but I really wanted to. I was sure I had a vocation.

THERAPIST: What happened?

MR. FLYNN: Oh, lots of boys want to be priests. That'd be all you heard, how the calling was the greatest thing that could happen to you. And it's true, if you thought you had it, you did get treated special. But once you're in high school and see more of what's going on, most of the boys don't go through with it.

THERAPIST: Are you a religious man?

MR. FLYNN: Nah, I haven't gone in years. Except for Christmas and Easter, of course.

One of my aims in this first formal therapeutic session was to determine what Mr. Flynn could do with words, and how fixated he was on the immediate problems that confronted him. If he had suffered from the typical or classic form of depression, it would have been difficult to get him to talk of anything but his immediate pain. But I was able to lead him quite easily into speaking about his upbringing. Once he began to do that, I, of course, noted what he was describing, but was even more interested in what I could gather of the affective atmosphere in which he grew up. What I had heard so far corroborated the idea that the patient's primary psychological damage was related to the development of the subjective sense of self and to faulty affect attunement.

I told Mr. Flynn that I wanted to make the most of the time we had to work on his problems, and would see him two or three times a week, and that it even might be necessary to have double sessions. He demurred at first, repeating that he wanted to use the time to rebuild the bathroom for his son, as well as do some other construction work to make Lenny's care easier. He also expressed pessimism that whatever it was we were doing would not help. Using what he had told me about his youth as a guide, I kindly but authoritatively told him that he was on medical leave and that medical matters took precedence. As I expected, his need for a strong person who would protect him and help him to reorganize his life—in other words, the need to form an idealizing transference—let him fall in line with my suggestions without further objection. I had become Doctor Superior.

With little prodding from me, Mr. Flynn continued to describe his developmental years. After deciding against the priesthood, he switched his high school curriculum from a liberal arts track, which was giving him great difficulty, to a vocational one he liked much better. He liked to fix and make things; and, as he spoke about it, it was obvious that he obtained great satisfaction from such achievements. An opportunity to get a job led him to quit high school before graduating. As he was expected to do, he then left the orphanage, the only home he had ever known. He rented a room in a different neighborhood, one close to his employment. He was not aware that the drinking problem he then developed was a reaction to this uprooting. He did not remember feeling lonely or missing the people at the orphanage. As far as he was concerned, that was simply a phase of his life that was now behind him.

It was at this point that I began, for the first time, to intervene with more than comments meant either to stimulate his associations or show that I understood what he was saying. Without, of course, using technical terms, I explained to him his need for affective expression and the effect that primal repression had had in arresting an important aspect of his development. I talked to him about the feelings and emotions that, had his development in this area not been impaired, he would probably have experienced, and pointed out how an atmosphere that discouraged expression of them had left him literally bereft of words to describe what were basically vasomotor bodily reactions. Comprehension dawned almost visibly in his face. He had not realized that the tension and restlessness that seemed to drive him to bars in those years was loneliness and despair at losing the tie to the only family he had known. I spoke of how a child is expected to develop and of the interaction of affect and cognition; and he began, at first hesitantly but soon with more confidence, to identify the affective consequences of his upbringing and their significance for his life.

I debated whether to bring up my impression that his current difficulties were of a similar nature, that some aspect of his affective reaction to his son's tragedy was not finding direct expression and was, instead, being displaced into his anger at work and at his colleague Paul. I decided against it, for the moment at least, thinking that more could be accomplished by fostering Mr. Flynn's affective maturation.

Roger Flynn never became so dependent on alcohol that his work suffered, but he did spend much of his free time in several local bars drinking beer until he felt that he had had enough to let him sleep once he got home and into bed. He never drank alone, only in taverns, but he made no effort while there to make contact with any of the other patrons or the bartenders. He had told me that once out of school he never read a book, except for technical manuals, but now I learned that he did not care for even movies, radio, or television. We speculated on how the entertainment offered by these media depends to a great extent on the viewer or listener's affective identification with a fictional protagonist—something Mr. Flynn could not readily achieve.

Mr. Flynn's reliance on alcohol ended as suddenly as it had begun when he met his wife-to-be. Also a recent high school dropout, she worked in the office of the company that employed him as an apprentice machinist. They were brought together by the fact that it was his job, before closing, to bring her forms for jobs completed in the shop, wait while she processed them, and then carry them back to his boss for filing in the customer's records. This took about twenty to thirty minutes every day, during which time they gradually got to know each other. It was Nancy who took the initiative in the conversations, overcoming Roger's shyness to the point that he suggested they go out after work. It was the first date he had ever had. Nancy obviously liked him, but she made it very clear that her Baptist upbringing made intolerable association with anyone who smoked or drank. Roger stopped both habits as suddenly as he had begun them. He was later surprised when he heard other people at work make a big fuss about quitting the cigarette habit; they suffered so much, while it never bothered him. I was able to explain to him that alcohol and smoking had been only makeshift substitutes for what at the time he did not know he needed: a relationship with a human being who cared for him and, especially important, who needed him to care for her. This now made a lot of sense to him.

Roger and Nancy married about a year and a half after they met. Both were nineteen years old at the time. He had literally not one person to invite to the wedding. Nancy's brother served as his best man. He would have liked to invite Sister Mary L., but the ceremony took place in a Protestant church, and he knew that she could not attend.

SESSION NINE: THE RESOLUTION OF PATHOLOGICAL
SHAME—PROMOTING INTEGRATION

MR. FLYNN: I don't know if this is getting us anywhere, doctor.

THERAPIST: I thought you said last time that you were sleeping better and felt less irritable during the day.

MR. FLYNN: Maybe that's from being on vacation, like.

THERAPIST: Hmm. [*No response from Mr. Flynn.*] You know, sometimes it happens that a patient will challenge the worth of therapy at a point where something is coming up in his own thoughts he wants to avoid talking about. Offense being the best defense, if you can keep me busy justifying therapy, we don't have time to talk about what's really bothering you.

MR. FLYNN: I didn't want to make you mad.

THERAPIST: Do I sound as if I were mad?

MR. FLYNN: I guess I'm all confused.

THERAPIST: You've been doing fine so far. If you're confused today, it means something is coming up. Give it a chance. [*No response from Mr. Flynn.*] Was there anything we talked about in some of the sessions that stayed on your mind?

MR. FLYNN: The religion business, I guess. I haven't really stopped thinking about it since we talked about the home and all. I don't know why it should bother me. I gave that up long ago.

THERAPIST: You know, I've been wondering about that, too. Here you were, in a religious atmosphere, the nuns were the most important people in your life, serving as an altar boy, thinking about being a priest, and then in high school you just "sort of gave up the idea of the seminary." How did it really happen? [*Mr. Flynn blushed.*] Bingo!

MR. FLYNN: [*Laughing a little in spite of himself*] I suppose I didn't want to talk about that.

THERAPIST: This is a tough one, huh?

MR. FLYNN: I just couldn't go to confession any more, and if you can't receive the Host, there's no point in it.

THERAPIST: You can't very well hope to give the sacraments if you can't receive them, can you?

MR. FLYNN: That's right

THERAPIST: So, why couldn't you go to confession?

MR. FLYNN: I guess this is what I don't want to talk about. I've never told this to anybody.

THERAPIST: Let's see, you stopped going to confession—you must have been about fifteen or sixteen years old.

MR. FLYNN: Yeah, in high school.

THERAPIST: Well, usually what troubles boys at that age are sexual feelings and masturbation.

MR. FLYNN: [*Very quietly*] How did you know that?

THERAPIST: As I said, every normally developing boy suffers some agonies about that.

MR. FLYNN: We always heard how bad it was. That if you touched yourself, you were risking your soul, that you'd go crazy. If anybody ever got caught doing it after lights out, all the other guys made fun of him. When I started doing it, I couldn't stop. I felt bad, but I'd do it every chance I got that I didn't think I'd get caught. I was sure they could tell on my face what I was doing.

THERAPIST: You were in a difficult situation. You were under tremendous tension, brought up the way you were, with very little understanding of how children feel and the closeness they need. It's no surprise that when you found a way to relieve the tension temporarily by playing with yourself that you used it.

MR. FLYNN: I thought only really bad-off kids would want to do that. It was like a disease. Thinking about it was already a sin.

THERAPIST: Just the other way around. An adolescent boy who is not beset by masturbatory urges is most likely in real trouble.

MR. FLYNN: I just couldn't face admitting it so I stopped going to confession. I must have been too guilty.

THERAPIST: I don't think it was the guilt, the feeling that you had sinned. Your contrition and the penance take care of that. I think it was the shame involved in telling anyone, even a priest, what you felt and what you were doing. Letting someone else know how sexually excited you were. Not *doing* something wrong, but, as you saw it, letting someone know that there *was* something wrong with you, that seems to me to have been the problem. Doing wrong produces guilt. Feeling that there's something wrong with you generates shame.

MR. FLYNN: We heard it every day, what a bad thing it was to do that.

THERAPIST: I think it was not just the act of masturbation that was so shameful to you, but the excitement it betrays. I think, as we've been talking about, you learned very early on not to get excited because there was no one there who would get excited with you, share your feelings, and make them an understandable part of yourself.

MR. FLYNN: Well, that's true. Anyone got out of line, bam!

THERAPIST: Yes, excitement was considered a disturbance, a getting out of line. After a while you learned to squelch those feelings before they got too far. Yet, when you grow up sexually, suddenly there is all that excitement. You couldn't stop it, so you just made sure no one knew about it, even the confessor. The fear of embarrassment governed your life.

I had now begun to bridge his early development with what I thought was presently undermining his well-being: the fear of being shamed.

MR. FLYNN: I just thought I wasn't normal. That I was the only one. That I had lost my faith. Otherwise, I wouldn't be doing that.

THERAPIST: That must have been quite a blow to you since you felt strongly enough about your religion to think of entering the seminary.

MR. FLYNN: I don't know how I felt about it then. It was just one more thing that didn't turn out. Nobody wanted me, not even God.

THERAPIST: [*After a long pause, as we both comtemplated what he had said*] Then Nancy came into your life.

MR. FLYNN: Yeah. I couldn't believe it. I didn't trust her for a long time. What did she want with me? But it worked out, I guess.

THERAPIST: And then you had Lenny.

MR. FLYNN: I think that was the happiest day of my life. [*His face clouded over.*]

THERAPIST: And then this had to happen.

MR. FLYNN: [*Crying softly, then collecting himself*] I'm sorry, but every time I think about it—— He was going to have it all. A good home. Parents. A chance to be a kid. Everything I never had, for Chrissake!

THERAPIST: How did you and your son get along when he was little?

The mourning process for his son as he was before the injury could now begin, and I aimed to move it along in manageable increments.

MR. FLYNN: He was a good boy, always a little wild, but a good boy. He never cared much for school, except for his music lessons. He could play piano when he was real little. Then he took up the trumpet, that's what he really liked. He won contests all over the state. He went with the band to the governor's place once. He got to play a solo by himself.

THERAPIST: What was your relationship with him like?

MR. FLYNN: He didn't listen much to me. But I always figured that was natural, boys not listening to their parents. We always had to listen and never had any fun. He didn't have to, having real parents, I mean.

THERAPIST: When you feel loved, you feel safe and don't have to do everything you're told. There isn't always the feeling that if you don't please, there's no knowing what's going to happen.

MR. FLYNN: Yeah. Like being told you'll be put in the juvenile home.

THERAPIST: Lenny could afford to be a boy, to let his emotions come out, to get excited about things.

MR. FLYNN: [*Bitterly*] And look where it got him!

THERAPIST: And look what it got you. I think you let yourself hope and dream about your son and then felt betrayed when this happened to him.

MR. FLYNN: You think it's going to be different for them, that what you went through wasn't all for nothing——

THERAPIST: You know, I think your having to come to grips with Lenny's being in a wheelchair is tough enough, but it's something to which you'll adjust—for his sake. What you can't handle is the shame you feel personally that this happened. It's as if Lenny's misfortune makes you look foolish for ever having had dreams and hopes for his life. Like dreaming you'd be a priest and then everyone would love and respect you, only to have what you considered to be such a shameful thing happening to you. All you want to do under those circumstances is hide.

MR. FLYNN: I never thought of it that way.

THERAPIST: Exactly. When you don't have the chance to develop words to describe your feelings, they govern you—instead of you gaining reasonable control over them. Not the kind of control where you force them not to happen, but the kind of control where you understand what's happening and you're able to go with the flow and manage it.

MR. FLYNN: I was never much of a talker.

THERAPIST: The problem is not so much talking to other people. The trouble is that you can't talk things over with yourself inside your head. Without words it's hard to think things through, to consider different possibilities. I think that's what happened to you at work. For you it became a repetition of your adolescence, imagining that others, if they knew what had happened, would be laughing at you. At one time the contrast between your wishes to be a priest and what was going on sexually seemed to be too much for you. Nobody ever helped you to understand that what was happening was human, normal, and neither bad nor basically shameful.

MR. FLYNN: No, we never heard that. All you heard was how bad it was. We never knew priests were like other people, like they do now, a lot of 'em leaving and getting married, and all that.

THERAPIST: I think something like that happened to you at work also. Somewhere you imagined that people would laugh at your misfortune. That people like Paul, with healthy children, would make fun of you for thinking you could be like them. And the more humiliated you felt, the more you couldn't talk to anybody about it, probably not even to your wife.

MR. FLYNN: No, I never talked to her about my troubles at work, she has enough of her own. I just told her I was having stomach trouble, that's why I got off of work.

THERAPIST: When you're ashamed, you feel all alone, and think that others have as low an opinion of you as you have of yourself at that point.

SESSIONS SIXTEEN TO TWENTY-FIVE: TRANSFORMATION AND THE TERMINATION OF THERAPY

Mr. Flynn himself became more aware of his feelings and volunteered the association that, although he was not in a wheelchair, he was in his own way as paralyzed as his son. He was first angry and then mournful as he contemplated what he had missed affectively in the years that had gone before. Although he then first blamed the nuns for inhibiting his emotional growth, he came to realize that they were probably as frightened of their feelings as he was. He thought more kindly of what they had done and tried to do for their charges. It was clear to me that his turning away from his church had been a painful experience. I was not surprised when he announced that he was thinking seriously about talking to a priest who said mass on television for shut-ins, those too sick to attend Church. I learned from him that over the past few years he often "just happened" to have the television tuned to that particular channel while he was puttering around in his basement workshop on Sunday mornings, while his wife attended services at the Baptist church.

He asked me if I thought he was foolish for thinking that he had been led to me so that I might free him to return to God. "No," I said, "it seems to me that you never felt you left God, but rather that your shame made you feel that God had left you. Now that you can talk about it, and you know what happened to you, you're the one who can really decide what to do about religion and cease to be dominated by your fear that no one can or wants to understand you, not even God."

Mr. Flynn did make a general confession and reinstated himself as a practicing Catholic. He felt at peace with himself and wondered if he should plan to go back to work before his sick leave expired. The patient's ability to turn to the religion that had sustained him in his early years indicated to me that he felt that he was acceptable once more, that he had been understood and had rejoined humanity. It also signaled the beginning of his separation from me. The idealizing transference he had formed had served its purpose by letting him mature affectively, and he could now look to his religion—a more mature, abstract, internalized source of selfobject experiences—for support in times of stress.

I could now view his work situation with him without his getting so angry, and bring him to the point where he could see how his feelings of being all alone and helpless in his despair had made him unable to tolerate the everyday problems and irritations that always had been and always would be part of his job. He became ashamed of how he had behaved, of what a fool he had made of himself, especially vis-à-vis Paul. This gave me the opportunity to work with his sense of shame in the here-and-now, rather than only in retrospect. Very much as the family physician had worked with Mrs. Kruger (see chapter 4), I helped Mr. Flynn to think out loud about how he might handle his feelings at work, and how he could now better manage his emotional reactions without rejecting his awareness of them.

Prior to being permitted to return to work, he needed to get clearance from the physician at the health service, and that in turn required a statement from me to the effect that I thought Mr. Flynn would be able to resume his full duties. I told him that one thing left to do before I could write such a letter was to settle the matter of his embarrassment with Paul.

I again talked about the idea that one should not swallow shame, that it is a signal that a connection has been broken and needs to be reinstated—the sooner the better. I explained that there was a difference between feeling ashamed of his own affect, and his having behaved in ways that, no matter what the reason for that behavior, were indeed alienating and understandably led to his being ashamed. The former we had handled in our sessions as he learned to form or re-establish connections with his affective potential. The latter could be resolved appropriately only when he took steps to rectify the situation and, I hoped, re-established the broken bond with Paul. As I told Mr. Flynn, it was my conviction that only if he got this situation cleared up would he have a chance to function unimpaired.

With fear and trepidation, using a trip to the factory to pick up his paycheck as his "excuse" for being there, he did contact Paul and talked to him about returning to work. He did not go into details, but explained himself to Paul by saying that he had not been himself because his son "came back sick from Vietnam." Paul, Mr. Flynn reported, was very happy to hear that he was coming back, commiserated with him about his son, and understood perfectly why he had been having a difficult time.

Once returned to work, Mr. Flynn told me that everything was going along fine. It was as if the previous months were like a bad dream that had never really happened. It was hard for him to believe that he could ever have let himself deteriorate so badly.

I continued to see him once a week for three months and then once a month for a year. He not only maintained his new-found equanimity but saw that his son improved right along with him. As Mr. Flynn was better able to structure a life for himself and no longer expected his son to provide him with a vicarious existence, the young man was able to go forward in adapting himself to his handicap. It was a great day when Mr. Flynn was able to tell me, with tears in his eyes, that his son had turned on the stereo for the first time since his return home. It was not long before Lenny made plans to resume his musical studies.

Mr. Flynn did not come to see me of his own volition; he was mistrustful and not introspective, and, in essence, challenged me to try to find out what was wrong. All that I knew in the beginning was that his personality change was probably not caused by gross neurological or other somatic disturbances. The next question, then, was whether a psychosis was present, but neither his history nor his present interaction with me pointed in that direction. If a non-psychotic, psychological problem was responsible for his difficulties, what developmental level of the self system was involved?

According to Mr. Flynn's history, as he spoke about it in the initial interview and as it was written up in the record supplied by his employers, he exhibited basic tension control and adaptation to life's exigencies—indications of a stable core self. His symptomatology was not neurotic, nor did he evince much capacity for self-examination and introspection. It was therefore likely that his difficulties were located in the area of the formation of the subjective self. His history and my observation of how he functioned as I elicited his story corroborated the idea that the weakness in his self system lay in the area of affect attunement. The absence of appropriate validation, especially in the area of affect development, had left him vulnerable to later traumatization.

In terms of the developmental spiral, his son's injury was an insult to Mr. Flynn's self system, leaving him, like Lenny, helpless and incompetent. There was nothing that Mr. Flynn could do to "fix it," the basis of his self-esteem in almost all areas of his life. As his self-esteem sank, the decisions he made led to less and less adaptive behavior, to further lowering of competence, and so on. When he came for therapy, he was well along the way to a serious depressive retreat, though he was fighting angrily, but counterproductively, against that outcome.

The deficits in affect attunement during those times of his life available to memory tended to corroborate my initial hypothesis regarding the etiology of his present problems, and pointed to the area where I had to step in and actively promote his affective development before he could be helped to restore his self-esteem, and with it a cohesive sense of self.

Once his assumption that he would be misunderstood was resolved, Mr. Flynn formed an idealizing father transference. I became the father he never knew, the father who could understand him and help him to grow. Using the leverage of the transference and his present advanced cognitive capacities, I was able to help him gain considerable insight into his affective difficulties. As a result, he remobilized his development in those areas, a course leading to much-improved functioning and the resolution of his depression. The transference, though not resolved analytically, was shifted to a trust in a more abstract, internalized ideal.

9

Narcissistic and Borderline Personality Disorders

Disavowal and the Divided Self-Concept

Another group of patients whose problems center around the failure of affect attunement are the so-called narcissistic personality disorders. As best as one can reconstruct the development of these patients, as children they did not respond to the misunderstanding of their affective needs and communications as had Roger Flynn. Instead of manifesting the effects of primal repression and arrested affective development, these children offset traumatic disappointment by learning to rely on their own efforts to promote substitutes for the selfobject experiences they really required. Not simply passive and resigned, as Mr. Flynn had been as a child, these people even as infants apparently became very skillful at changing course and actively responding to what the adults around them wanted or needed from them. Seemingly giving up hope of being understood, they opted instead for the attention they were able to recruit with their achievements.

Around the age of two, when the preoperational phase of cognitive development introduces symbolism and the possibility of fantasy, these children reinforce their defensive sense of self with grandiose fantasies of omniscience and omnipotence. The end-product is an outer shell of self-confidence based on cleverness, intelligence, and effective manipulation of the environment, with a center that is vulnerable and insecure. Any threat to their effectiveness, and hence to their sense of competence, exposes these children to the danger that their early need for responsiveness and affirmation will reassert itself, leaving them open to a repetition of the disappointment and humiliation that gave rise to the defensive self in the first place.

The watershed for the character development of these children comes around the age of six years or so, when, according to the developmental timetable, concrete operational thinking and the possibility for logical thought mandate that grandiose fantasies retreat in favor of the recognition of and adaptation to a culturally shared external reality. The realization that others have an independent existence, and that one is not the center of the universe, demands that the child drastically change his perspective. He must reorient himself and find his place in a world in which he is only one among others, and a small one at that.

However, now to relinquish their defensive sense of superiority would expose these children to the very humiliation that they have fought hard to avoid. That their present situation might offer very different possibilities for fulfillment is, of course, immaterial: their fears of traumatic disappointment are based on patterns of expectation experienced earlier, ones that have not been influenced significantly by further maturation. Thus, these children face a seeming dilemma. Simply to deny the reality of their limitations at this stage of development would not be adaptive and, indeed, might portend a psychotic retreat from reality. But to accept their relative helplessness to control the world around them would expose them to the depression that they would have suffered had they not been able to develop that exaggerated sense of self that they are now being asked to relinquish. But cognitive maturation offers a third possible solution. Neither denying, nor fully accepting the reality of their limitations, these children *disavow* it: that is, they recognize and subscribe to the reality of their circumstances cognitively, but not affectively.

On the cognitive level, the narcissist-to-be accepts the world's judgment that he is "only" a child, but—by keeping his fantasies to himself—can maintain the belief that his real self is very different from what others see. The child may modify fantasies ("See how powerful I am" may become "I will be powerful and do marvelous things when I grow up. Then everyone will see my true self and will have to love me") and then use his considerable intellect and available talents to make these fantasies come true. It is not surprising that members of the professional élite—successful business people and artists, physicians and lawyers, as well as the movers and shakers of the political establishment—are found in this group of patients; nor that their often highly rewarded adaptation to the needs of the world fails to bring them either a healthy sense of achievement or a sense of wholeness or cohesiveness. The integrity of the narcissistic person's self system is maintained only at the cost of splitting the self-concept. The triumph they experience when their achievements are acclaimed, and the preferments that they win in the social order, maintain their grandiose position but do not address the underlying sense of worthlessness and insecurity that made this attitude necessary in the first place. They present themselves for therapy with the complaint that all their success has not brought them happiness in their relationships—that is, no one understands them and/or in spite of all their success, they feel like frauds—that is, they don't understand themselves. Small wonder! Such a person's whole life has been spent in concealing from himself—and everyone else—the continuously needy and rejected part of the self-image. To discover that aspect of one's character is the equivalent of repeating the early trauma; it is to be exposed once again as truly worthless, incapable of recruiting an empathic response. It is indeed paradoxical that these people have been labeled *narcissistic*. This term has moral overtones, implying that their suffering is based on an inordinate love of the self, a love that must be overcome and brought into line with reality. Such is not, however, the situation. The demanding behavior of these patients, when in evidence, does not come from an overweening sense of self-love:

their brazen expression of entitlement only conceals the unconscious conviction that they are neither lovable nor admirable. Because patients with so-called borderline disorders often display a
similar need to have their way at all costs, these two quite different problems are often confused with one another. The narcissistic
patient's demanding nature is in the interest of maintaining an
inflated or grandiose sense of self so as to avoid depressive feelings, while the borderline patient's disregard for the needs of others is based on a more primitive and much less stable organization
of the self system.

Narcissistic Personality Disorder: Esther Romberg

"Outside, hooey! Inside, phooey!" is the way Dr. Esther Romberg
summed up her reason for coming to see me. Although she had tried
several careers and been successful in all of them, she still felt, at
the age of thirty-three, unsatisfied. Married and divorced twice, she
had found each husband "not enough" for her. She began psychotherapy at twenty-five and left treatment after six months; a second
attempt with a different therapist was also terminated abruptly.
One therapist she experienced as being competitive with her; the
other "just sat there." She complained that nothing seemed real; she
felt like a spectator of her life.

When I asked her to tell me more about herself, she said that she
was the third of five children and the only daughter. Her father,
who had died three years previously, had been a rabbinical scholar;
her mother managed a wholesale grocery business founded by Dr.
Romberg's maternal grandparents.

She was intellectually precocious and received her undergraduate
degree before she was twenty. Graduate studies in French and European history led to a master's degree in both fields. She had the
opportunity to pursue doctoral studies abroad on a prestigious
scholarship, but chose instead to remain in the United States and
marry the chairman of the English department at her university, a
divorced man eighteen years her senior. She then taught evenings

in a nearby college, continued her academic work and, in due time, was awarded a doctorate. She felt that her thesis, which dealt with a minor but interesting figure in French literature, could be turned into a successful *roman à clef*. Her husband had connections with a publishing house, and her manuscript was given a reading. She received a scathing critique and became enraged.

She decided not to remain in a field that did not properly appreciate her. In any case, she had by that time become aware of the limitations of both an academic career and her marriage. Regarding the former, what had looked so glamorous at first now bored her. As for the latter, she was no longer impressed with her husband and decided that what she had thought was love had been only infatuation. The teen-age children from his first marriage, who lived with their mother in a nearby community, were all in difficulties of one kind or another, and her husband expected her to be an interested participant in their lives, making their problems her own—a role she did not relish at all. She herself had no wish for children and resented this intrusion into her life. Her husband's periodic and increasingly prolonged episodes of sexual impotence, which had set in shortly after they were married, did not matter much to her. She had continued to take lovers for short periods of time, much as she had always done before marriage. One of these, a highly successful trader on one of the financial exchanges, whom she met when he took a class she was teaching, appealed to her more than others had, and a romance blossomed. She divorced her first husband and married this man.

After the life of a faculty wife and teacher, she enjoyed the hectic pace and the instant gratification of her new existence; it all seemed very exciting. Although she had been raised in middle-class comfort, the luxury in which she now lived was something she had never imagined. She enjoyed it for a while, but what really stimulated her was the power her husband and his friends wielded. The commercial world revolved around their activities; they made things happen that ordinary mortals only read about in the newspapers. What intrigued her even more was that, once she got to know them, her husband and his friends—though clever, industrious, and daring—were, as far as she was concerned, appallingly limited. She considered some of them to be downright stupid. She reasoned that she ought to be able to master what these people were able to do, especially when she had the opportunity to learn the fine points of the game from a man who already knew them all.

So she enrolled in a training program to qualify for membership in the exchange and had her husband review his trades with her every day and explain his reasoning behind them. Eventually she was hired by a firm to do backroom work, and then moved on to trade for her own account. Although she discovered that she was not the kind of person who, like her husband and his friends, could take the huge risks that would make or break millionaires in a matter of days or weeks, she succeeded in doing very well indeed.

However, to her chagrin, after a few years she realized that she once again was losing interest in both her work and her spouse. Like many of his colleagues on the fast track, her husband had acquired a drug habit that was becoming unmanageable. Her interest in him waned. She thought of him as shallow and preoccupied and, furthermore, saw that he would probably soon be unable to perform the daily financial miracles needed to support either their life style or his various drug dependencies; and so she divorced him.

At this point, Dr. Romberg interrupted her story, looked at me with a half-worried, half-mischievous expression, and said, "I'm not a very nice person, am I? I'm a user, I use people." "Well," I replied, "don't we all? The problem seems to be that the use you make of people doesn't get you what you're looking for." She clapped her hands together delightedly and, suddenly looking like an adoring child, said, "I knew you were the one for me! Oh," she caught herself, "there's something else. I lied to you about being referred by Dr. W. It was simpler than telling you the whole story on the phone."

She had decided to call me after hearing me give a lecture to which her most recent paramour, a psychiatrist and former student of mine, had taken her. She felt that what I had to say not only made sense but seemed tailormade for her situation. She liked how I spoke and conducted myself, especially admired how I handled the questions, some hostile, that were asked during the discussion period. The more she thought about it in the next few days, the more she convinced herself that I could help her where other therapists had not been able to do so. The complimentary things her lover told her about me only increased her determination to see me "by hook or by crook." I said that it sounded as if she had not only sold herself on coming to see me, but also had decided that I would not want to see her, and that she could gain admission only through trickery, using the name of the eminent Dr. W. as leverage.

Here I began to enter the developmental spiral in the self-esteem segment. With a patient like this, the stage of collaboration is reached quickly: as soon as Dr. Romberg realized I could understand her, she volunteered associations that readily guided me in evaluating whether I was on the mark with my interventions.

The first few times in my career as a therapist that I received such laudatory reactions from patients I felt it was necessary to check to see whether they were making fun of me. By the time I saw Dr. Romberg, I recognized that such naked flattery as hers is the hallmark of a readiness to mobilize a particular form of an idealizing transference, genuine in itself but also meant to reassure the therapist that the patient will respect and cater to the therapist's need for self-esteem. It immediately suggests how such a patient learned to ensure attachment early in life.

Esther Romberg spoke at length, with bitterness, of how she had been robbed of her childhood. Her father distanced himself from the family with his biblical research, which occupied him from morning to night. When he came home from the house of studies, he was besieged by students, colleagues, and petitioners, all of whom wanted to talk with or be counseled by this widely known and highly respected scholar. She adored her father and remembered waiting, for hours it seemed, outside his study door in the hope that when he came out he would look at, perhaps even speak to, her. Mostly, however, all he gave her was an absent-minded smile.

Here I interjected: "Now I can better understand your reluctance to take a chance on waiting outside *my* door and hoping for the best." She beamed.

Her brothers, insofar as they took an interest in biblical studies, received some attention from father, but she, being a girl, was her mother's responsibility. Her mother, however, was seldom home during either the day or the evening. The maternal grandfather, having been successful in business, but not in producing any male heirs, was pleased to see his daughter marry an obviously bright, promising rabbinical scholar who, it was anticipated, would bring honor and respect to the family in return for the support that it was understood would have to be provided for him. At the same time, the maternal side of the family treated the rabbi with a certain disdain, for, when all was said and done, his wisdom did not put anything on the table. Having done her duty by marrying him, the mother preferred to have as little as possible to do with her husband; and the two lived peaceably together, maintaining outward appearances but going their separate ways.

The mother remained, as she had been before her marriage, associated with her father's business and, as his health failed, more and more took charge of it. In the evening, when not occupied with friends or community activities, she preferred to be left to herself. Her children were cared for by various housekeepers and maids, none of whom lasted long once they found that they were expected to function as parents to these bright but undisciplined youngsters.

School brought order into Esther's life. For the first time she could remember, what she did or did not do mattered to someone—to the teacher, who expected her to achieve and to conform to a predictable set of rules. Praise was forthcoming when Esther was successful, while punishment followed when she misbehaved or failed to do her work. At first it did not matter to her whether she was praised or punished; that someone cared enough about her to take the trouble to do either was heady enough. It did not take long, however, for her to become, as she said, "addicted" to success. The possibility of being singled out for praise, of having her work held up as an example, of reciting out loud to the amazement of her peers was a powerful incentive. She never found school either boring or difficult. Her academic career was an uninterrupted triumphal march until her doctoral thesis was rejected for publication.

I commented that school provided a stable frame of reference for the formation of her identity. She leaned forward excitedly and marveled how well I already understood her. We ended the session soon after, agreeing to a twice-a-week schedule for therapy.

THE IDEALIZING TRANSFERENCE

My impression that this patient's longing for a respected parental figure, whom she could trust to have an interest in her, had already led to the formation of an idealizing transference was borne out by her subsequent behavior. Looking for my approval, Dr. Romberg first undertook a study not only of what I had written and published but of the references I cited in those articles. This was not a mirror transference: she was not seeking my validation for her achievements. Nor was it an alter ego transference: she evinced no need to be accepted as a fellow traveler in the field. It was homage, pure and simple. She read what I had written in order to appreciate me more. I squirmed a little inwardly when she unabashedly praised me in words that were a little too close to some of my own youthful grandiose fantasies. I was able, however—as Kohut (1971, chapter 10) has advised in such situations—to maintain an empathic stance and thus accept with equanimity what my patient was saying.

Probably the worst thing a therapist can do when a patient needs to idealize him or her is immediately to assume that the patient's declaration of love and admiration is a screen for hostility and then to insist that the patient search inwardly and find it.* Nor is it advisable to distance oneself from the patient's hero worship by immediately linking it to the past. For example, in this case it would have been easy to show Dr. Romberg that her attitude toward me was a recapitulation of her need to unite with her otherwise distant father by at least sharing in his glory. Instead, the attitude I took was for the most part to listen quietly to her praise and, when she became flustered by the intensity of her feelings, to assure her that she was only doing what had been asked of her: to be open about everything that she was experiencing. In other words, I tried to show her that neither one of us needed to be shamed by honest feelings, honestly expressed.

That Esther Romberg, unlike Jim Zurf or Roger Flynn, could

---

*Therapists who were analyzed and were analyzing before Kohut made his contributions remember only too well the kind of misunderstanding that occurred when this happened. Eventually the patient did get angry, not because of having found the hidden wellspring of his or her aggressive drives, but because of the frustration of not being permitted to express in the transference the unqualified loving admiration that a child has for a protector.

experience and express nuances of affect was of course very impor
tant. Her therapy was geared to letting her express her feelings
rather than helping her to formulate them. It is much easier to talk
to and with patients like Dr. Romberg because they are not only
acquainted with their own emotions but are usually also able to take
into account the affective message implicit in the therapist's comments and respond to it.

During this phase of her treatment, her wish to please me permitted her to overcome the initial shame involved in voicing the fantasies that had sustained her in her loneliness, and to trace their
development.

SELFOBJECT FAILURE

One incident she recalled vividly was coming home from kinder-
garten and feeling wonderful. Laughing excitedly, she came into the
house and exuberantly tossed her beret at a coatrack, but it sailed
past its intended goal, through the open door of the kitchen, and
landed on a platter of meat sitting on the kitchen counter. The
woman who was their housekeeper at that time, a buxom, maternal-
looking person whom Esther had rather liked, angrily turned on her
and gave her a tongue-lashing for being a spoiled child. It wasn't
bad enough that she (the housekeeper) had to do all the work,
Esther had to go out of her way to make it harder for her, and so on.

The housekeeper's response to Esther was a classic example of the
traumatic empathic (selfobject) failure in childhood that Kohut
often spoke and wrote about. Esther comes in all excited and happy,
and then there is a mishap. The adult not only neglects to take into
account the affective message the child is sending through her exuberance, but incorrectly attributes motives to the child that permit
her (the housekeeper) to use the child as a conduit for expressing
her own emotional concerns.

RETREAT INTO FANTASY

What might have rectified the situation, but what her character
pathology—that is, her inability to relinquish her grandiosity—did
not permit her to do, would have been Esther's affective acceptance

of the adult's superior position. Had she been able to apologize, she might in this way have mollified the adult and hoped to win forgiveness. Instead, dreadfully humiliated and unable to explain herself, Esther retreated to her room and fantasied revenge. She would grow up and become very important and very rich. The housekeeper, by now old and sick, would come to her for help. Esther would be generous with her, and the old woman would break down and humbly apologize for her inconsiderate behavior years ago. Intellectually Esther knew an apology was called for. But, unable to subordinate herself and put herself at the mercy of the adult, she fantasied a role reversal: the adult would apologize to her. Spinning various versions of this daydream had a calming effect. At the same time, however, that she was soothing herself with her fantasies, she now recalled that in another part of her thoughts she had also become aware of the idea that, formulated in a sophisticated fashion, would have been something like, "No one really cares about anybody. Everyone is concerned only with himself."

Of course, as is usually the case, such dramatic recollections from childhood are composites; and it is probable that Esther formulated her world view over a period of time and based it not on just one dramatic experience. She presented many similar examples of how she was either misunderstood or ignored while she was still attempting to make affective contact with members of her household. She defended herself unconsciously against being retraumatized by disavowing her need for emotional understanding. Consciously she would be aware of such thoughts as "Who cares about them anyway? They don't count. Someday I'll . . ."—and off she would go into a soothing, compensatory fantasy.

Usually I dealt with such recollections as the one about the housekeeper by focusing on the affective aspect of the experience, expressing how I thought she might have felt, and then waiting for her reaction.

THERAPIST: Here you were all excited and happy, and suddenly found yourself the target of anger. I think you might well have been ashamed, as we all tend to be when the response we get is the diametric opposite of what we had hoped for.

DR. ROMBERG: I can still remember the hot feeling.

THERAPIST: We're especially vulnerable when we're not on our guard and something like this happens.

DR. ROMBERG: It wasn't long before I made sure that I wouldn't get caught unawares.

THERAPIST: Well, you're certainly being open here with me.

DR. ROMBERG: I trust you. Once I trust someone, they have all of me. I never really had that with either Bill or George [*her two former husbands*], but with my friends, anything goes.

THERAPIST: When you trust someone, you become more the person you wanted to be but couldn't afford to become.

Since the defense of disavowal is maintained by not talking, to oneself or others, about the event that threatens to create painful affect, silence on the therapist's part only plays into the defense. Even if the therapist's hypotheses turn out to be mistaken, it is important for the patient to hear the therapist deal verbally with the issues involved. Although Dr. Romberg responded quickly to this technique, many patients take much longer to become able to talk about what they fear; but even if such patients do not respond verbally, it helps them to hear that the therapist can do so.

GROWTH THROUGH TRANSMUTING INTERNALIZATION

Esther Romberg had been able as a child to retreat into fantasy to cope with her disappointments and frustrations. Such patients can deal with metaphor and analogy; with them I can say or imply, "It is as if———" when I interpret the meaning of experienced affective needs. Hence I was able even in the first session to give Dr. Romberg such an interpretation when I explained her felt need to manipulate me into giving her an appointment as being a consequence of the frustration she experienced at her father's study door. It made sense to her for me to say, in effect, "Your need for me is as strong as a little girl's for her father, but now that you are not as helpless as the little girl you once were, of course you will use everything at your command not to re-experience that awful tension only to be disappointed." In doing this, I already set in motion what became the dynamic curative component of her treatment—the stage of transformation that Kohut (1971, 1984, 1987) has called *transmuting internalization* (see pages 143–44).

Some patients, like Esther Romberg, each in his or her own way, implicitly say to the therapist, "I will merge with you, and then your strength will be my strength, and that will let me cope and be satisfied." The other side of that coin is the justified, paralyzing fear/wish that if that process were to occur, one would surrender one's self—lose oneself in the therapist's stronger personality. The therapist's job is to let the patient experience that his or her need, when properly understood, is not an impossible dream, nor does it have to become a nightmare in its fulfillment. Although I made a specific comment to Dr. Romberg when I connected her present situation to me with the memory of herself and her father, from a broader perspective I was also saying to her: "Look at how I think about you and your behavior. You talk from the viewpoint of the so-called objective observer—let's say, a lawyer or a moralist—and find yourself guilty of being a liar and a manipulator. That is certainly a position one can take, and it is not without value to have the strength to judge yourself as the world might do. However, I take a different, but equally valid, developmental point of view. Yes, you manipulated me, but why? Because once upon a time, when you should have been able to recruit an affective response, your needs were not met, and so perhaps you got the idea that there was something wrong—not with your father but with you. That, given the choice, people you needed and wanted would ignore you, and that it was up to you to figure out ways that would offset this defect in yourself, to create situations that would trap those who would not voluntarily choose to be with you and help you. The question is not whether you behave properly, but whether you really are so unlikable and unlovable as you imagine yourself to be; whether there might not be ways of dealing with your needs that will be more satisfying in the long run so that you won't feel that what you get doesn't count because it was obtained fraudulently."

Some little bit of that implicit message got through to the patient: perhaps the realization that someone could think of her differently from the way she expected to be thought about. That little bit of insight became part of her cognitive strength. When it happened dozens or hundreds of times in treatment, she began to think developmentally about herself: "Now here I've gone and done it again—the little girl just won't believe that she's good enough for anybody." Then when she came to the therapy session, she would report not simply her behavior but also an explanation of it, which represented her insight into the reason behind it. Eventually, analysis of behavior preceded action, and instead of simply reporting the repetition of old patterns, she found she could exercise control and prevent re-enactment of self-defeating patterns. When, finally, the need for conscious evaluation of behavior in terms of its developmental antecedents faded into the background, she was left with choice—the ability to weigh the affective consequences of behavior realistically and to act accordingly. In other words, she was able to exercise her free will (pages 102–3).

THE BASIC SUSTAINING FANTASY

Withdrawing further into herself when at home, Esther became an avid reader. She told me she thought that she was looking for an explanation of why people are the way they are. She recalls being offended, even at the age of nine or ten, by books in the children's section of the public library. She knew the relationships portrayed in them were not true to life. What she did like were the myths and fairytales in which everything took place at high intensity, and hate, greed, revenge, and jealousy played as much a part as did love and devotion. She found herself taking part in these stories in fantasy, and eventually created an ongoing saga that she expanded with bits and pieces of new tales she read. Generally she was the misunderstood princess who won, through her virtuous character and brave deeds, the love and admiration of an apologetic king, queen, and court. She blushed as she told me this, and I speculated aloud that perhaps these fantasies were not all in the past. She nodded and, with some difficulty but a determination to be honest with herself and with me, explained that she still played out such fantasies daily, modifying the old scenarios to fit whatever situation she happened to be in at the moment.

THERAPIST: Here, too?

DR. ROMBERG: [*With bitter humor*] I am going to be the patient you like best of all as you come to realize how bright I am, and how devoted I am to you and to your ideas.

THERAPIST: Then I would finally understand what you have to offer and appreciate you. [*Dr. Romberg remained silent, but nodded affirmatively.*] It's not easy to bring together these two parts of your mental life that you have kept apart for so long.

Being able to speak about her ongoing fantasy marked a turning point in the treatment. Now that she could step back from and observe her need to idealize me, we could explore this need as a father transference which activated an earlier longing to be recognized as an important person in her father's life.* In this connection, I was able to explain to her that her lack of satisfaction in daily life, in spite of her accomplishments, was related to the fact that nothing she could accomplish could match the glory of fantasy achievement unencumbered and unmodulated by everyday reality.

RESOLUTION OF AN IDEALIZING TRANSFERENCE

As my work with Dr. Romberg progressed, her idealization matured and became less childlike. For a short time she entertained the idea of becoming a psychiatrist and psychoanalyst. Although I neither discouraged nor encouraged her in this idea, I helped her to understand its various meanings. In part, she wanted to please me; but, more important, she wished to be like me. This was the beginning of a short-lived alter ego transference. Because she expected me either to ignore or to ridicule her for her wish—the response received when as a child she expressed an interest in Hebraic studies—she also experienced considerable shame in this phase of the transference. Once she could recognize that I was neither for nor

*I suspected that behind the wish for her father's acceptance lay an even earlier rejection by her mother, but Dr. Romberg gave no evidence of being ready to deal with that. Kohut (1977, chapter 1; 1984, chapter 1) has suggested that the earliest and most devastating trauma often remains beyond the reach of therapeutic reconstruction. Therapists usually deal with the adverse consequences of a patient's further frustration that occurred when he or she turned to the *other* parent for help and once again was disappointed.

against her ambition, but interested only in helping her to think through what was best for her, she could deal more objectively with this idea. There was an element of competition: she recalled a time around the age of five or six when she tried to urinate standing up and, half squatting, persuaded herself that with practice she could develop a stream like her brothers'. For Dr. Romberg, then, to be like her brothers, or now to be like me, meant acceptance and an end to loneliness. Once she understood its meaning, her interest in psychiatry and psychoanalysis as a profession waned, though she remained an interested consumer of the literature.

Reading had remained a significant part of her life; it was the bridge between her private life and her public existence. A voracious reader of novels, biographies, and technical literature on various subjects that interested her, she had accumulated a tremendous fund of knowledge about human motivation, which she used in dealing with those around her. As a result, her relations to others had an artificial quality. Priding herself on being able to anticipate what other people expected or hoped for from her, she used her understanding to manipulate them. As we talked about this, she was contemptuous and cynical: how easy it was for her to make things come out to her liking. Her tone was defiant, daring me to criticize her.

I would ask her to recall incidents that would illustrate what she was talking about, and was then able to point out to her that the examples of manipulation she was giving me demonstrated that, in most cases, she proceeded to use her insight in a way that was also helpful to the people involved. She got what she wanted, but the others also benefited. The problem was that she really did not enjoy these transactions because, having consciously brought them about, she thought they did not count. To her objection that if she had not planned her moves she might well not have gotten what she wanted, I replied that what she said might well be true, but that was life. Other people do have interests and priorities and expect them to be taken into account. She happened to be expert at that, and it is a highly rewarded skill. What made it seem phony was her longing for acceptance just for being herself, something she did not have from her parents. As a matter of fact, I continued, babies and children are also "manipulating": that is, by their affective communication, by their very needs, they are sending messages that in turn address the needs of the adult, who gets pleasure from playing a part in the growth of the child and is rewarded by the positive emotional bond that develops as a result. It was unfortunate for her—but in its own way just as much, if not more so, for the adults involved— that her parents could not benefit from all she had to offer them.

"Do you get pleasure from me?" she asked. "Yes, I certainly do," I replied. "What we're doing gives me great gratification and pleasure. This is what it's all about for me." She smiled shyly and cried quietly for a while. It was a moving moment for both of us.

As she became increasingly bored by her occupation as a financial trader, she realized that she was at a point where she could maintain her life style by devoting an hour or two a day to her work, but that this was not enough for her. She was unwilling to return to university life and, once she understood its transference meaning, realized that the profession of a psychotherapist was not really to her liking either. As she cast about for what else she might do with her life, I asked whether she remembered anything about how she had made her decision to study French and history and to teach at the university level. Actually, she told me, she had originally wanted to become a writer, but chose the other fields because she soon became dissatisfied with the teaching and the people she met in her English courses. She did enjoy the study of foreign languages and later combined it with an interest in history. Since childhood, writing represented power and admiration to her. Having felt undesirable for so long, she found that through writing she could have a new identity—one independent of her mundane self. As an author she could be what she wanted herself to be: loved, admired, and honored.

She had participated, at around age ten or eleven, in a weekly short-story contest for children sponsored by a local newspaper. Each week a panel of judges selected what they considered to be the best story, which was then published, with a small monetary prize awarded to the young writer. She entered this contest often, and won more than once. She enjoyed seeing her stories in print, but was flabbergasted when—and she recalled the scene exactly—a boy from another class, whom she did not know, hesitantly asked, as they were both walking up the school stairway, whether she was *the* Esther Romberg who always had her name in the paper. She said she was, and the fellow told her he really liked to read her stories. They never talked again, but that was perhaps the most glorious moment in her life.

While she had never really thought of other people reading her work, now it dawned on her that she had become an author; and, wonder of wonders, the tone of admiration and awe in that boy's voice reflected how she felt about the writers of the books she devoured. She experienced a feeling of triumph—the result of suddenly finding herself exceeding anything she might have imagined or hoped for—an experience whose repetition she had pursued ever since. In this context, it became much clearer why the critique of her manuscript had devastated her so.

Shortly after telling me this story from childhood, she brought in the doctoral thesis in question and asked whether I cared to look at it. After its rejection, she had put the manuscript in a trunk and until now had not taken it out again. She compared it to an unsightly rash that she had wanted to cover up: she could know about it, but not anyone else. I agreed to read her work as soon as I could.

I had at the outset no particular interest and certainly no expertise in the subject of her book—nonetheless, I quickly found myself fascinated by it. I thought it extremely well written, eminently publishable, and of general interest, and told her so. "Well then, look at this," she said, pulling out of her purse a letter she had been carrying around in anticipation of this moment. It was the critique that had laid her so low. I read it, and then asked her to read it aloud. As she heard the words, it became clear to her that the writer of the letter had been in a rage and probably had not done more than briefly look at her manuscript. What he was so angry about we could not know—perhaps the editor was angry at the patient's husband, who had interceded for her, or at women or women writers; but, in any case, it seemed obvious that the critique had nothing to do with the merits of what she had written. As we pieced together what happened at the time, Dr. Romberg recalled that she had looked at the editor's letter, realized it was a rejection couched in no uncertain terms, and, furious at being so humiliated, had put away both letter and manuscript. Her shame was so great that she could not read the critique thoroughly or go back to it some time later to look at it more dispassionately. To be rejected, no matter how unfairly, was for her a repetition of the trauma she had suffered in childhood, and threatened her with a disorganization of the self system that had to be handled emergently even if unsatisfactorily.

Within months she submitted the manuscript to other publishers; and about a year later, with some revisions, it was published as a book. In the meantime she had decided to apply to law school, feeling that the practice of law would answer her need to make things happen and feel effective, give her an outlet for her skills as a writer, and offer an appropriate forum for her dramatic, exhibition-istic propensities.

RESOLUTION OF TRANSFERENCE

As she began her new studies, the transference shifted to what Kohut (1971) called the mirror phase of the grandiose transference. Not the early need of the infant for a validating merger or blissful union with the adult, but a need to have her performance validated by an affectively attuned, appreciative correspondent. She would report to me her daily activities in the classroom, much as she might have wanted to but was not permitted to do as a child. She found me an interested and appreciative listener. When, for example, she told me how she had been the only one to arrive at a certain correct answer to some question the teacher had asked of the class, I might say, "How did that make you feel? Did you get sort of both a proud and embarrassed glow inside?" Her eyes would light up, feeling that I really understood how she had felt. Sharing in her pride, I vali-dated (mirrored) her experience and so strengthened her sense of self worth in a way that her previous lonely successes had not been able to do.

Her personality change in this atmosphere was clear. She became much softer and less challenging, without, however, losing her ef-fectiveness. People she had known who had always liked her also noticed this change and commented positively on it.

On one occasion she was preparing a brief for a mock trial in the classroom and was talking to me about her strategy. It involved a case of alleged medical malpractice; and, knowing something about the issues involved, I pointed out some flaws in her argument. She took note of my comments and thanked me. When she returned for her next session, there was a marked alteration in her demeanor. She was cold and aloof. When I asked her about this change, she denied it, claiming she was just so busy now that she could not concentrate on what we were doing, her thoughts were elsewhere. I suggested that what I had said in the last session had set off this mood: that is, meaning to be helpful, I had come across as critical and led her to feel attacked and endangered. Once I acknowledged that I had hurt her, she relaxed visibly and gained access to the feelings she had suppressed at the time of the session and thereafter, which corroborated what I had said. With that experience as a springboard, the examination of the episode with her thesis and some other similar ones became available for being worked through. When she no longer needed to disavow her feelings in this area, she became much more able to titrate her reactions to criticism, real or imagined. Many of her fellow students were aggressive individuals who habit ually belittled their peers and, if possible, made them feel insecure. She noted how she was much more able to avoid rising to their bait and to brush off their hostility as being part of their personalities that did not need to affect her self-esteem or called for retaliation.

As she saw herself changing, becoming more comfortable with herself and others, functioning more happily and expressing a contentment that she had not known before, her idealization of me returned in the form of gratitude for all we had accomplished and for what she felt I had been willing to endure in the process. As before, I neither minimized her gratitude, nor hastened to reassure her that, far from suffering, I had enjoyed working with her, but, instead, waited to see what would come up.

TRANSFORMATION AND PSYCHOSEXUAL MATURATION

The idealization at this point, in the fourth year of her treatment, was, expectedly, much less infantile than the first manifestation of this transference, and gave way to increased wishes to be close to me physically as well as psychologically. Sexual dreams and conscious longing for me in the form of "I know perfectly well that we are patient and doctor and that everything would be ruined if we went beyond that, but if we weren't, and you met me socially as I am now, would you want me?" I rephrased her question, suggesting that she was saying that, now that she no longer had to cope with the sense of being depreciated, and felt secure in her identity as a person, she could afford to want to be recognized as a woman. The erstwhile sense of inferiority she had attached to her femaleness was a pseudo explanation she had given herself. She, like many little girls deprived of appropriate affect attunement during critical times, blamed that neglect on the fact that she was not a boy. Under these circumstances, it was important to deal with her present sexual longing for me, as Kohut (1977) has emphasized: not as the repetition of an oedipal *conflict,* for there was no evidence in dreams and associations for that; but as the initiation of a healthy oedipal *phase* in the transference. It was an aspect of development she had not had a chance to experience because of the trauma of the pre-oedipal years, to say nothing of the fact that her family situation did not, in any case, permit the expression and working through of oedipal sexual feelings. Dr. Romberg's push to act out sexual longings with me faded as she became occupied with the belated satisfaction she felt in being a woman.

CONCLUSION OF THERAPY

She had become friendly with a fellow student, a man two years her junior, who had also left an academic career to study the law. They became increasingly involved; but, for the first time that she could remember, she delayed sexual relations until it was clear to both of them that they would get married. As she reviewed her relations with other men and her two former husbands, Esther Romberg was aware, as was I, that this was a very different type of man. The two of them were committed to one another, and their gratification lay much more in doing for the other than in enhancing themselves. Although she had always been orgastic, her sexual response had been of the same quality as that derived from the masturbation she had practiced as a child and as an adolescent to relieve tension and soothe herself. The only real warmth she ever felt in sex was with an older woman, her gymnastics teacher in high school, with whom she had a relationship for two years. Esther was the passive partner in the predominantly oral sexual play between the two of them. Although she responded to clitoral stimulation, what gave her the deepest pleasure was when her lover would play their private game of cat and kitten and would lick Esther's entire body. This warm, sensuous, cared-for feeling she had never had before or since, until she re-experienced it in sexual intercourse with the man to whom she was now engaged. It seemed to us that her need for a mother who cared for her enough to want to touch her body—a need that had been answered in her homosexual relationship—had now become incorporated in her love for her husband-to-be.

She became fearful that I would leave her now that I was no longer the only man who counted in her life. She herself volunteered that what she was going through was typical of adolescent girls who want their fathers to give them their freedom without having to relinquish the parent's love. Her insight dissipated her anxiety.

Even before her marriage, Dr. Romberg became aware of a heretofore unsuspected wish for children. She and her fiancé decided that they would try to conceive as soon as possible because she was getting to the age where a first pregnancy becomes somewhat problematic. She did become pregnant shortly after they were married; the tests for fetal abnormalities were negative; and she also learned that her child would be a girl. This last bit of news made her very happy. She finished the academic year, took her examinations, and delivered a healthy six-pound baby two weeks later.

Motherhood agreed with her, and when she was able to resume her sessions with me she reported glowingly about her baby and their relationship. She thoroughly enjoyed caring for the infant herself with minimal outside help. Initially she had planned her return to school at a time when her daughter would have been about nine months old; but as the time for the start of the new semester approached, she decided that she could not leave the baby, not only because it would have been too much like repeating her own history, but also because she did not want to give up the pleasure of being with the child all day long. She postponed her return to law school indefinitely, and planned to try to have another child in the next year or two. She and her husband were planning to share child care, which, she thought, would enable her to complete her studies when her children reached school age. In the meantime, she had computer equipment installed that enabled her to pursue her financial trading in her home. During the two or three hours a day she was occupied with this, the baby was cared for by a housekeeper. Dr. Romberg did not resent having to deal with financial instruments now that this was no longer the focus of her life.

With this opportunity to give to her baby what she herself never had, Dr. Romberg felt she had finally healed the wounds that originally brought her to therapy, and that she could terminate treatment. I agreed, and after about six weeks of further work, during which nothing surfaced that contradicted the advisability of her decision, we parted with the understanding that, if the need arose, she could feel free to come back. Since that time I have received annual greetings from her, accompanied by pictures of her daughter, first alone and then later in the company of her new baby brother. Dr. Romberg writes that all has remained well, and she continues to be happy with her life.

Tension Intolerance and the Borderline Personality: Tina Pearl

The diagnostic category of narcissistic personality disorder should apply only to a patient whose main defense against traumatic disappointment and disorganization of the self system is the disavowal of affective longing. In everyday language, however, the term *narcissism* carries a pejorative connotation that often confuses therapists when they see someone as cooperative, eager, and insightful as Esther Romberg, thinking that *narcissism* more aptly applies to someone like the demanding lady, a total stranger, who telephoned me at home at six one Monday morning and, neither apologizing for the time of the call nor introducing herself, told me she wanted to see me later that day. I said that unfortunately I had no open appointments that day. Before I could inquire whether this was an emergency that called for immediate referral, or whether something could be scheduled later in the week, she interrupted me and brusquely demanded, "So, when do you eat lunch?"

Intrigued, I suggested that I would arrange to see her after my regular office hours. When Tina Pearl arrived at my office, I witnessed a remarkable phenomenon. Although she carried no more paraphernalia than did any other patient—a magazine, a raincoat, and a pocketbook—she succeeded, within seconds after entering, in making my office look as if a bomb had hit it. She herself looked disorganized, and so was her life.

As I later put it together when she had become my patient, from childhood on she had learned that a girl without a husband was nobody, and that nothing she might do much mattered until she "caught" or "trapped" one. Programmed in this fashion, she dutifully went through school, got reasonable grades, and entered college with the specific purpose of finding someone there who would marry her. Emotionally shallow, but attractive and flirtatious, she attached herself to a shy, isolated premedical student who became infatuated with her, and eventually proposed. She left college before graduating in order to accompany her new husband to another city where he was to begin his medical education. Faced with a need to get a job and help support the two of them, she found that she had no skills to offer the working world. She answered advertisements for jobs such as that of receptionist, filing clerk, or restaurant hostess. She soon found that these positions required that she be punctual, helpful, and at least somewhat interested in what she was doing. But this was too much for her, and she resolved her occupational problem by becoming pregnant, in this way forcing her parents and her parents-in-law to supply all the support for her and her student husband. From her not well-to-do-family, she was able to extract a better apartment and, when the baby came, full-time help to take care of the infant. The tactics she used on the older generation were applied even more successfully to her husband. She insisted that upon graduation he go into practice as quickly as possible, rather than train for the specialty in which he was interested. She refused to have any more children, and spent her days shopping and in the company of friends with similar life styles.

She told me this in a tone of angry self-righteousness. She seemed genuinely oblivious to the needs and feelings of others and dealt with life as if it were a constant battle in which she had to seize by any means what the world would otherwise withhold from her. It was tempting for me to identify myself with what I imagined Mrs. Pearl's husband and child must be suffering and then to confront her critically with the implications of her "narcissism." I did not feel this way with Dr. Romberg; yet she, too, rode roughshod over anyone or anything that stood in her way.

THE ABSENCE OF FANTASY AND THE THREAT OF DISORGANIZATION

What made the difference between a Tina Pearl and an Esther Romberg was that the latter was able to take into consideration and deal with the existence and needs of other people—indeed, was hyperalert to their signals. Dr. Romberg had, at least on the cognitive level, decentered her self; Mrs. Pearl had not. Although Mrs. Pearl was not psychotic and had no confusion between self and others, object and subject, in terms of adapting to the environment, in personal relationships, she made no such meaningful differentiation. It was not that she was thoughtless; but, as with an infant, others' needs simply did not exist for her. Without such an awareness of a possible conflict between her wishes and those of other people, fantasy life, in the sense of a private preserve, never had a chance to develop. When subject to tension, all that Mrs. Pearl experienced was unbearable frustration and the need to eliminate it. Even minor disappointments would produce rage attacks, followed by depression if her temper tantrums did not have the desired results. Her sense of entitlement was, however, not in the interest of maintaining a defensively grandiose sense of self but was instead directed at holding together a fragile self system organized on a much more primitive level. Patients like Mrs. Pearl are trying to protect themselves not against the shame and humiliation of disappointment, but against an even more devastating fear of disorganization of the self system—against the experience Kohut (1971, 1977) called *fragmentation*. It is the clinging, grasping, desperate behavior produced by the fear of fragmentation that is the hallmark of what, when observed in adults, is often called *borderline behavior** (see also page 131).

In a patient like Mrs. Pearl, who had no capacity to sustain herself through fantasy, there is no buffer between the patient and what he or she perceives to be a hostile world. They lack what in biology is called the *self-righting tendency* (Waddington 1966; Fajardo 1988): that is, the ability to resist disruption in goal-seeking behavior— they lack resiliency. They are easily overstimulated or under-stimulated, and, once traumatized, do not seem to be able to mend the injury and recover. These patients have no way to deal with frustration, tension, disappointment, and pain, except to demand compliance from the world. And because, no matter how much they get, their sense of worthlessness and imminent self-fragmentation is so overweening, all they can do is demand more and more. Unlike the Esther Brindlings of this world, patients like Tina Pearl are not soothed by the therapist's effort at understanding them in the light of their self-development. On the contrary, words are ineffective. These patients feel they must have a merger with the therapist that eliminates the therapist as an individual, much as Mrs. Pearl had apparently been able to do with her husband.

But the fact that her husband's subordination to her needs did not make for a satisfying life for her, suggests that this strategy does not work either. It is small wonder that the therapist confronted by such a patient becomes anxious and wants to be anywhere but with that person—as, indeed, I periodically felt when working with Tina Pearl. Without being oblivious to how one feels about a Mrs. Pearl, one must keep in mind—in terms of the empathic viewpoint—that such a patient is doing only what we all must: namely, maintaining

*The diagnosis of borderline pathology was originally formulated to describe patients who defend themselves as best they can against a psychotic regression: that is, they are on the borderline of psychosis. But I believe there is another group of patients whose desperate but only marginally effective behavior makes us think of "borderline." These are people like Mrs. Pearl who seem in no danger of psychotic regression, however bizarre their behavior may sometimes be. Since the idea that one exists in relation to other selves seems to have no meaning for these patients, they are often confused with those suffering from the problems associated with the more developed narcissistic personality disorders.

"Borderline" also applies to a group of patients, often ones who have been sexually abused or physically brutalized as children, who resort to dissociation, a form of defensive withdrawal. The result is a type of fragmentation of the self system which, in its most severe form, leads to the formation of multiple personalities. Access to this psychopathology requires specialized techniques, and I have not dealt with these types of patients here.

a sense of self as best she might. Tina Pearl's basic sense of worth-lessness was apparently imparted to her early enough to create a significant arrest and/or deformation in the core sense of self, pre-cluding both the development of a reasonably stable, subjective sense of self and the ability to see herself as an individual in relation to others (Stern 1985). Like a little baby, all she could do was cry; and like a baby in severe distress, her crying was not plaintive, but angry.

Once the therapist realizes the terror of fragmentation which is chronic in such patients, their behavior becomes less threatening. The possibility of establishing a therapeutic relationship with them is enhanced if the therapist can find something to like in the patient: thus, from the beginning, I admired Mrs. Pearl's unmitigated gall and what it said about her determination to survive.

THERAPEUTIC FAILURE

With patients like Tina Pearl, one has to accept the fact that, for long periods of time, months and sometimes years, all the patient can tolerate is an echo of himself or herself: what Kohut (1977) has called *empathic immersion.* Eventually this may build enough of a structured self that the patient can take the next step and form a selfobject transference that will ultimately lend itself to interpreta-tion. The psychoanalyst Gerald Adler (1979, 1985) discusses an interesting group of impulse-ridden patients who are unable to re-create a mental image of the therapist's appearance, his words, or his office to sustain them between sessions. When, over time, they can be helped to do this, transference-directed insight therapy becomes possible with them.

I was not able to achieve this with Tina Pearl. I tried my best to avoid going beyond what she could tolerate (Kohut 1971, pp. 283–93). If she was distressed because a woman friend had not called when expected, I would limit myself to echoing, "It certainly sounds as if you are distressed because your friend did not call you as she had promised to do." This would calm her temporarily, but then we would shortly have to deal with another injury to her self-esteem. After several years of treatment, she told me that her daughter was running into school difficulties, and that she and her husband had been advised to seek psychotherapy for her. Mrs. Pearl was indignant at the recommendation and very angry at her husband for going along with the idea. Mrs. Pearl felt that it was the school's fault that her daughter had become a discipline problem. As tactfully as I could, I dared to disagree with her, hoping to save her child. Although she did arrange therapy for her daughter, Tina Pearl shortly thereafter decided that I was no longer being helpful to her, and discontinued treatment with me. Off and on, for the next few years, I heard that she had gone for brief periods to one or another therapist primarily to complain about me and how I had failed to understand her.

Although Mrs. Pearl's pathology was reminiscent of Jim Zurf's personality structure when he first came to see me, the latter's capacity for transmuting internalization of my selfobject functions made for a very different outcome. Mrs. Pearl's angry and desperate reaction to feeling misunderstood by me on that one occasion shows that our work together had not led to insight or transmuting internalization of function. At best it was temporarily supportive psychotherapy, strengthening her ability to function for the moment but leaving no increment of new structure in its wake.

Most of the patients who seek the services of a psychotherapist are suffering from the effects of interference with affective development on the basis of inadequate tension control, primal repression, or failed affect attunement. The last chapter of this book will be devoted to an examination of another type of patient—the psychoneurotic—who, though he or she has reached a high level of affective maturation, is brought to treatment by difficulties in the area of psychosexual development.

10

Psychoneurosis and Related Character Disorders

PSYCHOTHERAPY deals not only with patients who have suffered deficits and trauma during early maturation, but also with those patients who, in spite of having achieved satisfactory cognitive and affective decentering of the self system, are gripped by symptoms that often control and may threaten to destroy their lives. Such patients suffer from psychoneuroses or psychoneurotic character disorders.

So far, in respect to the developmental spiral, I have focused primarily on the aspects of competence and self-esteem associated with coping skills and psychological survival. The psychoneuroses involve the other broad area of competence—that related to reproductive behavior and the preservation of the species.

Psychosexual Development

Given the opportunity for contact with other human beings, the physical aspect of mating is usually not a problem for us. Our cognitive ability and flexibility let even sexually naïve partners negotiate the act of intercourse to a successful physical conclusion.* Very commonly, however, we do run into varying degrees of difficulty because of a psychological peculiarity built into our sexual development, one that is probably required by the need to develop and maintain an interest in sexuality during our long period of extrauterine maturation, so that when we finally reach puberty and reproductive viability, the requisite affective investment that will lead to sexual behavior will be present. Herman Roiphe and Eleanor Galenson (1902) and Johanna Tabin (1985) have reported that evidence of genital excitement is already present in the first year, and that pleasurable masturbatory behavior is normally observed in the second year of life. But in terms of other-directed psychological desire, two critical periods must be negotiated: one between three and six years of age; and another, at the time of puberty. Freud (1905), who first called attention to it, referred to this phenomenon as the *diphasic onset* of sexuality. It is during the first of these periods of sexual efflorescence, the oedipal phase of psychosexual development—when a child is sexually excited by the parent of the opposite sex and angry that the parent of the same sex stands in the way of this desire—that he or she is vulnerable to psychological trauma which may later eventuate in a neurosis.†

THE OEDIPAL PHASE

The oedipal phase of sexual development puts special strains on the self system by virtue of the fact that it comes at a time when

---

*There are occasional exceptions. Cases have been reported, for example, of couples who complained of infertility but were found to be performing anal intercourse, unaware that the vagina offers an opening for penile penetration.
†This scenario holds true for children raised in a Western culture where the relationship between the parents forms the nucleus of the family. In cultures where the powerful male or female of the family is someone other than the parent, the child's sexual interest may be directed differently.

the child is not yet prepared to deal with the sexual feelings that preoccupy him or her. At the beginning of this period, although the child is capable of imagination and, therefore, of symbolic thought, the latter is idiosyncratic and prelogical—thoughts and words still have magical power, and the child equates them with deeds: to wish something is to make it happen. Although the child is beginning to use the vocabulary of adults, the words do not necessarily have the same meaning. For example, "bad boy" may mean "naughty" to the parent, but the misbehaving little boy to whom it is addressed equates the term with permanent banishment. If the little boy who has misused a toy is punished by having it taken away, he may readily assume that his, to him, forbidden sexual fantasies will result in his penis being taken away—a fate that he assumes overtook his little sister or the neighbor girl whom he saw naked. Angry when disciplined for some misbehavior, he terrifies himself further with thoughts of revenge, a revenge he fears will really hurt the people he needs most in the world; and so on.

In the case of the little girl, there is the sense that something is missing which should be there. The unconscious belief as to why this is so can take various forms: good, powerful people, like mother, have a penis, but bad little girls who have played with their genitals had it taken away; there is something there that will grow; it was there originally but taken away as punishment and could be restored if she is worthy, and so on. Girls in the oedipal phase also often have the fantasy that instead of a penis the father will compensate them when they grow up by marrying them and giving them a baby (see also pages 300, 302–3).

The child's fantasies must be offset by the steady, reassuring, ameliorating influence of caregiving adults. Their verbal and affective communication moderates the excesses and confusions of the child's mental life during this time of transition between the learning of language and verbal skills and the eventual conceptual grasp of how the society in which the child lives is organized, how its systems of rewards and punishments actually operate. Parents have many opportunities to counteract a child's excessively exciting and frightening sexual fantasies with a more benign version of familial relationships.

Take, for example, a boy in the oedipal phase whose father is about to go on a business trip: "Mommy, do you like me better than Daddy?" "Of course I like you, dear, but that doesn't mean I don't like Daddy. I love you both." "Daddy was mad at you the other day." "Oh?" "When you weren't ready to go and he thought you'd be late to the party, he yelled at you." "Yes, well, you know Daddy, he always thinks we'll be late." "Are you mad at him?" "Sure, I get mad at Daddy when he irritates me, and he gets mad at me, too, sometimes, but that's life. We forget those little arguments very quickly. They don't mean anything."

"Daddy, if your plane crashes into the ground, then I'll be Daddy, won't I? Then I'll sleep with Mommy in the bed." "First of all, my plane is not going to crash. Secondly, boys don't marry their mommies. But I do hope you'll find someone as nice as your mother to marry when you grow up." "When I grow up I'm going to marry my friend Mike." "Boys don't marry boys. Boys marry girls, and girls marry boys." "How tall is God?" "Eight miles. Now here's my taxi. I've got to go or I'll miss my plane. Give me a kiss good-bye. See you in two days. Be a good boy. Help Mom."

SECONDARY REPRESSION

Ideally, with reasonable psychological support, psychosexual maturation proceeds beneath the surface right along with one's more visible affective and cognitive development. The oedipal phase comes to a close at about six to seven years of age with the child's capacity to manipulate concepts logically. One can now begin to do for oneself what one has heretofore needed one's parents to do: compensate for frightening fantasies with the knowledge gained from both direct and vicarious experience. More often than not, however, the incestuous and aggressive wishes of the oedipal phase are not simply eliminated but are defended against by secondary repression (page 124).

Repression (following Freud's [1915*b*] custom, I shall use *repression* interchangeably with *secondary repression* and *repression proper*) permits us to go on with our lives relatively free of the ambivalent struggle with incestuous wishes that occupied us during the oedipal years.

While forbidden sexual interests and wishes cannot be eradicated completely, their affect can be changed from pleasurable and positive to distressing and negative by an anxiety signal that is set off whenever these impulses strive for expression. This change in the affective import of ideas and memories constitutes the process of repression. It affects not only external behavior but also the intracerebral activity or behavior we call thought. It prevents forbidden fantasies or memories of actual childhood sexual experiences from attaining the symbolic representation, especially verbal expression, required for recall and consciousness. What is repressed cannot be thought, much less talked about. Without language and its capacity to form a network of meaningful associations between past, present, and future, it is difficult if not impossible to sustain the significance and vitality of any occurrence.

Repressed fantasies—that is, fantasies barred from association with words by the anxiety signal aroused whenever such a connection is attempted—do not participate in the ongoing development of the self system and lose a considerable portion of their efficacy. As a result, if all goes well and the repression is adequately maintained, the intense genital excitement attached to the parent of the opposite sex is attenuated and, after a period of relative sexual quiescence, referred to as the *latency period*, directed in adolescence to other people. This is not to say that the early fantasies ever completely disappear. On the contrary, as Freud found, oedipal longings persist in everyone's dreams and enter into everyone's eventual sexual choice. They need not, however, interfere with healthy maturation but, instead, can confer a desire and excitement on the sexual act that makes it one of the greatest pleasures we can experience. Not infrequently, however, this happy outcome fails to materialize.

If the parents, beset by unresolved problems from their own psychosexual development or for other reasons, are unable to maintain an understanding and helpful attitude toward the sexually assertive and competitive oedipal child, the latter finds it difficult successfully to repress and attenuate earlier sexual desires. The strong upsurge of affect attached to sexual feelings at a time when the still immature cognitive apparatus is poorly equipped to handle it promotes a conflict between what the child has been taught to expect of himself or herself and the relatively unmodified longing for the excitement of earlier days. This conflict is especially marked when the child has been sexually overstimulated or actually seduced early in life. Commonly, then, the oedipal phase ends in a conflict between prohibition and desire. This conflict may later be reactivated and escape from repression. The psychoneurotic symptom or character trait that may then form serves as a second line of defense against the forbidden impulses.

NEUROSIS

It was Freud who recognized that a neurotic symptom—whether in the form of an anxiety attack, a hysterical somatic conversion, a compulsive ritual, an obsessive thought, or a phobia—is always a symbolic representation of a forbidden incestuous wish that cannot be successfully contained. Neurotic symptoms tend to develop when an oedipally conflicted person—one for whom sexuality, or sexuality under certain conditions, always signifies incest—is faced with an upsurge of sexual demands. The stress can be an internal psychological one, such as the hormonal intensification of sexual desire at puberty, or an externally precipitated one, such as a proposal of marriage. The symptom then serves to remove the affected person from sexual temptation while at the same time expressing or acting out the forbidden sexual wish in a symbolic manner. A classic example from Freud's writing is the young woman brought by her mother for consultation because she suffered from convulsions. Freud observed the young woman in a seizure and recognized immediately that it was not organically caused, but was a dramatic enactment of sexual intercourse. Neither the patient nor her mother was aware of the significance of the patient's pelvic thrusts and ecstatic moaning during the "seizure." Her hysterical symptom indirectly satisfied the patient's wish to have sexual intercourse, while at the same time it punished her for that desire by invaliding her, tying her to her mother, and lessening the likelihood of her being able to form a heterosexual attachment.

From the viewpoint of practice, Freud's insights into the nature of psychoneurotic pathology and its manner of treatment are still valid today. Freud recognized that neurotic symptoms are so powerful because the fears behind them still exist in prelogical and preverbal form and cannot be dealt with rationally by the adult. To Freud, the obvious cure was, therefore, to bring these primitive fantasies and their origin into consciousness where they could be talked about as often as necessary until they could be laid to rest, much as one would resolve any other problem in daily life. What stood in the way of any such direct approach to the patient's difficulty was, of course, precisely the fact that the organization or structure of the fears and wishes in question had been arrested at a point where words and deeds were considered to be one and the same— the preoperational (Piaget 1969) level of thought. Therefore, any straightforward attempt on the part of a therapist to help a patient talk about the problem only increases the latter's anxiety and the defensive effort to keep what is hidden from reaching self-awareness.

Freud, letting himself be guided by his patients, learned from experience that if he minimized intellectualization and refrained from pressuring the patient to focus on the symptoms as such, and, instead, accepted whatever the patient had to say, then a relationship developed in which the patient would find reasons to reactivate old patterns of expectation and re-experience with the analyst (transfer) the unarticulated desires and fears that had led to symptom formation in the first place. He could then help the patient to recognize what was happening and to find the words needed to describe his or her reactions. In this way (in my scheme of things), inchoate affect is transformed into feeling and emotion, enabling the patient to think openly about what had heretofore been hidden. The analyst can now, as the parent had been unable to do, deal with the patient's thoughts in an accepting, understanding, and explanatory fashion. The patient is then able to work through earlier, forbidden, needs: that is, he or she may resolve them or once again repress them, but in the latter case with more chance of success than before. This change both alleviates the need for the neurotic symptom and gives the patient the chance to make adult decisions regarding the sexual and other previously conflicted aspects of his or her life.

The Analysis of a Psychoneurotic Man: O. W. Neubach

I had never spoken to him—his secretary had made his first appointment—but just from his name I imagined that Otto Waldemar Neubach would be an elderly, heavy-set German widower, with a plumbing business and a depression. So I was momentarily startled to find a slim, impeccably attired young man sitting in my waiting room. He looked up with a friendly smile and asked, "Dr. Basch?" pronouncing my name as only a German-speaking person is able to do. I greeted him, and he shook my hand vigorously, at the same time explaining by way of apology that he had just come back from Europe and had therefore not been able to call me personally to introduce himself and set up our first meeting. He spoke English fluently, but had a hint of accent—Germanic, but not quite.

I asked him to come into the consulting room and invited him to sit down. He paused midway between the door and the chair to exclaim over the view from my window, remarking how interesting it must be to follow the lake through the seasons; he then complimented me on my furniture, about which he made some discerning comments. I gave an acknowledging smile and made a "thank you" noise, and let it go at that. When he had settled himself, I simply looked at him expectantly. He began by saying how pleased he was that I must still speak German. He had looked me up in a directory of medical specialists and so knew I was born in Berlin, but he had no idea about how old I was when I came to the United States, or whether German had been my first language. He clearly expected some reply from me and, when none was forthcoming, added that he had come to his conclusion regarding my fluency in German when he heard me pronounce his name, which, he added, "like yours, is subject to most peculiar distortions by the English-speaking tongue." As I still made no attempt to pick up on this conversational gambit, he, for the first time, looked uncomfortable. "Is there anything you want me to say?" he inquired. Before I could have replied, he added, "Of course, you need to know who I am and why I am here, right?" I said, "Please go ahead."

It is often striking how much information is conveyed by a prospective patient's appearance, general demeanor, tone of voice, and choice of expression. It is no big trick to hear depression in the way a Dr. Osgood sounds on the telephone; to postulate just from the appearance of a fellow like Bob Granger that he is probably at odds with his parents; to sense the envious despair behind the angry outburst of an Al Gertz; or to see the need for attachment in an Esther Romberg's fulsome praise. Paradoxically, Otto Neubach gave me a sense of what might be troubling him in those first few seconds of our initial greeting precisely *because* his behavior and appearance gave no hint that he was at all troubled. Nor did I detect any false notes as we went through the introductory process prior to settling down for the initial interview. He demonstrated friendly, competent, adaptive behavior and positively radiated charm, tact, and a healthy self-esteem. This, I thought to myself, might be the answer to an analyst's prayer—an honest-to-goodness neurotic. If I was correct, it would mean that the main defense to be dealt with would be repression (secondary repression); and that, in turn, calls for a particular therapeutic stance.

ANALYTIC RESERVE

From the moment I met Mr. Neubach, I maintained a reserve I did not show with the other patients I have discussed. Indeed, as in the previous cases I have described, I can be far from taciturn. With many patients, right from the start, with a view to potentiating a therapeutic relationship, I do not hesitate to do most of the talking. I may actively help patients to organize their ideas and mobilize their affects, and often go to great lengths to explain what I think is happening and what it might mean. Now, suddenly, I became a turtle. Mr. Neubach reached out to me, and I withdrew into my shell.

It was not that I was unfriendly or disliked this young man; on the contrary, I found him to be most congenial and had to restrain my impulse to respond in a sociable manner to his overtures. This change in attitude calls attention to an important issue: namely, that though there is nothing inherently unfriendly in the therapist-patient relationship, the therapist's function is not to befriend the patient, but to do everything possible to restore and/or promote the healthy organizing function of the patient's self system. I did not reach out to Jim Zurf week after week, month after month, to show him I was his friend but to enable him to have another chance to develop a capacity for tolerating affective transactions and thus, in turn, to rework other aspects of his arrested growth process. If, as I suspected, Mr. Neubach suffered from a psychoneurosis, then he was not in need of someone who could help him to organize his self system and to use it productively; he would already be doing a good job of that.

As Freud taught, and as the experience of psychoanalysts has since repeatedly confirmed, the psychoneurotic is suffering from an intrapsychic sexual conflict: that is, he or she is caught between the need both to gratify and to sublimate an incestuous wish. Much of what a therapist says to such a patient must be assumed to have a dual meaning: one meaning given to it by the goal-directed activity of a basically healthy, mature self; the other reflecting some neurotic need that the patient is trying to meet indirectly.

In an ancient joke about the profession, two analysts pass each other on the street: one says, "Good morning," and his colleague thinks to himself, "I wonder what he meant by that." Outside of the therapeutic situation the concern with possible hidden meanings behind the most superficial interchange is, of course, ridiculous; and this joke is an effective jab at parlor psychiatry. And even with most patients in the therapeutic situation, it is often a serious mistake not to accept communications at face value. "I love you" should not be automatically translated into "he hates me." Although I had no idea what the import of Mr. Neubach's questions might be, I did have an inkling about his possible pathology. Therefore, his indirectly asking me to tell him more about my birth and origins, my feeling about and for the German language, and my aesthetic proclivities, as reflected in my office furnishings, made me think not, "I wonder what he means by that" (there is no point in wondering what repressed material may mean until that meaning reveals itself in the ongoing analytic process), but rather, "Some day we'll figure out why he wants to know that." And so as not to place unnecessary obstacles in the way of that desired result, I chose not to answer him.

The other technical effect of analytic reserve is that it gives what is hidden a better opportunity to reveal itself. I went to great lengths to help the other patients I have discussed to control their anxiety lest it interfere with our relationship and their being able to use my help. With neurotic patients, however, it is necessary to use one's technique to generate anxiety sufficient to "undermine" a patient's defensive maneuvers and bring the underlying material to the surface. Since, in such cases, the relative anonymity and reclusiveness of the analyst render ineffective the socially adaptive but at the same time defensive measures of the self system, it is more likely that the warded-off fantasies that are deemed to be asocial and guilt-provoking will emerge in some fashion.

As I evaded his attempts to bring me into his orbit, Mr. Neubach did become mildly anxious: the patient's ability to handle reasonable amounts of anxiety is an important criterion for undertaking an analysis. I noted approvingly how effectively he brought that anxiety under control when he sensibly answered his own question as to what I might want him to tell me—obviously, who he was and why he was coming to see me.

THE PATIENT'S PRESENTING COMPLAINT

Mr. Neubach now went on to tell me that he was an electrical engineer and a partner in a computer manufacturing company. He had been spending much of his time abroad, selling and installing his firm's products. In the past year or so, he had noticed that, whenever he had to make a presentation to his partners and their executive staff, he found himself unaccountably anxious. His hands trembled, sweat soaked his shirt, and he was sure that his voice came out in a high-pitched quaver. Yet no one else seemed to react to him differently; and when he asked his secretary, who accompanied him to the meetings, whether she had noticed anything untoward about his performance, she told him that she had not.

As far as he knew, he had no reason to be anxious; his work had been going very well, and his personal life was untroubled. He had hoped that, during an upcoming trip to Europe, away from his home office, his malady would have a chance to disappear as mysteriously as it had come; but, just in case it did not, he investigated the possibility of getting some treatment for what he assumed must be an emotional disorder. He then read about various methods of therapy and made some circumspect inquiries among his friends who had had psychological treatment of one sort or another. Since psychoanalysis made the most sense to him and also seemed to address problems like his, he decided that, if it became necessary, that was the avenue he would explore first. My name surfaced on several occasions, and he took the trouble to look up my credentials and to talk further to several people about me. He decided that if he did not get better he would come to see me after his European trip.

His presentations on the continent went well, he had no symptoms, and he thought that whatever was responsible for his nervousness in the previous months had indeed cleared up by itself. However, two weeks before his return, he found himself once again unaccountably anxious, and now not just in meetings but unpredictably throughout the day. He had difficulty sleeping; and when he finally did doze off, he had terrifying dreams whose content he did not remember upon waking, but which left him with the feeling of having been pursued. At that point, he called his secretary and told her to get in touch with me to arrange a consultation for him as soon as possible after his return. When she let him know that she had done so, his anxiety diminished and he was able to sleep better.

INITIATING THE ANALYSIS

Having told me this much, he paused and asked me if I thought he was doing the right thing to come here. I said it certainly sounded that way. "Will you work with me?" he asked, and then added, "Do you have time for an analysis? I know you must be very busy."

I said that, from what I had heard so far, I would agree that psychoanalysis was the treatment of choice, that this involved four visits per week for an indefinite period of time, and that the treatment should proceed with a minimum of interruptions. I wondered whether his schedule would permit him to make such a commitment. He asked when I took my vacations and how long they were. I told him, and he said that he no longer had to be out of town for lengthy periods. If I could give him four appointments at the beginning of the week, he would plan to start out-of-town travel on Thursday afternoons. His European trips could be arranged in conjunction with my vacation periods in such a way that he would only lose a week or two during the year. Of course, he volunteered, if and when that happened, he would pay for the appointments he missed.

I then told him what my fees were and the times I had available, and we settled on a mutually agreeable schedule.

Throughout this initial interview, Mr. Neubach demonstrated that his concept of self was appropriately decentered. He could remain aware of his needs without neglecting or negating what he accurately perceived were mine. In other words, he showed the empathic understanding indicative of the affective maturity that one typically finds in the neurotic patient.

MR. NEUBACH: Do you have any questions you want to ask me?

ANALYST: No, I don't.

MR. NEUBACH: What do we do now?

ANALYST: Try to say everything that comes into your mind— everything that you think and feel. Continue to be as open and straightforward about yourself as you have been so far.

MR. NEUBACH: What if my thoughts are technical ones, facts about my business?

ANALYST: In our work, there are no exceptions. Whatever thoughts and feelings come to your mind should be said, and we will then follow wherever they lead. If you were unilaterally to pick and choose what to say, eliminating this or that for whatever reasons may occur to you—it's repetitious, it's boring, it's private information about other people, and I can think of a million other rationalizations for dismissing thoughts—then our work would inevitably be compromised for a shorter or longer period of time. Whatever help I can give you is dependent on your cooperation in letting me know whatever is going on inside your head at any given moment.

MR. NEUBACH: Just like it says in the book.

ANALYST: Just like that.

MR. NEUBACH: Should I lie on the couch?

ANALYST: Whenever you are ready to do that, yes.

MR. NEUBACH: All right, I'll try it. I might as well get started. [*He walked to the couch, took off his jacket, hung it over a chair, and lay down.*]

Undertaking an analysis is a serious commitment for both therapist and patient. Was I too quick to start an analysis with Otto Neubach? After all, I knew hardly any details about his past and present life: Did he have brothers or sisters? Was he married? Had he ever had sexual intercourse? Had he accidentally killed a playmate in a game of cowboys and Indians? Did he have a foot fetish? I also knew that none of these or a million other details I might gather over dozens of interviews would matter one iota in the decision whether to analyze. Even if I had obtained relevant clues to what interfered with his development by taking a detailed history at the outset, any such history, no matter how extensive, would not allow me to ascertain how these experiences came together and predisposed him to the anxiety that brought him for treatment. I knew that not only were the "facts" I needed in order to understand the meaning of Mr. Neubach's anxiety hidden from view, but that they would remain hidden until bit by bit they became available for study as he eventually, in the transference, reactivated those hopes, wishes, and fears that had at one time threatened the organization of the self system and, therefore, had been eliminated from further consideration by repression.

In cases like this, I hold to Freud's dictum that the only test of psychoanalysis is a trial of psychoanalysis. It is much more informative to have the details of the patient's history emerge in the context of the analysis than to elicit them by direct questioning, for how and when they surface spontaneously gives the analyst invaluable clues about their significance for the patient. For instance, the patient who comments on his having seen a man, whom he assumes to be a new patient, leave my office just before his appointment, and then later in the hour or the next day wonders if he has ever mentioned that he had been told that he had an older brother who died before he was born, has said a great deal more than if this information came out in a routine family history taken during his initial visits. Indeed, when supervising psychoanalytic candidates whose cases are assigned only after a thorough history has been taken by members of the clinic staff, I have observed so often as no longer to be surprised how, unconsciously, those patients manage to leave out or distort the aspects of their past lives that would bring them too close to the source of their difficulties. What the candidate and I really need to know comes out only in the process of the analysis.

While Otto Neubach was telling me the story of the onset of his difficulties, I became increasingly convinced that the anxiety he was experiencing was indeed being generated by a neurotic conflict. I came to that conclusion when I saw that his affective and cognitive maturation seemed to be unusually successful, that he gave no evidence of having overt problems in his daily life, and voiced no complaints about his relationships that might account for his anxiety. I decided, therefore, that, in all likelihood, anything short of psychoanalysis would fail to unearth and help him with his symptoms. I was prepared to spend several more sessions with the patient both to hear more about his past and present circumstances and to present the advisability of an analysis to him for his consideration. When, however, he himself volunteered his readiness and need for psychoanalytic treatment, I had no hesitation about accepting him. It was my impression that this man would have seen any equivocation on my part at that point, no matter how well meant or carefully explained, as my reluctance to treat him, because I either rejected him as a person or had some doubt whether I could deal with him appropriately.

There are, of course, situations where either the presenting problem, the patient's capacity for introspection and tolerance for anxiety, and/or the patient's commitment to the process and its demands on time and money, and, above all, to the emotional investment, are questionable. Under such conditions, one proceeds more slowly before suggesting, much less starting, an analytic process.

A patient may start on the couch and find it too much to tolerate. I have had patients who were either overstimulated or paralyzed by the regression resulting from the recumbent position and the absence of the analyst's facial expressions. No permanent damage has ever followed. I suggest that such a patient sit up, and we talk about the problems that have arisen from the attempt to use the couch.

Occasionally, then or later, such patients try the couch again, and it works out. More often, we continue our work face to face.

In the first four or five analytic sessions, Otto Neubach told me about himself and his family background. He stemmed from a family of wealthy manufacturers in the northern part of Germany. His grandfather, Waldemar, the founder of the firm, served as an officer in a Prussian regiment during the First World War and died a hero's death on the Russian front. His grandmother never recovered from the loss and led a hypochondriacal, bedridden existence. The patient's father, Eberhard Neubach, was raised by a man he called Uncle Otto. "Uncle Otto" was not actually a blood relative but the executive vice president of the family business, and a close friend. There never was any question but that Eberhard, like his father before him, would become an engineer and eventually take over the presidency of the firm. A year after taking the helm, Eberhard wooed and won a renowned beauty, the only child and heiress of a wealthy family in their social and business circle.

In 1934, Eberhard was in South America on business when he received a cryptic telegram from Uncle Otto saying that he must come immediately and directly to London for a business meeting with representatives of a certain English company. Since no such meeting had ever been planned, it was clear that something untoward had happened that precluded Eberhard's return to Germany, and in those times that usually spelled "Hitler."

The patient's father hastened to England and was met by Uncle Otto, who said that he had been tipped off by a former employee, a man now high in the hierarchy of the Nazi regime, that, because his wife was of partial Jewish ancestry, Eberhard was on the list of those who would soon have their property expropriated under the racial purity laws. The Nazi official advised Uncle Otto that Eberhard Neubach should immediately divorce his wife if he wished to escape the fate planned for him. Eberhard indignantly rejected this suggestion, a decision that Uncle Otto had anticipated and for which he had begun to plan.

In order to avoid being called in for questioning, Eberhard Neubach returned to South America and continued to conduct the business that had originally brought him there. His wife "went on vacation" to Paris and eventually was able to join him. On his return to Germany, Uncle Otto liquidated as much of the business as could safely be done and, under various guises, placed the money obtained in foreign banks. In the next twelve months, other members of the Neubach family, Uncle Otto and his wife, and the families of several other trusted managers who had been let in on the plan, also left their homeland and joined the exiles in South America.

This small band now did its best to re-create in its new surroundings what had been left behind. With the funds Uncle Otto's foresight had made available to them, they bought a ranch which they ran with native help, and on whose grounds they constructed several houses, one for each of the families that had fled. This replicated the circumstances under which they had lived in Germany. Eberhard and Uncle Otto began to look for possible business opportunities in the new country and soon founded a construction company which within a few years promised to become every bit as successful as the old business had been.

Otto, my patient, was born in 1938, the first and, as it turned out, the only child of his parents. He was named Otto in honor of both his father's one-time guardian and Otto von Bismarck, the Iron Chancellor, a man whose memory was revered in the family as the founder of modern Germany. Some of my patient's early memories were of being taken into the *Ahnen Galerie,* a long hall in which were hung oil paintings of his paternal ancestors. There he was told the story of the family's former glory, to which was added the confident expectation that when, God willing, the band of criminals who had wrested power from Germany's legitimate ruling class would be deposed, they would return to reclaim their rightful place. To that end, his parents and the families accompanying them had established a government-in-exile, so to speak. They spoke German among themselves and used the native language only when necessary to communicate with outsiders. The main meal of the day was taken communally with the adult members of the four or five families gathered in the main house, and the protocol of former years was strictly observed. Although not formally associated with a church, prayers were said at mealtime by the male elders. Uncle Otto, when it was his turn, always managed to put in a few words suggesting to the Almighty that He might wish to consider restoring the monarchy to Germany.

My patient experienced his environment as warm and protective, his mother as kind and loving, his father as more strict but fair. Uncle Otto was called "Uncle Opa," *Opa* being the affectionate term for grandfather. Around the little boy was German music; he was read to from German children's books; and wherever he turned, he heard talk of the good old days and the restoration of order and civility that would surely come in the not-too-distant future. For playmates he had the sons and daughters of the household servants; the children of the other families were already adolescent and were either away at school or else did not have much to do with him.

In 1940, close to his third birthday, the native maid who had acted as his nurse was given other duties; and, so that he might learn French as his second language, the nineteen-year-old daughter of a refugee French family who had settled near them was engaged to be his nanny. From his playmates and the servants he was, of course, picking up a good knowledge of the native Spanish dialect. My patient-to-be was a happy, contented little boy. Raised very much as his father and grandfather had been raised before him, he took for granted the privileges his origin conferred upon him, and accepted as a matter of course the future obligations to state and family that accompanied his birthright.

This idyllic existence was shattered when he was between five and six years old. His mother and father had a serious automobile accident while being driven to the capital city to attend a yearly week-long reception and gala given by the country's president. His father was only badly bruised, but his mother was severely injured and suffered extensive burns and broken limbs. She remained in a hospital in the capital city for half a year. Her progress was unsatisfactory; she remained bedridden and developed lung and liver abscesses. It was clear that she would never recover, and she requested that she be brought home to live out with her family whatever time remained to her.

My patient did not recall how he felt during his mother's absence, but he remembered vividly the changed atmosphere of the home when his mother returned from the hospital. Everyone was expected to walk on tiptoes, voices were hushed, and it seemed as if the only topic of conversation, day in and day out, focused on the invalid's state: what was her color today; what had she eaten; had she slept, and if so, for how long; did she seem a little stronger today; what did the doctor have to say on his last visit, and so on. His mother called Otto to her bedside as often as her strength permitted. She talked to him about his activities, his studies with the tutor who had been engaged to begin his education; and occasionally she was able to read to him or play the simple card and board games they used to enjoy. When she realized that she could not go on much longer, she spoke seriously to little Otto about her impending death and the sorrow she felt at having to leave him. He remembers crying because of her serious tone and her sad face, but not really comprehending what she was saying. He was able to acknowledge the full extent of his loss only much later when he read again and again the letter she had left for him to read when he reached adolescence. In it she said goodbye to the boy she would never see, but who could now better understand her parting words. At that time he cried bitterly and felt the pain of her absence much more than he had been able to do at the time of her actual demise.

What was much more dramatic and frightening for him at the time of his mother's death was the transformation in his father. This man who had radiated authority and self-confidence now collapsed in his grief. Eberhard isolated himself in his quarters, refused to eat most days, left all decisions to the aging Uncle Otto, and lost interest in everything around him, including his son. Eventually he was taken to a sanatorium run by an order of Catholic nuns, where he stayed for several months. Apparently he received some form of psychotherapeutic assistance and recovered sufficiently to resume his place at the head of the family and his business. Caught up in the daily activities of his ever-expanding enterprises, and his spirits bolstered by the defeat of the Nazis, which opened the possibility for a return to his homeland, he became again much more like his former self, or so it seemed to my patient. Otto, aged seven at that time, was placed in an English school in a nearby town where he was boarded with the family of the headmaster during the week, returning to the ranch on weekends and holidays. His nanny, who had been the adult closest to him throughout the two years of turmoil in the family, became his father's secretary, and so was able to maintain contact with the boy.

Otto remembers his years in the English school as happy and exciting ones. His already trilingual brain easily overcame the handicap of knowing no English when he first entered his new surroundings. For the first time, he had playmates with backgrounds similar to his own, and he readily fell in with their activities. His father, true to the plan formulated years before, instituted proceedings to reclaim the family properties in Germany and, after some years, succeeded in doing so. This triumph was tempered by the fact that Uncle Otto died shortly after the news of this accomplishment reached them, and never again saw his beloved country free of the Nazi incubus. In due time, the now sizable South American holdings were sold so that the money could be used to rebuild the German factories that had been severely damaged by Allied bombings. It was decided that, owing to postwar conditions in Germany, Otto, then twelve years old, should be sent to either Switzerland or the United States to continue his education. Since it was assumed by all and accepted by Otto that he would become an engineer and follow the footsteps of his forebears, and since at the time the United States afforded the best training in this area, he was enrolled in a prestigious Eastern preparatory school. Prior to their return, Eberhard married his secretary, Otto's former nanny, and brought her to Germany as his wife.

Otto's life progressed uneventfully. He spent the long summer holidays and the Christmas vacations with his family in Germany, and completed high school and undergraduate studies in mechanical engineering in the United States. It was expected that he would now return to the family's machinery business with a view eventually to succeeding his father. Otto, however, had different ideas. He had become fascinated with electronics and computers and asked for further support to undertake graduate studies in that area—a plan to which his father, not unaware of the future importance this field would have for all businesses, agreed.

Otto met two likeminded young men in graduate school, and the three spent many hours fantasizing about how they might win fame and fortune by improving the state of the art. Their daydreams began to take on reality when Otto hit upon an ingenious idea that promised to simplify the manufacture while increasing the capacity of a particular computer component. He and his two fellow students decided to apply for a patent and go into business for themselves. Otto went to his father to seek financing for this venture. Somewhat reluctantly, his father agreed, looking at his son's plans more as a youthful fling than as a serious enterprise. In return for his investment, Eberhard exacted a promise that if Otto's idea did not pan out he would devote himself to expanding the fledgling subsidiary of the family business that had been set up in North America. But Otto and his partners succeeded beyond their wildest dreams. They found themselves in the forefront of a rapidly expanding new industry and took full advantage of their opportunity. Within a few years, instead of working for his family, Otto enlisted his father's help in founding European subsidiaries for the manufacture and distribution of his own very successful product.

What Otto Neubach told me about his family circumstances and upbringing further confirmed my belief that his anxiety originated in a neurotic conflict. Patients with a psychoneurosis tend to come from stable backgrounds that are neither confused nor confusing. Their families are embedded in a social milieu in which their place is clear, and where the obligations and privileges of each person and each one's relationship to the larger whole are unambiguously spelled out. Their parents' sense of identity and purpose provides an ambience in which a child's early affective and cognitive development can proceed unhampered. In such an environment, a child is neither a burden on an already overtaxed relationship nor in the position of being overburdened by parents who depend on him or her to define themselves. In this sort of atmosphere, the maturation and eventual decentering of the self can proceed relatively smoothly—as certainly seemed to be true of my patient. What Mr. Neubach did not tell me about his past life was also suggestive; that is, he made no mention of his present or past sexual relationships or lack thereof. I sat back and waited for matters to unfold.

The patient fell easily into a pattern of recounting for me what had happened to him in his life between sessions. In the context of these recitals, he filled me in on details of his past he had not previously mentioned. I learned that he had never been married; that he had close friends, both male and female; that there was another group of women whom he dated with whom he had sexual intercourse. He did not go into great detail about his relationships because most on his mind was the fear that his anxieties at work would recur. As I expected, based on the relief he experienced from just knowing his secretary had obtained an appointment with me, he found that he functioned very well in the sorts of meetings that had previously triggered his anxiety states. He was full of praise for me and for psychoanalysis.

I thought of him as being in a positive idealizing father transference, drawing strength from his association with me, just as in childhood the presence of the parent banishes the fear of the dark. There was no need to say anything about this transference. As Freud (1913; 1916–17, p. 443) said, as long as the transference is the ally of the analytic process—that is, is stimulating the patient's associations—one leaves it to run its course, and does not interrupt. This is not always easy to do, especially for a beginning therapist. While therapists know that one must tolerate and work with the negative feelings a patient may direct toward one, even though one has not given the patient cause for them, it is often more difficult to learn to restrain oneself from fending off patients' strong positive emotions one feels are undeserved. There is the temptation to be self-effacing and appropriately modest; to introduce reality, and thereby protect oneself from the patient's disappointment when, inevitably, he or she comes to know the therapist's shortcomings (see also pages 244–45).

Another neurotic patient of mine once bemoaned the fact that he had wasted a good deal of time playing cards in his college years, and contrasted that with what he assumed must have been my undeviating devotion to my studies. I interjected, with the intention of showing him that we were not so different and that he need not be so hard on himself, that I knew very well how tempting it was to while away the hours at the card table and had had much the same experience as he when I was a student. Indignantly, he took me to task for this intrusion of my reality. "What does that have to do with me?" he asked. "I need you not to have played cards at college." He was quite right.

During the first months of Otto Neubach's analysis, I said little, except to ask here and there for clarification when I lacked the necessary factual knowledge or circumstantial background to understand what he was telling me. When he realized that I really meant what I said—namely, that he should give his mind free rein and say everything that occurred to him—he told me a great deal about his business activities. He was obviously proud of what he had accomplished, and enjoyed my interest in his achievements. In about the third month of his treatment, he began to make seemingly innocuous observations about the building in which my office was situated. At first, he would comment positively on such things as the architecture and decor of a building like mine, one built in the 1920s. Gradually this changed to a feeling that the building was not safe. One of the elevators made a funny noise: what if it failed? I had only one exit from my office: what if there was a fire and I was trapped? This led him to associate to the ultramodern building to which his company had just moved and the luxurious suite he occupied. Shortly thereafter, upon entering my office, he looked at a picture on my wall and asked whether it was new. I said nothing. He lay down and went into his customary recital of the events of the previous day, but this led nowhere and soon he ran out of anything to say.

ANALYST: You took note of the picture when you came in.

MR. NEUBACH: I just can't remember having seen it before.

ANALYST: Yes?

MR. NEUBACH: [*In an irritated tone very unusual for him*] Yes, nothing.

ANALYST: You sound irritated.

MR. NEUBACH: I'm sorry, I didn't mean to offend you.

ANALYST: What are your thoughts about my picture?

MR. NEUBACH: It's just not my taste.

ANALYST: You don't like it.

MR. NEUBACH: I'm not claiming to be an expert.

ANALYST: But you don't like it.

MR. NEUBACH: It is sort of nondescript. This isn't any of my business. How did we get into this anyhow?

ANALYST: How did you? Why do you think you might have seen this picture for the first time today?

MR. NEUBACH: I'm buying the art for the new offices, maybe that's it.

ANALYST: You hadn't mentioned that before.

MR. NEUBACH: I guess I forgot. When I leave here today I'm commissioning some paintings for the reception area. That's probably why I noticed your painting. It's perfectly natural.

ANALYST: But anxiety provoking for some reason.

MR. NEUBACH: Oh, damn! I just remembered I forgot something else today—your check. [*Silence.*]

ANALYST: Yes, say what you're thinking.

MR. NEUBACH: It's positively indecent. Just as I was writing it out yesterday, I got the word that they had made a mistake on figuring our bonus. It is even bigger than I thought it would be. It went through my head that the extra amount I'll be getting is more than I will pay you in a year.

ANALYST: And so this is the best painting that I can afford.

MR. NEUBACH: It's ridiculous. I'm looking to you for help, why should I have so much more?

ANALYST: It made you anxious. Perhaps you fear that I will resent your success.

MR. NEUBACH: For all I know, maybe you're rolling in money and are laughing at me. A friend of mine is in treatment with an analyst in California who must own half of Los Angeles. He doesn't need to work, he just wants to.

From this point on, the patient became increasingly concerned with whether he was diminishing me through his achievements. This preoccupation, however, did not affect his actual functioning in his business, where he continued to be anxiety-free and highly productive. Sometime later, when I was a few minutes late for one of his appointments, he speculated whether I gave extra time to the woman patient who preceded him, and liked her better. As he talked about this, his voice was not angry but, rather, had a wistful, longing quality. I suggested this meant that he wished he could change places with her; that if he were a woman, and not a successful young male rival, he would be no threat to me and I would want to spend more time with him.

I wish to emphasize that I was interpreting the affect in the transference and not the content of his associations per se. Mr. Neubach had made comments before about other patients, including the one he was talking about now: he wondered whether I liked one better than another, whether a pretty woman was more interesting to me than he was, or whether I was put off by a scruffy-looking man in my waiting room, and so on. But none of these comments called for a response from me except to urge him to follow his thoughts wherever they led. What made an interpretation both called for and possible here was that, in the transference, he was re-experiencing something from the past, with the original affect now attached to the person of the analyst.

In this instance what I said, to the surprise of the patient, caused him to become tearful and to recall poignant memories from the time after his mother's death when his father was withdrawn and eventually hospitalized. The patient himself made the connection between his wish to be with his father, to have his father back, and hearing the other adults talking about the sisters—that is, the Catholic nuns—with whom his father was now living. Maybe he thought that if he were a girl—that is, a sister—he would be reunited with his dad. This conjecture seemed to me a not unlikely possibility.

His company was going public, and he wondered aloud whether I would become a member of his board of directors; alternatively, he played with the idea of assigning a large block of stock to me, or perhaps he would give the bulk of his money to a psychoanalytic institute of which I would become the director. He was clearly uncomfortable with his ever-increasing success and the wealth that went with it. I pointed out to him that he was behaving as if his growth were taking something away from me: that we were on a teeter-totter—if he was up, I was down.

What we reconstructed was that Mr. Neubach was reliving in his relationship to me the interruption of his psychosexual development in the oedipal phase, a time during which his mother had been ill and died, followed by his father's withdrawal into depression. The patient seemed to have been much more affected by his father's collapse than by his mother's demise. In the absence of his father's presence and interest in his burgeoning competitiveness and masculinity, the little boy apparently felt frightened by the changes in himself. It was probable that the fear that his success and increasing wealth would lead me to resent him represented a belief that he was somehow responsible for his father's regression. He behaved as if there was room for only one man in the family; and in that case, he would gladly retreat if that was what it took to restore his father's strength. In terms of his psychosexual development, Mr. Neubach was in what is called a *negative oedipal phase.* Frightened that his competitiveness had harmed his father, he offered to sacrifice himself.

THE TRANSFERENCE OF THE NEUROSIS INTO THE ANALYTIC SITUATION

Mr. Neubach now found himself preoccupied with thoughts of me and my childhood. Once again, the question of my background and when I came to the United States occupied him. He pressed me hard on what sort of childhood I had had, what my parents were like, and other such issues. I focused both on the urgency behind his questions and on the fact that they were coming up at a time when his relationship to his father during those crucial years after his mother's death was in the forefront of the analysis.

He could, of course, easily have found out what he wanted to know about me. Running a sophisticated company, he was no stranger to how one obtains a background check on prospective employees. That, plus friends he had who were directly or indirectly involved in psychoanalysis or associated professions, could probably have given him more information about me than I remembered about myself. But he did not do this. What mattered to him was that I tell him, and in telling him give him something he needed to know that went far beyond the facts. We got closer to what was troubling him when he casually mentioned that he might have to miss a session with me in order to cover an out-of-town appointment for which one of his partners, who was Jewish, had scheduled himself without realizing at the time that it fell on one of the High Holidays. "Unless," he said, "you're not going to be here either." I remained silent. "I can't remember if you took off for the Jewish High Holidays last year," he added. I said nothing. Irritated, he now began to argue with me. After all, this question had nothing to do with analysis; it was just a matter of logistics. He simply needed information to make plans, and so on. I still made no comment. Angrily, he said, "If you don't tell me, how do I know that you won't charge me for the appointment, even though we're both not here?" Quickly he added, "I'm sorry I said that. I apologize." I made no reply, and he then remained silent for some minutes. Suddenly he sat up. He was very pale. He did not look at me but said, in a very stilted manner and in an unaccustomedly heavily accented English, "I've just thought of something I cannot possibly tell you. Excuse me please." He stood up, seemed a little unsteady, took a second to catch his balance, and left the room.

He missed the next two appointments without notifying me, something that had never happened before. I made no move to call him. In this instance, Mr. Neubach's behavior offers a dramatic example of the principle that the analyst must not be tempted into disrupting a transference neurosis with socially appropriate concern in a misguided attempt to help the patient. The missed appointments were as much part of the analysis as any verbal associations he might make; and, as with the latter, I waited to see what would happen rather than interfere with the process that was unfolding. (This approach would be contraindicated in a patient whose primary difficulties were the result of failures of early affect attunement or other attachment problems. In such cases, I often call the patient to find out what is happening; not infrequently, as I did with Jim Zurf [chapter 7], I offer alternate appointments or pursue the issue then and there on the telephone.)

On the third day, Mr. Neubach came in and, instead of going to the couch, sat down on the chair across from me. He said that he had entertained the idea of just not coming back, but had decided that would be insulting and cowardly. Rather than run away, his honor demanded that he come back, tell me what he had to say, face to face, so that I would be the one to end the analysis rather than he. I looked at him expectantly. Steeling himself as if for a blow, he said that last time he had not finished his thought. When he accused me of planning to charge him unjustifiably, he had thought but could not say, "which would be a typically Jewish thing to do." He paused, turned his head slightly to the side, and said, "You have every right and reason to slap me." I said, "Why don't you lie down and tell me about this?" Tears formed in his eyes, and he lay down. When he was able to speak, his thoughts went in two directions. One dealt with his horror at finding himself having an anti-Semitic thought, something that linked him to the very Nazi rabble his family so despised. Where it came from he had no idea; but since it was his thought, he bore the responsibility for it and was prepared to be punished. He took himself to task for having such suspicions about me when I had been so helpful, patient, and good to him. I wondered to myself whether something about his mother, who had had a Jewish grandmother, was coming up, but there was no evidence for that notion in his associations.

The other aspect of Jewishness that he came to talk about was something he had wondered about off and on for a long time. How could the Jews of Germany have let themselves be led to the slaughter? Why didn't they either flee or fight? Why couldn't they have done what his family did? Once again, it would have made no sense analytically to introduce reality by explaining to him the vast difference between his privileged family and the situation of the average Jew in Germany during Hitler's time. Instead, I suggested to him that his initial wish to know about my background when he first entered analysis was symbolic of his fear that, like his father, I was not really strong—self-possessed on the outside and vulnerable on the inside. Initially idealizing me, as he had his father, he was now convinced that, like his father, I would ultimately also fail him when he became assertive and competitive. What he needed, but thought he could not have, was a strong father who could stand with him, encouraging him in his assertiveness instead of being damaged by it.

This theme recurred in various ways throughout the next few months. For example, although always well dressed, he came in one day in an especially elegant suit. He said nothing about it, but at the end of the hour, as he was getting up from the couch and putting his jacket back on, he commented that a button on his sleeve was open. He rebuttoned it and left. There was something awkward and forced about this; and the next day I asked him if he, too, had noticed something out of the ordinary at the end of the session. He acknowledged that he had. He had been diffident about telling me that he was now buying his suits from a bespoke tailor in London.

He wanted me to admire his new clothes, but feared I would resent being presented with one more sign of his affluence. When he paused to button his sleeve, he became aware that he thereby was calling attention to the quality of his jacket, for on domestically tailored men's suits the decorative sleeve buttons are simply sewed on. He then recalled that he must have unconsciously planned to do this when he was playing around with the suit the night before, and managed to "forget" to button his sleeve correctly. He himself was able to interpret both his wish to have me admire, perhaps envy, him and his fear that I would be disheartened and crushed, and therefore lost to him by myself not owning such an elegant garment. That behind the buttoning and unbuttoning lay curiosity about the relative size of our genitals and his wish to have a bigger penis (a better suit) than mine, was something he was not yet ready to deal with; that only came up later in the analysis.

Through the interpretation of many such episodes, bit by bit, we were able to make conscious for him and so resolve the ramifications of his fear that I, in the father transference, could not tolerate him if he were strong and competitive.

Eventually, when we had worked through this issue and he was satisfied that I was strong enough so that his fears of destroying me were unfounded, heretofore unconscious memories of sexual curiosity and sexual exploration in childhood emerged. This meant to me that he had resolved his negative oedipal feelings—the feelings that, in order to preserve his father, he had to retreat from his own masculine development—and could enter a different phase of treatment. He now recalled that there was a barn in which he and the other children of the ranch played and where he had first seen animals copulate. It was also there that he would hide and spy on some of the older boys and girls who played a game in which they exposed their genitals to one another. Ashamed, but with increased understanding of why it was so, he could now tell me that sexual intercourse was possible for him only if he first stimulated himself with pornographic pictures and watched pornographic films during the actual sexual activity. He then recalled with disgust how he and his playmates would go into this same barn and observe rats' tails hanging down from the rafters where the animals nested. Some of the older boys took delight in climbing to the exposed roofbeams, trapping the unsuspecting animals, and cutting off their tails. My patient was both frightened and fascinated by this display. These memories put us in touch with his castration anxiety, his fear of loss of masculinity as punishment for his sexual curiosity. Such anxieties are normal and expected in males at this time of their sexual development. Ideally, they are handled by the experience of actual punishment for transgressions being not as terrible as the child's fantasies make it out to be. My patient, however, during the period of his mother's illness and father's distance from him, was left very much to his own devices and to the all-or-nothing fantasies that beset a child's mind at that age.

These recollections were followed by a dream in which he was with a woman who takes off her clothes to reveal an extra breast with a long nipple, similar in appearance to a cow's udder. The patient is frightened and disgusted in the dream, but the woman tells him not to worry, that it is normal. The woman in the dream reminded Mr. Neubach of a patient of mine whom he thought of as somewhat masculine, and whom he found mildly attractive. These associations led him to thoughts of homosexuality and some adolescent fears that he might be a homosexual because he found the physique of some of his male friends attractive. He thought about lesbians and the use of dildoes. In this way a woman can become a man. I added, "As the woman in your dream did, through the protruding penis/breast."

He was curious about female genitals. Although he had seen the little girls of his peer group undressed in the barn, he was at the time sure that grown-up women were different. It turned out that he was convinced that adult women have a penis. He recalled that when he was lying on the floor playing, he would take every opportunity to try and look up his nanny's skirt as she passed, or he would spy on her when she was in the bathroom or getting undressed for bed in the room next to his. The few times he succeeded in catching a glimpse of her pudenda and saw only a black shadow, he was disappointed at not having seen more, but not dissuaded from his conviction that there was a phallus there to be seen.

These recollections and reconstructions from his childhood explained a great deal to him about his attraction to masculine-looking women, women he could think of as having a penis. He found himself dating different, softer, and, to him now, more attractive women. One of these, to whom he was turning more and more in preference to others, was not averse to having sex with him but did not appreciate his need to accompany their lovemaking with pornographic films. He was surprised and pleased that he was able to perform and enjoy himself sexually without such artificial stimulation. As he remembered retrospectively what those films meant to him, he realized they were not so much exciting as reassuring. What he looked for were the closeup shots of the penis going in and out of the vagina, a prominent feature of this type of movie. That the penis came out of the hole and was not lost inside the woman addressed a fear that had persisted until the analysis had been able to deal with his castration anxiety.

FALSE TERMINATION

After about two and a half years of treatment, the patient rather regretfully came to the conclusion that our work was about done. He was feeling and functioning well in all important areas of his life. He had wondered off and on why he had never married, but believed that fate had simply not yet put him in touch with the right woman. He felt, however, that there was no hurry in starting a family, and that he had plenty of time before settling down. In any case, this was not a matter for psychoanalysis. He thought that four to six weeks would be about the right amount of time to allow for our parting and working through any loose ends that might come up in the process. He asked me what I thought about his plan. Although I felt some vague apprehension, I thought it was perhaps my reluctance to let such an interesting and rewarding patient go on his way, and, seeing no reason for his not leaving, tentatively agreed with his plan. The Monday after this discussion, he came back devastated. The anxieties that had precipitated his beginning treatment in the first place had returned—not as bad as before, but definitely there. His chagrin soon turned to anger at himself, at me, and at Freud. It was all an illusion; he was just a frightened little boy after all; psychoanalysis was an addicting drug that threatened to make him dependent on me for the rest of his life. And what would happen to him if I died? As he began to talk, it hit me. In some unconscious way, the two of us had colluded in completely "forget-ting" that we still did not have an explanation for the anxieties that originally led him to come to see me. The return of his initial symptoms was a reminder that there was still work to be done.

It is not uncommon during the termination phase for a patient to re-experience in attenuated form some of the difficulties worked through in the analysis. It is a way of saying, "Do I really have to go? Can't I be a little kid and stay with you?" These recurrences are usually readily dealt with by examining the anxieties attached to "leaving home." My recognition that we really had not understood an important issue showed, however, that what was going on with Mr. Neubach did not fall into this category of termination anxiety.

I suggested to the patient that we take his anxiety as a message whose significance we had to decode through his associations. He was reluctant to do so, alternately pouting and making sarcastic remarks about his gullibility in having such faith in hocus-pocus. My acceptance of his regressive behavior, and acknowledging his disappointment as understandable, did not seem to help matters. After a while, I suggested that he tell me exactly the circumstances under which his anxiety had recurred. He sullenly said that it had happened, as before, at a meeting with his partners—the matters discussed were routine, his own areas of responsibility were not even particularly involved. "Was there anything different?" I continued to probe. "No, no, no," he insisted. "No big deal. Gil had to go out of town for a couple of weeks on a big installation, and he was filling us in on his projects here so that we could babysit them while he's gone." He then paused and said several times. "Yeah, Gil has to go out of town. Gil has to go out of town." "Hmm?" I said. "I never told you about Gil's wife, did I?" he asked. I said I did not remember his doing so. Ruefully, but also with some relief, he said, "Well, back to the old drawing board."

RESOLVING THE OEDIPAL CONFLICT

He then told me the story of how, about two years before he began analysis with me, he had become infatuated with a married woman. Vi, as he called her, is a French woman some years older than himself, married to his partner. He and Vi often saw each other at business-connected parties and clearly liked each other. Vi enjoyed the opportunity to converse in her native language with the attentive young man. She probably did flirt with him, and this set off what became an intense need on Otto's part to have her for himself. He was torn between his desire and the guilt he felt at betraying Gil who was also his friend. After some months, when Gil had to leave on a business trip, Otto took the opportunity to arrange a rendezvous with Vi at an inn in a nearby town, which both understood would mean that they would spend their first night together. That afternoon he smashed up his car. Though not seriously hurt, he took it as an omen and called off his tryst. The next afternoon he walked into the conference room and was stunned to see Gil, who had returned unexpectedly from his trip the evening before. Struck by remorse at what he had almost done to his friend, to himself, and to Vi, and tremendously relieved that he had not been discovered, he put out of his mind all thought of pursuing the affair any further. He remained true to his resolve. He could not be sure, but he thought his first anxiety attack in the boardroom occurred shortly thereafter.

On a hunch I asked him whether Vi was a nickname and, if so, what it stood for. "Violette," he said. "What was your nanny's name?" (I now realized that he had never called this woman anything except "nanny" or "nurse," when he was referring to his early years, or "my father's wife," when he referred to her in the present.) "Jacqueline," he said and, after a long pause, added thoughtfully, "Violetta was my mother."

It took almost another year to work through the vicissitudes of his oedipal desire for his mother, which had been in great part displaced onto his nanny. We could now also explain a heretofore-unmentioned resentment he had felt when it became clear that his father was romantically involved with Jacqueline. It turned out that the decision to educate him in the United States, while the rest of the family moved to Germany, was not entirely for scholastic reasons. He had become something of a behavior problem, expressing his resentment of his father's impending marriage through a passive, uncooperative, sullen demeanor whenever he was in the couple's presence. His father, assuming that Otto felt that his remarriage represented a betrayal of his feelings for Otto's mother, did his best to help the boy understand that such was not the case. The father's understanding helped, but it was clear that the separation rationalized on educational grounds was welcome to all. Otto learned to accept Jacqueline as his father's wife and behaved correctly when at home. His relationship with his father resumed its former closeness, but he never really felt comfortable with Jacqueline and avoided being alone with her.

The transference during the last year of the analysis was again directed toward me as father, now not a weak and helpless one but one who was both idealized and envied. He could recognize with little interpretation how the fantasies about my family and sexual life related to the competitive fears and excitements of his past. As we worked this through, he felt that he had made peace with his past and with his parents. He set the termination date some weeks after I would be coming back from a vacation and he would be returning from a trip to Germany. He felt that he would now be able to deal differently with the reality of his father's marriage to Jacqueline, and his visit turned out to substantiate his belief. This time we adhered to the termination date, and he left with both of us satisfied that we had completed what remained to be done.

Was it just good luck that Otto had a board meeting that set off an anxiety attack and signaled us that his first plan to terminate was premature? Not at all. If it had not been a board meeting, something else would have triggered the message. When the self system is prepared to deal with what repression has eliminated from consideration, that readiness will somehow let itself become known. If I had had the prescience to ask him the name of his nurse sooner and had taken a detailed history of his sexual life, could I have made the connection between his former paramour's name and its symbolic significance for the patient's oedipal struggle? Highly unlikely. When it is premature, patients manage to tell facts in such a way as to avoid useful analytic connections. Even if the therapist guesses a connection correctly, it does not—movies and novels about psychoanalysis to the contrary—suddenly lift the veil from the patient's eyes, letting him see what he needs to see in order to be free of his symptoms.

In neurosis, the curative trajectory of the psychoanalytic process—the reunion of repressed affect-laden experience with the words to express it—is, as I have emphasized before, from the affect to the word, not from the word to the affect. Until the affective memory in question is remodeled and transfered to the analyst in the here-and-now of the therapeutic situation, intellectual insight is of no help. Mr. Neubach's anxiety attack as he planned to terminate his analysis represented his readiness to relive the oedipal quandary with me as a father who could both support and constrain him. Had we not mobilized his feelings about the absent, weak father, he would not have been able to work through the negative oedipal anxiety in the analysis. Having resolved that problem, he had no way in which he could now evade taking the next step of letting me know that there was more to be done.

Analysis of the Oedipal Conflict in Women: Irma Waller

In the psychoneuroses—where the determining factors of the pathology and its treatment lie in the area of psychosexual development—though the method of approach is identical in the analysis of men and women, there are significant differences between what is uncovered. When considering the psychosexual development of women and the female oedipal complex, occasionally called the *Electra complex,* Anna Ornstein (1986) warns that it is important not to confuse oedipal problems with earlier problems in affective and cognitive development that convince the child that to be a woman is to be worthless. This negative sense of self for being female is generated by the girl's relationship with a mother who transmits to her child an often culturally generated conviction that to be feminine is to be defective. The neurotic woman does not suffer from a self-esteem problem. Rather, she is traumatized at a time when, still basically healthy, she reaches out sexually, assertively, and competitively to the parent of the opposite sex.

Freud compared the neurotic symptom to an abscess that exerts pressure on what would otherwise be normal adaptive processes, and interferes with them. Using a surgical analogy, he said that with analysis one drains the abscess and restores normalcy. The *symptom neurosis*—also called *transference neurosis*, or *psychoneurosis*—in which the pathology seems to be isolated from the rest of character development, is the classical or paradigmatic case for psychoanalytic treatment as described by Freud. Such patients are uncommon today— Mr. Neubach's pathology gave me a rare opportunity to work with such a case. The psychoneurotic women whom I have had the opportunity to treat have, for the most part, had hysterical *character neuroses*, not *symptom neuroses*. In patients with a character neurosis, the symptom does not stand apart from the rest of the self system but manifests itself in the way the patient adapts to the world. The women I treated functioned on a high level professionally and socially but found their relationships with men disappointing and frustrating. In analysis it became clear how oedipal guilt time and time again created situations that made fulfillment in the heterosexual area impossible for them. (I should add that the symptom does not make the diagnosis. Difficulty in establishing or maintaining satisfactory heterosexual relationships is one of the most common complaints of both men and women who come for therapy. The symptom in the context of the patient's overall development and current functioning is what needs to be evaluated in establishing a classification of the patient's pathology.)

In my experience, the course of the analysis of a female patient's oedipal conflict tends to fall into four phases. In the first, the patient uses the (male) analyst's interest, understanding, and willingness to be of help to re-create for herself the (usually satisfactory) pre-oedipal relationship she had with her father. It is during this first phase that she is often able to free herself from the frustration of the unsuitable relationship with a man which brought her to treatment in the first place. This relationship, usually only the latest in a series of basically similar ones, is an expression of both the patient's desire for sexual consummation and, since it is usually distressing and increasingly ungratifying, the punishment for such temerity. Once she has transferred to the analyst her unconscious hopes and wishes for acceptance and understanding, and found them fulfilled, it is only a matter of time before the second phase and tenuous sexual feelings for the analyst make their appearance. Initially, these usually take the form of trying to expand the relationship to the analyst: wanting to know more about him; wanting to be there for him when he has worries or problems; to be not "just" analyst and patient, but friends. There may be a time during which the patient's physical sexual feelings are directed toward men other than the analyst; but eventually these, too, are focused on his person. What the patient holds out to the analyst is not simply physical consummation, but an all-encompassing love that has no bounds. As Freud (1915d) pointed out, the love in the transference is genuine. (In the case of a woman with psychoneurotic problems in treatment with a woman analyst, the initial positive transference focuses on the analyst as the good, strong mother who will make up for whatever disappointments the patient experienced in childhood. Eventually jealousy and competitive feelings will make their appearance. Now the analyst becomes the withholding mother who could give her what she needs, but will not do so: that is, who has a penis but will not give it to her. Eventually rivalry with the analyst/mother takes the form of fantasizing what the analyst's relationship is with the man or men in her life, and the patient's wish to have him or them for herself. This is accompanied by guilt, and the fear that the analyst will now see for herself how bad the patient really is and withdraw from or otherwise punish the patient.)

The patient cannot recognize that her love is not for the analyst but for the analyst-as-father; the analyst must, however, keep this firmly in mind without interpreting it prematurely to the patient, lest she experience that explanation as the repetition of a traumatic rejection of her longing. This is easier said than done. Although, when this happens in an analysis, I now feel the awesome responsibility of having awakened such intense emotion in a fellow human being who has in effect placed herself totally in my hands, I was taken aback and frightened when I first mobilized this depth of longing in a patient.

MANAGING AN EROTIC TRANSFERENCE

Miss Waller was an analytic patient who, after considerable resistance to acknowledging the evidence of her sexual interest in me, came one day to the analysis radiating passion and saying that she now realized that I was right, that I was the man for her, and that she was prepared to give herself to me. It was early in my career, and I was totally unnerved. Fortunately, I had enough presence of mind to keep my mouth shut and avoid defending myself against her claim that it was I who all along had wanted to seduce her. She left the hour giving me a long, knowing look. It seemed that she had interpreted my silence as acquiescence, tempered by a shyness that time would overcome.

I quickly obtained an emergency consultation with one of my supervisors, convinced I had inadvertently derailed the analysis and quite at a loss about what I should do next. My consultant helped me to understand that what was happening was not an interference with the analysis but the emergence in the transference of some heretofore repressed wishes from childhood. To which I added, "Complicated, of course, by the reality that she is now a woman and not a little girl, and I am not her father but a man of about her age." "No," my supervisor said, "the reality is that, though she is not aware of it yet, while she is on that couch she *is* a little girl and you *are* her father. What a properly managed analysis brings out is the true—that is, the unconscious—reality that governs a patient's life. The rest is window dressing. Analysis is not a game like Monopoly where you pretend to invest in this or that, knowing all along that you are using play money. Analysis is for keeps. The patient's sexual feelings for you are as real and as exclusively for you as are those of any healthy little five- or six-year-old girl for her father. What is confusing the two of you is that she is also a grown woman and misinterprets her passion as originating in her present relationship and calling for an adult's solution."

That explanation helped me a great deal. It enabled me to focus with the patient on what she was feeling and to stop thinking that I had to address her need for me as me, in the same way I had to learn not to interfere with the need of the card-playing-student patient who had to see me as unrelentingly studious. When Miss Waller subsequently expressed her sexual desire for me and her wish to meet me outside the session, I acknowledged how strong those feelings were and encouraged her, as usual, to let her thoughts take her wherever they led. In a dream following this session, she portrayed herself and an unknown man in a motel. But though the dream was filled with sexual excitement, it ended not with intercourse but with her being held close while the couple slept together. She woke up from this dream feeling marvelously refreshed. The dream led to memories of being told by her mother when she was in second grade that she was too old to be spending time with her father in bed on Sunday mornings, and being banished to the playroom.

"PENIS ENVY"

I am, of course, compressing several months of treatment into a few sentences. Matters did not unfold so smoothly as I describe here, in part because I was then still a novice, but also because they never do, no matter how much experience one gains. However, my ability to accept Miss Waller's seductive overtures did ultimately lead to the next and third phase of the female's oedipal resolution. She became very angry that, in the final analysis, it was the man who had the upper hand. I controlled the relationship with her, just as her father had. This led to a heretofore unsuspected rage at several former lovers who had had problems with impotence. She had always been most understanding and had usually been able over time to help them regain potency. Now she was furious that she was dependent on their erection for sexual gratification. Through these memories, the patient was helped to become aware of what has been labeled, somewhat inaccurately, *penis envy*. The anatomical reality that men have penises and testicles, while girls have a clitoris and a vagina, does not exist for little children. For them, the world is composed of those with and those without a midline appendage; and the little girl has a sense that there is some-thing missing, that she is incomplete. What seems to happen in the neurotic woman's sexual development is that the guilt deriving from incestuous wishes—which in the boy leads to the conviction that were his desires known they would lead to his penis being cut off, leads the girl to believe that she once must have had a penis, but that her "badness"—that is, her sexual fantasies—caused her to lose it. Alternatively, some female neurotic patients in treatment uncover the belief that if they can only learn to be good—that is, freed of incestuous desire—they will be given or will grow a penis. The unconscious belief that she has been punished by being deprived of a penis is as ubiquitous and as focal for the analysis of the neurotic woman as is castration anxiety for the neurotic man. Because of the guilt feelings that precipitated these convictions, patients of both sexes try to fend off the anxiety created when memories are mobilized that lead to awareness of these fantasies. Often the resistance takes the form of accusing the analyst of making interpretations according to the book, finding what he has been taught to find, and so on. With the women's liberation movement, it is not uncommon for female analysands who have a neurotic character structure to label any interpretation of this longing for a penis as an example of "male chauvinism." One such patient, whose case I supervised, was adamant in insisting that dreams of losing things, of being damaged, and of being left out, had nothing to do with any wish for a penis. She did not feel in the least deprived. Her parents had brought her up to be proud and unashamed of her body. Indeed, they had been part of a back-to-nature movement and spent their summers in a nudist camp. The turning point in this patient's analysis came when she suddenly realized that, whenever she had thought of those vacations, her very vivid visual recollections were only of naked men and never included any women.

Observant parents can also attest to the reality of the female child's sense of deprivation at seemingly missing something. I was told of one little girl who, on observing her recently born brother being diapered, said, "That's right, Mom, cover it up so I won't have to see it."

OEDIPAL GUILT AND ITS RESOLUTION

Once in touch with her fantasies, Miss Waller became aware that the guilt for which she was being punished was the imagined oedipal triumph over her mother. Chagrined as she had been at being dismissed from the parental bed, she was relieved that her mother had reclaimed her father. But it did not last. As she relived the events in the analysis, she was able to understand that she believed unconsciously that her wishes for her father were responsible for her parents' divorce when she was about eight years old, an event that made her feel both powerful and guilty. This memory let us understand the adult pattern of her sexual relationships. She had repeatedly formed liaisons with married men whom she had abruptly to abandon when they declared their readiness to get a divorce and marry her. Her ambivalence toward her lovers represented the repetitious re-enactments of an unconscious conflict—a closed system. On the one hand, she wanted her father to herself; on the other, she suffered guilty torment when her lover (father) was ready to jettison his wife (mother) in order to be with her.

The fourth and final phase, the consolidation of what had been worked through in the transference regarding the longings and disappointments of her incestuous attachment, left Miss Waller free to see herself as a person in her own right—her life now governed by the hopes and ambitions of the present rather than those of the past.

The reader may wonder whether it should not have been obvious that a woman who comes for treatment, and gives evidence of having a psychoneurotic character disorder, is likely to have oedipal difficulties. Since that conjecture combined with a history of the sort of love affairs that she has had ought to lead the therapist straight to the relationship with the father, why not directly investigate and interpret that? To such questions, I can answer only that all I have seen in my own practice and learned about the work of other analysts has increasingly convinced me that the fewer preconceptions the analyst formulates based on what a neurotic patient can relate without resistance, the more likely it is that an analytic result will ultimately be achieved. For what is repressed cannot be directly fathomed and reveals itself only as it emerges in the transference neurosis, the new edition of the old problems as the patient relives them with the analyst. As with other patients, letting myself be led by Miss Waller, I stumbled after her until, in a roundabout way, I ended by finally understanding what the first session, or the first dream, was all about.

Although one sees few such cases, I cannot think of a psychoneurotic patient who has accepted my recommendation for and participated in a psychoanalysis who has not had a creditable result. I dare say that any other psychoanalyst properly trained in Freud's work would say the same thing. Given even a modicum of talent for that kind of work, the therapist who applies Freud's method, guided by his theory of how and why a neurosis develops, will produce exactly the results he promised. It never ceases to amaze and delight me how, when I am thoroughly confused by a patient, I can—like a pilot making an instrument landing in a dense fog—do what Freud said should be done, and eventually bring the analysis to a satisfactory conclusion. By the same token, unlike those cases where the primary defense is other than secondary repression and modification of the so called classical traditional analytic technique is called for, I have not succeeded in resolving an oedipal conflict when circumstances influenced me to try to take shortcuts or otherwise modify Freud's original psychoanalytic procedure. The account that follows will illustrate what can and what cannot be achieved in the treatment of a patient with a psychoneurotic character disorder who does not come into analysis.

Psychotherapy of a Case of Hysteria: Norma Newton

Miss Newton was thirty-three years old when I first saw her. She had been married at the age of eighteen and was divorced by the time she was twenty-one. For the next twelve years she lived in serial monogamy with several older men, each of whom, attracted by her striking appearance, superior intelligence, and capacity for empathy, would have been more than happy to marry her. Yet, though she remained on friendly terms with her erstwhile lovers, she had a pattern of breaking off the relationship whenever things reached that point. Her reason for coming to therapy was to try to find out why she could not marry, since she was coming toward the end of her childbearing years and longed for motherhood. As I talked further to her over a period of three or four diagnostic sessions, it became clear that there were other symptoms she had not mentioned and did not recognize as being problems. She was a fairly serious alcoholic, but called herself a social drinker. She was habituated, if not addicted, to several other drugs, but dismissed this, like drinking, as part of the movie-making milieu in which she worked. I later learned that she had an eating disorder, too, bingeing and vomiting on some days as often as a dozen times. She also had numerous physical complaints, including migraine headaches, dizzy spells, an annoying ringing in the ears, colitis, and various muscular aches and pains. Repeated medical investigation had shown no specific physiological problems that could account for these often painful and sometimes incapacitating symptoms.

The more I talked with Miss Newton, the more I was convinced that her basic character structure was a neurotic hysterical one: that is, her various somatic symptoms represented the symbolic expressions of oedipal rather than other selfobject problems. Accordingly, I suggested that the treatment of choice for her would be psychoanalysis. The patient understood and accepted my recommendation in principle, but asked if we could not maintain, for the time being, our schedule of once-weekly appointments since, though she had an extremely well-paying job, she had recently purchased and furnished a new residence and felt she could not undertake the financial obligation of an analysis for at least a year. I agreed to that. When her finances were once again in order, she was given a big promotion. Now, she said, much as she really saw the need to do so, she could not spare the time to come four or five times a week until she had mastered her new position; and so it went. I continued psychotherapy with her for about three years, during which time she managed never to come more than once a week. Yet in her sessions Miss Newton behaved like an ideal analytic patient: she was open, trusting, and cooperative; she was intelligent, introspective, and had no difficulty in making the connection between aspects of her present behavior and her childhood.

A PSEUDO-EROTIC TRANSFERENCE

Some months after first seeing me, she came to the office not dressed in her usual, businesslike, stylish manner as befitted an executive, but in a seductively low-cut blouse and a skirt that was split well up her thigh. As the hour moved on, I realized that she was totally oblivious to her appearance, and that the seductive intent of her outfit was not consciously available to her. My own reaction to her appearance was very interesting to me. My first impulse on seeing her was to smile indulgently as one would at a little girl playing "dress-up." Simultaneously, there flashed through my mind a scene I had witnessed a few days before. Near my office was a showroom where television sets were sold. To attract the attention of the passers-by, a set with a huge screen, tuned to some championship sporting event, had been placed in the window. A crowd, almost exclusively male, had gathered around the window to follow the game. Among these men I saw a little girl with a forlorn look, rhythmically tugging at the trouser leg of a man I assumed to be her father who, lost in the action of the game, was completely unaware of his child's entreaty.

Miss Newton's associations were to a class she had agreed to teach to aspiring film makers and to her fear that she would be seen as less than sufficiently knowledgeable, even though she realized that factually her concern was unfounded. "Will I be able to hold their attention and interest?" she wondered. At that point, about twenty minutes into the session, she suddenly seemed to become aware of how much of her leg was exposed. She blushed, and rearranged her skirt as best she could—not easy to do in an Eames chair. She apologized and offered a somewhat unconvincing rationalization for her choice of costume. Using both her associations and my own reactions to her appearance, I hazarded my impression that the revealing clothes were chosen unconsciously for my benefit because of the concern she then displaced onto her role as a teacher—namely, some fear about her ability to hold *my* attention and interest. Furthermore, I suggested it could well be that something from her childhood made her feel she had to choose this route to ensure she would not be neglected.

It became clear to us that I at this point represented her father, a charming alcoholic ne'er-do-well, who promised her much emotionally but never delivered. Yet she kept hoping that some day he would really be there for her, able to pay attention to her needs instead of using her for his own purposes. That he preferred her to her mother, there was no doubt. What money there was he lavished on his and her wardrobes. Then, dressed to the nines, they would go to his friends' houses, or to the gambling halls, poolrooms, and bars that he frequented, so that he could show off his beautiful little daughter.

A BLOCK TO THE FORMATION OF A TRANSFERENCE NEUROSIS

The fact that I did not pick up on her flirtatious invitation, or use her for my own voyeuristic purposes, but, instead, kept my nose to the therapeutic grindstone let her see me as the father she always wanted but never had, a father who would listen to and really care about her, rather than only use her for his own ends. Her positive transference to me relieved her of stress and tension to the point that her somatic symptoms for the most part disappeared. No longer in need of chemical soothing, she resolved to give up alcohol and other drugs and did so without much difficulty. Although our time together was limited, she was nevertheless able to recover aspects of her past history that clarified the vicissitudes of the triangular relationship between mother, father, and herself. Eventually, I think we both came to understand the outlines of her particular oedipal constellation. However, though what we saw of her oedipal conflict seemed clear, it was as if through a glass window. We could see Miss Newton's pathology so clearly precisely because it was not muddied by the passionate feelings, positive and negative, of a transference neurosis. We could see what had happened in the abstract, but it belonged to the past; it was not playing itself out in the here-and-now. Although I could observe the beginnings of the transference reactivation of older patterns, they did not have a chance to develop in all their complexity. By the time the next week's session rolled around, whatever was stirring had had ample opportunity to be sealed over or displaced onto everyday problems. This time element is a limitation of all therapy short of psychoanalysis when an oedipal conflict and its inadequate repression is causing a patient's problems (see also Basch 1980, pp. 105–10). What commonly then happens is illustrated by this case. Many significant gains were made, but the more basic feeling of dissatisfaction with herself and her life that had led her to alcohol and drugs in the first place did not change. My pointing out the need for analysis, as I said, found her in agreement, but one rationalization after another blocked her from carrying out her intentions to begin. My attempts to help her understand that the reasons she adduced for not starting an analysis probably indicated some fears about the process and what it might uncover were of no avail.

She eventually resolved this impasse by falling in love with a recently divorced man at her office. It was interesting to observe, as she described their courtship, that his relationship with her was similar to the one she and I had. He was interested and attentive, took her concerns seriously, and treated her as a whole person. She told him all she had told me of her childhood, her various addictions, and her sexual acting up. He heard it all without either condemning her or minimizing what she had experienced. He offered himself as someone who was ready to be at her side, facing whatever they had to together, with no illusions that everything was now going to be fine and wonderful. She realized that she had had relationships with similarly devoted men before—indeed, she seemed to attract them but only now could she let herself become fully committed to someone who loved and could help her.

Her announcement of both her engagement to this man and their intention to move to another city for professional reasons meant that her therapy with me would come to an end. To date I have not heard anything from or about her, and do not know how things have turned out. In retrospect, I believe Miss Newton's unconscious fear of the inevitable rejection involved in the resolution of the oedipal complex was so strong that she had to find a substitute for her father rather than an analyst. If she can get enough from her marriage to reinforce the repression of her incestuous feelings, her maneuver may succeed. Freud long ago said that the right marriage could be an excellent alternative to a cure by analysis.

Psychoanalysis and Psychoanalytically Oriented Psychotherapy

There is no doubt that Miss Newton gained a great deal from psychoanalytically oriented therapy. It is called *psychoanalytically oriented* because it is based on searching for an understanding of the unconscious motivation behind a patient's counterproductive behavior through an examination of that patient's verbalized introspections. But that is not yet psychoanalysis.

I realize that I am in the minority when I state categorically that when the principal defense is repression, psychoanalysis, the first form of insight therapy, is still the best therapy and the only one that leads to a curative resolution. Many therapists believe that they can join and resolve oedipal conflicts through less demanding psychotherapies. Some even assert that they can do so in a time-limited therapy of a dozen sessions, or even fewer. I question these assertions. At best, what happens is that a patient, as did Miss Newton, gains sufficient cognitive understanding, combined with a countervailing experience with the therapist, to offset her conflicts and improve her functioning. At worst, the patient, for the sake of the relationship and terribly dependent on the good will of the therapist, adopts his language and complies with his needs. What I have seen of the latter cases leads me to believe that whatever relief a patient gets from such acquiescence is usually lost when the relationship ends, not infrequently leaving the patient worse off than he or she was before.

However, it was most unfortunate that from its earliest days psychoanalysis and the resolution of the oedipal conflict became, for all practical purposes, synonymous. It was Kohut who uncoupled the method of transference analysis from the resolution of the oedipal conflict, thus expanding the scope of psychoanalysis. The great majority of patients therapists see today are not neurotic, and can benefit from a psychoanalytically oriented approach that is not focused on the resolution of repression and the transference of incestuous wishes. As I have illustrated, these patients are struggling not with the vicissitudes of psychosexual development per se but with other issues relating to the maintenance of competence and self-esteem; and they are protecting the self system with defenses other than secondary repression. In the treatment of many of these patients, psychoanalytically oriented psychotherapy can be extremely effective and, I should add, frequently produces an analytic result. For example, in Esther Romberg's case, the primary defense to be dealt with was the disavowal that protected her from reexperiencing the pain and humiliation of earlier disappointments suffered in childhood. Although we never met more than twice weekly and, rather than the patient lying on the couch, she and I sat facing each other, the work with her produced a psychoanalytic result: that is to say, the selfobject transferences—idealizing, mirror, and alter ego—were fostered, examined, and resolved. In this process the patient gained insight into the meaning of her relationship to me, and that insight led in turn to a fundamental restructuring of her self system.

It is not the nature of the patient's pathology, the setting in which the treatment has been conducted, or the specific interventions used by the therapist that determine whether a psychoanalytic result has been obtained. If it is insight into and resolution of the transference which has brought about the therapeutic result, then that treatment qualifies as psychoanalysis.

Epilogue

TODAY we have available a systematic approach to the psycho-logical dimension of human existence. It is certainly gratifying for me to teach a theoretical orientation to human development and functioning that permits students entering the field to progress far more rapidly toward their goal of becoming effective practitioners than could I and my peers when we began. But it is equally reward-ing to watch experienced therapists take a new lease on their profes-sional lives once they are free to understand and respond to what their patients are trying to tell them. So, for example, just a few days ago, a colleague who had consulted with me over a period of some months when he found himself at an impasse with a patient—a man who reminded me very much of Roger Flynn—pulled me aside at a social gathering and said that he just wanted me to know how comfortably and effectively he is now able to work with all his patients. And, he told me—his face beaming—that his patients, old and new, are responding dramatically to his new-found under-standing, opening up to him in ways he had never before seen.

These are exciting times for psychotherapy. Freud's concept of the therapeutic transference—when freed from the doctrinaire res-trictions of his biological speculations about instincts, and informed by what is now known about the nature, origin, and development of the self system—permits the psychotherapist to observe what patients reveal about themselves, and then to deal creatively with those findings. Yet the implications are broader.

There will always be persons suffering from conditions that require the services of a skilled psychotherapist. But—as shown by
both the pediatrician's interaction with Billy Kruger's mother, and
my contact with Al Gertz—what we have learned about the benefits
of therapeutic intervention based on an empathic understanding of
another's communication has a much broader application and need
not be limited to the formal relationship between therapist and
patient.

And so opens a new era in dynamic psychotherapy—a century
after the field was founded. Freud's dream of a psychology that
would truly be a science of human nature is now within our reach.

References

Adler, G. 1979. "The Myth of the Alliance with Borderline Patients." *American Journal of Psychiatry* 136:642–45.

———. 1985. *Borderline Psychopathology and Its Treatment.* New York: Jason Aronson.

Arnheim, R. 1969. *Visual Thinking.* London: Faber & Faber.

Arnold, M. B. 1960. *Emotion and Personality,* vol. I. New York: Columbia University Press.

Atwood, G.; and Stolorow, R. 1984. *Structures of Subjectivity: Explorations in Psychoanalytic Phenomenology.* Hillsdale, N.J.: Analytic Press.

Bacal, H. 1983. "Optimal Responsiveness and the Therapeutic Process." In A. Goldberg, ed., *Progress in Self Psychology,* vol. I, pp. 202–27. New York: Guilford Press.

Basch, M. F. 1975a. "Toward a Theory That Encompasses Depression: A Revision of Existing Causal Hypotheses in Psychoanalysis." In E. J. Anthony and T. Benedek, eds., *Depression and Human Existence,* pp. 485–534. Boston: Little, Brown.

———. 1975b. "Perception, Consciousness, and Freud's 'Project.' " *The Annual of Psychoanalysis* 3:3–19. New York: International Universities Press.

———. 1976a. "Theory Formation in Chapter VII: A Critique." *Journal of the American Psychoanalytic Association* 24:61–100.

———. 1976b. "Psychoanalysis and Communication Science." *The Annual of Psychoanalysis* 4: 385–421. New York: International Universities Press.

———.1976c. "The Concept of Affect: A Re-examination." *Journal of the American Psychoanalytic Association* 24:759–77.

———. 1977. "Developmental Psychology and Explanatory Theory in Psychoanalysis." *The Annual of Psychoanalysis* 5:229–63. New York: International Universities Press.

———. 1978. "Psychic Determinism and Freedom of Will." *International Review of Psycho-Analysis* 5:257–64.

———. 1980. *Doing Psychotherapy.* New York: Basic Books.

———. 1981. "Psychoanalytic Interpretation and Cognitive Transformation." *International Journal of Psycho-Analysis* 62:151–75.

———. 1983a. "Empathic Understanding: A Review of the Concept and Some Theoretical Considerations." *Journal of the American Psychoanalytic Association* 31:101–26.

———. 1983b. "The Perception of Reality and the Disavowal of Meaning." *The Annual of Psychoanalysis* 11:125–54. New York: International Universities Press.

———. 1983c. "The Significance of Self Psychology for a Theory of Psychotherapy." In J. D. Lichtenberg and S. Kaplan, eds., *Reflections on Self Psychology,* pp. 223–38. Hillsdale, N.J.: Analytic Press.

———. 1985. "New Directions in Psychoanalysis." *Psychoanalytic Psychology* 2:1–13.

———. 1988a. "The Teacher, the Transference, and Development." In K. Field and B. Cohler, eds., *Learning and Education: Psychoanalytic Perspectives.* New York: International Universities Press.

———. 1988b. "The Selfobject Experience of the Newborn." In A. Goldberg, ed., *Progress in Self Psychology,* vol. IV, pp. 101–4. Hillsdale, N.J.: Analytic Press.

Beebe, B.; and Sloate, P. 1982. "Assessment and Treatment of Difficulties in Mother-Infant

Attunement in the First Three Years of Life: A Case History." *Psychoanalytic Inquiry* 1:601–23.

Beebe, B.; and Stern, D. 1977. "Engagement-Disengagement and Early Object Experiences." In N. Freedman and S. Grand, eds., *Communicative Structures and Psychic Structures,* pp. 35–55. New York: Plenum Press.

Beigler, J. 1957. "Anxiety as an Aid in the Prognostication of Impending Death." *American Medical Association Archives of Neurology and Psychiatry* 77:171–77.

Bertalanffy, L. von. 1967. *Robots, Men and Minds: Psychology in the Modern World.* New York: George Braziller.

———. 1968. *General System Theory.* New York: George Braziller.

Bowlby, J. 1969. *Attachment: Attachment and Loss,* vol. I. New York: Basic Books.

———. 1980. *Loss: Attachment and Loss,* vol. III. London: Hogarth Press.

Bower, T. G. R. 1977. *A Primer of Infant Development.* San Francisco: W. H. Freeman.

Brandt, H. F. 1945. *The Psychology of Seeing.* New York: The Philosophical Library.

Breuer, J.; and Freud, S. 1893–95. *Studies on Hysteria.* In *The Standard Edition of the Complete Psychological Works of Sigmund Freud,* vol. 2. London: Hogarth Press, 1955.

Brothers, L. 1988. "A Biological Perspective on Empathy." *American Journal of Psychiatry* (in press).

Broucek, F. 1979. "Efficacy in Infancy: A Review of Some Experimental Studies and Their Possible Implications for Clinical Theory." *International Journal of Psycho-Analysis* 60:311–16.

———. 1982. "Shame and Its Relationship to Early Narcissistic Developments." *International Journal of Psycho-Analysis* 63:369–78.

Buck, R. 1984. *The Communication of Emotion.* New York/London: Guilford Press.

Buckley, W., ed. 1968. *Modern Systems Research for the Behavioral Scientist.* Chicago: Aldine Publishing.

Campbell, J. 1982. *Grammatical Man.* New York: Simon & Schuster.

DeCasper, A.; and Fifer, W. 1980. "Of Human Bonding: Newborns Prefer Their Mothers' Voices." *Science* 208:1174.

Davis, M.; and Wallbridge, D. 1981. *Boundary and Space: An Introduction to the Work of D. W. Winnicott.* New York: Brunner/Mazel.

Demos, V.; and Kaplan, S. 1985. "Motivation and Affect Reconsidered: Affect Biographies of Two Infants." *Psychoanalysis and Contemporary Thought* 8:4.

Detrick, D. W. 1986. "Alterego Phenomena and Alterego Transferences: Some Further Considerations." In A. Goldberg, ed., *Progress in Self Psychology,* vol. II, pp. 299–304. New York/London: Guilford Press.

Dorpat, T. L. 1985. *Denial and Defense in the Therapeutic Situation.* New York and London: Jason Aronson.

———. 1987. "A New Look at Denial and Defense." *The Annual of Psychoanalysis* 15:23–47. New York: International Universities Press.

Eccles, J. C. 1970. *Facing Reality: Philosophical Adventures of a Brain Scientist.* New York and Heidelberg: Springer-Verlag.

Ekman, P., ed. 1973. *Darwin and Facial Expression.* New York and London: Academic Press.

Ekman, P.; Levenson, R. W.; and Friesen, W. V. 1983. "Evidence for Autonomic Reactions in Specific Emotions." *Science* 221:1208–10.

Fajardo, B. 1988. "Resilience in Development and Analyzability." Unpublished paper.

Field, T. M. 1985. "Neonatal Perception of People: Maturational and Individual Differences." In T. M. Field and N. A. Fox, eds., *Social Perception in Infants,* pp. 31–52. Norwood, N.J.: Ahler Publishing .

Field, T. M.; Woodson, R.; Greenberg, R.; and Cohen, D. 1982. "Discrimination and Imitation of Facial Expressions by Neonates." *Science* 218:179–81.

Fields, W. S.; and Abbott, W., eds. 1963. *Information Storage and Neural Control.* Springfield, Ill.: Charles C Thomas.

Freud, A. 1937. *The Ego and the Mechanisms of Defence.* London: Hogarth Press.

Freud, S. 1895. *Project for a Scientific Psychology.* In *The Standard Edition of the Complete Psychological Works of Sigmund Freud* (hereafter *Standard Edition*), vol. 1, pp. 281–397. London: Hogarth Press, 1966.

———. 1900. *The Interpretation of Dreams.* In *Standard Edition,* vols. 4 and 5. London: Hogarth Press, 1958.

———. 1905. *Three Essays on the Theory of Sexuality.* In *Standard Edition,* vol. 7. London: Hogarth Press, 1953.

———. 1910. "The Future Prospects of Psycho-Analytic Therapy." In *Standard Edition,* vol. 11, pp. 139–51. London: Hogarth Press, 1957.

———. 1912. "The Dynamics of Transference." In *Standard Edition,* vol. 12, pp. 97–108. London: Hogarth Press, 1958.

———. 1913. "On Beginning the Treatment." In *Standard Edition,* vol. 12, pp. 121–44. London: Hogarth Press, 1958.

———. 1915a. "Instincts and Their Vicissitudes." In *Standard Edition,* vol. 14, pp. 108–40. London: Hogarth Press, 1957.

———. 1915b. "Repression." In *Standard Edition,* vol. 14, pp. 141–58. London: Hogarth Press, 1957.

———. 1915c. "The Unconscious." In *Standard Edition,* vol. 14, pp. 159–204. London: Hogarth Press, 1957.

———. 1915d. "Observations on Transference-Love." In *Standard Edition,* vol. 12, pp. 157–71. London: Hogarth Press, 1958.

———. 1916–17. *Introductory Lectures on Psycho-Analysis Part III.* In *Standard Edition,* vol. 16. London: Hogarth Press, 1963.

———. 1917. "Mourning and Melancholia." In *Standard Edition,* vol. 14, pp. 237–58. London: Hogarth Press, 1957.

———. 1920. "Beyond the Pleasure Principle." In *Standard Edition,* vol. 18, pp. 7–64. London: Hogarth Press, 1955.

———. 1921. *Group Psychology and the Analysis of the Ego.* In *Standard Edition,* vol. 18, pp. 65–143. London: Hogarth Press, 1955.

———. 1923. "The Ego and the Id." In *Standard Edition,* vol. 19, pp. 3–66. London: Hogarth Press, 1961.

———. 1926a. *Inhibitions, Symptoms and Anxiety.* In *Standard Edition,* vol. 20, pp. 87–179. London: Hogarth Press, 1959.

———. 1926b. "Psycho-Analysis." In *Standard Edition,* vol. 20, pp. 259–70. London: Hogarth Press, 1959.

———. 1927. "Fetishism." In *Standard Edition,* vol. 21, pp. 152–57. London: Hogarth Press, 1961.

———. 1933. *New Introductory Lectures on Psycho-analysis.* In *Standard Edition,* vol. 22, pp. 7–182. London: Hogarth Press, 1964.

———. 1937. "Constructions in Analysis." In *Standard Edition,* vol. 23, pp. 255–69. London: Hogarth Press, 1964.

———. 1940. "An Outline of Psycho-Analysis." In *Standard Edition,* vol. 23, pp. 141–207. London: Hogarth Press, 1964.

Gedo, J. E. 1979. *Beyond Interpretation.* N.Y.: International Universities Press.

———. 1988. *The Mind in Disorder.* Hillsdale, N.J.: Analytic Press.

Gleick, J. 1987. "Using Chaos to Make Order." *Smithsonian* 18:122–34.

Goldberg, A. 1988. *A Fresh Look at Psychoanalysis: The View from Self Psychology.* Hillsdale, N.J.: Analytic Press.

Gould, J. L.; and Gould, C. G. 1981. "The Instinct to Learn." *Science 81* 2:44–50.

Gould, J. L.; and Marler, P. 1987. "Learning by Instinct." *Scientific American* 256:74–85.

Hadley, J. L. 1983. "The Representational System: A Bridging Concept for Psychoanalysis and Neurophysiology." *International Review of Psycho-Analysis* 10:13–30.

————. 1985. "Attention, Affect, and Attachment." *Psychoanalysis and Contemporary Thought* 8:529–50. Madison, Conn.: International Universities Press.

Hartmann, H. 1939. *Ego Psychology and the Problem of Adaptation,* D. Rapaport, tr. New York: International Universities Press, 1958.

Haviland, J. M.; and Lelwica, M. 1987. "The Induced Affect Response: 10-week-old Infants' Responses to Three Emotional Expressions." *Developmental Psychology* 23:97–104.

James, W. 1890. *The Principles of Psychology,* vols. I and II. New York: Dover Publications, 1950.

Jones, E. 1953. *The Life and Work of Sigmund Freud,* vol. I. New York: Basic Books.

Klein, G. S. 1976. "The Vital Pleasures." In *Psychoanalytic Theory: An Exploration of Essentials,* pp. 210–38. New York: International Universities Press.

Knapp, P. H. 1987. "Some Contemporary Contributions to the Study of Emotions." *Journal of the American Psychoanalytic Association* 35:205–48.

Kohut, H. 1959. "Introspection, Empathy and Psychoanalysis." *Journal of the American Psychoanalytic Association* 7:459–83.

————. 1971. *The Analysis of the Self.* New York: International Universities Press.

————. 1977. *The Restoration of the Self.* New York: International Universities Press.

————. 1984. *How Does Analysis Cure?* Chicago and London: University of Chicago Press.

————. 1987. *The Kohut Seminars,* M. Elson, ed. New York and London: W. W. Norton.

Kohut, H.; and Wolf, E. S. 1978. "The Disorders of the Self and Their Treatment: An Outline." *International Journal of Psycho-Analysis* 59:413–25.

Korzybski, A. 1933. *Science and Sanity.* International Non-Aristotelian Library Publishing. Lakeville, Conn.: Institute of General Semantics, 1948.

Lashley, K. 1958. "Cerebral Organization and Behavior." In H. C. Solomon et al., eds., *The Brain and Human Behavior,* pp. 1–18. Baltimore: Williams & Wilkins.

Levin, F. M.; and Vuckovich, D. M. 1983. "Psychoanalysis and the Two Cerebral Hemispheres." *The Annual of Psychoanalysis* 11:171–197. New York: International Universities Press.

Lewis, H. B. 1981. "Shame and Guilt in Human Nature." In S. Tuttman, C. Kaye, and M. Zimmerman, eds., *Object and Self: A Developmental Approach.* New York: International Universities Press.

Lewis, M.; and Goldberg, S. 1969. "Perceptual-Cognitive Development in Infancy." *Merrill-Palmer Quarterly* 15:81–100.

Libet, B.; et al. 1979. "Subjective Referral of the Timing for a Conscious Sensory Experience." *Brain* 102:193.

Lichtenberg, J. D. 1983. *Psychoanalysis and Infant Research.* New York: Analytic Press.

Lifton, R. J. 1986. *The Nazi Doctors.* New York: Basic Books.

MacLean, P. D. 1985. "Brain Evolution Relating to Family, Play, and the Separation Call." *Archives of General Psychiatry* 42:405–17.

Nathanson, D. L. 1987. "A Timetable for Shame." In D. L. Nathanson, ed., *The Many Faces of Shame,* pp. 1–63. New York/London: Guilford Press.

Ornstein, A. 1986. "Selfobject Transferences and the Theory of the Development of the Feminine Self." Unpublished manuscript.

Papoušek, H. 1969. "Individual Variability in Learned Responses in Human Infants." In R. J. Robinson, ed., *Brain and Early Behaviour,* pp. 251–66. London: Academic Press.

Peterfreund, E. 1971. *Information, Systems and Psychoanalysis. Psychological Issues,* VII, nos. 1/2, monograph 25/26. New York: International Universities Press.

Piaget, J.; and Inhelder, B. 1969. *The Psychology of the Child.* New York: Basic Books.

Powers, W. T. 1973. *Behavior: The Control of Perception.* Chicago: Aldine Publishing.

Reiser, M. 1984. *Mind, Brain, Body: Toward a Convergence of Psychoanalysis and Neurobiology.* New York: Basic Books.

Roiphe, H.; and Galenson, E. 1982. *Infantile Origins of Sexual Identity.* New York: International Universities Press.

Rosenblatt, A. D.; and Thickstun, J. T. 1978. *Modern Psychoanalytic Concepts in a General Psychology.* New York: International Universities Press.

Schwartz, A. 1987a. "Drives, Affects, Behavior, and Learning: Approaches to a Psychobiology of Emotion and to an Integration of Psychoanalytic and Neurobiological Thought." *Journal of the American Psychoanalytic Association* 35:467–506.

———. 1988. "Reification Revisited: Some Neurobiologically-Filtered Views of 'Psychic Structure' and 'Conflict.' " *Journal of the American Psychoanalytic Association* 35 (supplement).

Socarides, D. D.; and Stolorow, R. D. 1984–85. "Affects and Selfobjects." *The Annual of Psychoanalysis* 12/13:105–19. New York: International Universities Press.

Stechler, G.; and Kaplan, S. 1980. "The Development of the Self." *The Psychoanalytic Study of the Child* 25:85–105. New York: International Universities Press.

Stern, D. N. 1984. "Affect Attunement." In J. Call, E. Galenson, and R. Tyson, eds., *Frontiers of Infant Psychiatry*, vol. II, pp. 3–14. New York: Basic Books.

———. 1985. *The Interpersonal World of the Infant.* New York: Basic Books.

Stern, D. N.; Hofer, L.; Haft, W.; and Dore, J. 1985. "Affect Attunement: The Sharing of Feeling States between Mother and Infant by Means of Inter-modal Fluency." In T. M. Field and N. A. Fox, eds., *Social Perception in Infants*, pp. 249–68. Norwood, N.J.: Ablex Publishing.

Stolorow, R.; and Brandchaft, B. 1987. "Developmental Failure and Psychic Conflict." *Psychoanalytic Psychology*, 4:241–53.

Sullivan, H. S. 1940. *Conceptions of Modern Psychiatry.* New York: W. W. Norton.

Tobin, J. K. 1985. *On the Way to the Self.* New York: Columbia University Press.

Tolpin, M. 1971. "On the Beginnings of a Cohesive Self." *The Psychoanalytic Study of the Child* 26:316–51. New York: International Universities Press.

Tomkins, S. S. 1962–63. *Affect, Imagery, Consciousness*, vols. I and II. New York: Springer Publishing.

———. 1970. "Affects as the Primary Motivational System." In M. B. Arnold, ed., *Feelings and Emotions*, pp. 101–10. New York: Academic Press.

———. 1980. "Affect as Amplification: Some Modification in Theory." In R. Plutchik and H. Kellerman, eds., *Emotions: Theory, Research and Experience*, pp. 141–64. New York: Academic Press.

———. 1981. "The Quest for Primary Motives: Biography and Autobiography of an Idea." *Journal of Personality and Social Psychology* 41:306–29.

Vygotsky, L. S. 1934. *Thought and Language.* Boston: MIT Press. Paperback edition, 1962.

Waddington, C. H. 1966. *Principles of Development and Differentiation.* New York: Macmillan.

Watson, J. 1985. "Contingency Perception in Early Social Development." In T. Field and N. Fox, eds., *Social Perception in Infants*, pp. 157–76. Norwood, N.J.: Ablex Publishing.

Weiss, P. A. 1973. *The Science of Life.* New York: Futura Publishing.

White, R. W. 1959. "Motivation Reconsidered: The Concept of Competence." *Psychological Review* 66:297–333.

Whyte, L. L. 1960. *The Unconscious Before Freud.* New York: Basic Books.

Wiener, N. 1948. *Cybernetics.* Cambridge, Mass.: MIT Press, 1961.

———. 1956. *The Human Use of Human Beings.* Garden City, N.Y.: Doubleday.

Winnicott, D. W. 1965. *The Maturational Processes and the Facilitating Environment: Studies in the Theory of Emotional Development.* New York: International Universities Press.

Winson, J. 1985. *Brain and Psyche.* Garden City, N.J.: Anchor Press/Doubleday.

Wooldrige, D. E. 1963. *The Machinery of the Brain.* New York: McGraw-Hill.

———. 1968. *Mechanical Man: The Physical Basis of Intelligent Life.* New York: McGraw-Hill.

Index